PARKER SON AND BOURN WEST STRAND

**Thalatta!**

The great commoner

PARKER SON AND BOURN WEST STRAND

**Thalatta!**
*The great commoner*

ISBN/EAN: 9783741169311

Manufactured in Europe, USA, Canada, Australia, Japa

Cover: Foto ©Andreas Hilbeck / pixelio.de

Manufactured and distributed by brebook publishing software (www.brebook.com)

PARKER SON AND BOURN WEST STRAND

**Thalatta!**

# *THALATTA!*

OR

THE GREAT COMMONER

# *THALATTA!*

OR

# THE GREAT COMMONER

## A POLITICAL ROMANCE

> "Oh, emptiness of fame!
> Oh Persic Zoroaster, lord of Stars!"
> PARACELSUS

LONDON
PARKER SON AND BOURN WEST STRAND
1862

*[The Author reserves the right of Translation.]*

LONDON: PRINTED BY W. CLOWES AND SONS, STAMFORD STREET,
AND CHARING CROSS.

## PREFATORY NOTE.

THE substance of this sketch—written several years ago—originally appeared in *Fraser's Magazine;* and I cannot allow the present opportunity to pass without returning my grateful thanks to the friend who now occupies its editor's chair,—the most brilliant and thoughtful of living historians.

The age of dedications, like the age of chivalry, has departed. Had those pretty solemnities been still in fashion, I should have ventured to inscribe a political story to Mr. Disraeli; not merely because loyalty to one's leader is the first, and most neglected, of political virtues; not merely because that leader is to us in England, what Tully was to his countrymen in Rome, "*optimus omnium patronus;*" but because I recognise in him, as in the politicians with whom he is associated, when dealing with social and religious controversies, a breadth of aim and generosity of sentiment, which I do not find in their opponents, and which comprise the best and most sterling elements of " Liberalism." *The enfranchisement of the people, the abolition of church-rates,* and similar phrases, have become the deceptive and delusive beacons of faction; but when the advocates of a really national and unsectarian system of education desire an exponent of their policy in the House of Commons they are forced to turn to a Tory; Tories alone, it would seem, are prepared to resist the fanatical legislation of the modern puritan; and —when the National Church is menaced by the intemperance of Prelates, and the rancour of a partisan theology—to utter words of warning, reproof, and moderation.

I may add that the title of the sketch is slightly altered. That under which it at first appeared — *Thalatta! Thalatta! A Study at Sea*—was pronounced by the critics to be unpardonably affected. Perhaps it was—at least they said so—and it is the duty of a writer to accept with humility, and obey with alacrity, the decisions of our periodical Mentors. The present title indicates, I hope, with sufficient exactness the motley character of the contents, the hardy sea-life of the north, and—English politics. I use the word *politics*, as it was used by Hobbes in *Leviathan*, in its oldest and widest sense.

A French translation—by M. Ch. B. Derosne of Paris—has been completed, and is about to appear.

S.

*December*, 1862.

# CONTENTS.

|  | PAGE |
|---|---|
| PROLOGUE .. | .. 1 |
| I.—THE DAWN | 7 |
| II.—AUTUMN DAYS .. | 17 |
| III.—THE SNOW | 51 |
| IV.—CONFESSION | .. 111 |
| V.—THE ELECTION .. | .. 165 |
| VI.—DEFEAT | .. 221 |
| VII.—THE SETTING SUN | .. .. 283 |
| EPILOGUE .. | .. 361 |

# *THALATTA!*

## PROLOGUE.

*For me the favouring breeze, when loud
It pipes against the galley's shroud,
Makes blither melody.*

IT has been a lovely morning tide; but the noon is sultry and lowering, and a picturesque ridge of storm-charged cloud stretches along the sea-line in our wake. To-night we shall have a blow,—a lash of rain, and the wind rattling among the rigging. But now it is calm as Eternity, or as that still marble face which has never deigned even to smile upon our pain. O violet-eyed Evadne, grant us thy peace! Let us know the truth once and for ever. The bleeding heart may break, but death is preferable to this intolerable toothache. We pray for rest,—rest, rest,—*in æterna pace*. But the still maiden stirs not, answers not; only looks with those clear cold eyes—cold and elemental as the winter stars—right away past us into the outermost horizon. Oh, my wintry

## PROLOGUE.

heaven, for whom wait you? The old heroic ages have departed, and do not return any more. But in one breast there still beats knightly faith, and truth, and loyalty, and they are all laid at your feet. Bend your eyes, and kill us, if you will, with passion, or mockery, or tender tears; but do not remain for ever so inaccessibly, so snowily, divine.

Such was the Confession of Faith which I had addressed to a mortal Saint Cecilia about a fortnight before the date at which this narrative commences. I am naturally eloquent, I believe; yet I do not deny that I may have polished the speech a very little since its delivery. Evadne, though an exceedingly sensible girl, who would never dream of marrying a man without knowing his rent-roll and referring him to her mother, is still on certain speculative points charmingly capricious and sentimental. Bending her superb eyes, in answer to my appeal, "You are a knight," she said, "and a true knight must do his devoir before he wins his lady. Find first the Holy Grail, and when you return to Belgravia do not forget this souvenir," and she presented me with a fairy gauntlet, a wonderful little pink-coloured, lavender-scented Parisian kid-glove (No. $6\frac{1}{4}$), which I kissed devoutly. "But if I return not?" "Then I will weep for you," replied the maiden, with heavenly composure. This was altogether very consolatory; but Evadne was mildly inexorable as any saint, and I was forced to quit on the quest. I had not the most distant conception who or what the Holy Grail might be, or where he, she, or it was to be met with; and none of my club-friends, I found, were better informed. The Arthurian knights, however, when in search of the supernatural, commonly went north; and as it was now the middle of June, a yacht voyage to Norway I fancied would be an exceedingly pleasant way of passing the time. So here I am,—in the first place, in search of the blessed Grail, and in the second, provided with rods and guns for the salmon and wildfowl of the Scandinavian fjords.

I must write an account one day of life on board a yacht:—like Cerito's dancing, it is the poetry of motion. Not yet embalmed in a poem, indeed; but this happens because the poets are bilious, and when at sea keep mostly to the cabin. The morning is pretty far advanced before I rise,—for I like to lie and listen to the water as it whistles, and whispers, and plashes, and gurgles restlessly on the other side of the thin board which keeps the ocean out of my crib. Good heavens! I waken sometimes in the deep of the dead night, and feel with a chill sense of terror that there is only a fir-plank between me and the mysterious creatures of the deep who follow in the wake of the ship, and, with cruel stony eyes, wait for us outside. But the morning light scatters the mists, and Ponto and I leap overboard, where he sometimes nearly drowns me outright with his rough dog-play. Now, Ponto, let us pass the *Lily*—purest and stateliest of the virgin flowers which live in holy singleness of heart, and therefore likest of any to that blessed Lily at home—and so we beat the water with our shaggy paws, and shoot away like salmon. But, as the morning breeze ruffles her snowy plumage, she steals silently from us, and leaves us there, alone by ourselves, in the very heart of the ocean. Superb! A man can never stretch his limbs except in the sea. On the shore he is the victim of the tailor, and what with boots, braces, and gaiters, is as much a prisoner as if he were lodged in Newgate. But in the sea every limb gains an ampler sweep, a lordlier freedom, and the owner feels that he has returned for a while to his native element. Yes, native, no doubt. Men must have sinned foully, and fallen far, ere, chained to the prosaic and unpliant earth, they were forced to relinquish for ever the stormy caresses of the white-edged waves. See, the *Lily* lies-to; the white pennant streams from the gaff to intimate that breakfast is on the board: again we strike out, and clambering over the gunnel into our little cozy nest, speedily shake ourselves dry.

So here in the poop—note-book in hand—I am settled for the day. Among the brilliant coloured shawls and rugs that strew the deck, I must look uncommonly like the immortal Kubla Khan—without his harem, the Lord be thanked! I like comfort; and if a man loves an arm-chair, and a quilted coverlet at home, I see no reason why he should not have them on board his yacht. Hermit crabs, and sea-anemones (or "inemies," as Dan calls them), are very well in their way; but a man needs his wine and his weed even when naturalising. I don't chance to be a muscular Christian; and the conveniences, if not the pomps and vanities, of this wicked world, retain a strong hold on my affections. Dear little *Lily!* you are as white and innocent as the poet's "Lily" in the beautiful old idyl. Don't listen, therefore, my darling, to the Norland rover that would wile you away with him to your doom. He will tell you the strangest sagas of the yellow-haired sea-kings and their brides, and his hollow whispers are sweeter than the lascivious murmurs of tropic seas: but, indeed, he is very hard, and icy, and pitiless at heart. Take care, take care: I heard him whisper even now; thrust him back, and cast off his deceitful kisses, or you are lost for ever. You cannot fancy how merciless the beautiful creature is: he will smile, and fondle, and wanton, and the children may pull his ears, and stroke his whiskers, and smooth the lustrous fur; and then all at once he will leap upon you like a wild tiger-cat, as he is, and will rend you limb from limb.

Dan, our "skeely skipper," is coiled up somewhere among the rigging, darning, as he calls it, a pair of sail-cloth breeches, so compacted of shreds and patches, that not a single thread of the original garment can now remain; and as he "darns," recreates himself with an interminable "Song of the Sea," which is longer than the sea-serpent, and takes nearly a voyage to unravel. It unrolls itself "without haste, without rest," like the music of a broken-winded hurdy-gurdy, or the waves that lap against the vessel o' nights; and at intervals, through the monotonous solidity of the narrative, a dash of spray, in the shape of a chorus or refrain, breaks out, and is taken up mechanically by any of the crew within hearing—

>          Y——o! H——o!
>             Trip and g——o!
>          Over the water
>             Cheerily r—o—w!

Ponto occasionally joins in with an eccentric and commiserating howl; but at the present moment he is standing erect on his hind legs, his head between his shaggy fore-paws, and gazes wistfully, now at the loaded gun beside me, and then over the gunnel at a pair of red-throated divers who cross in our wake. "Down, Ponto, down; you don't go over at present, sir. We are writing a romance."

# I.

# THE DAWN.

# CHAPTER I.

### MARE TENEBROSUM.

———◆———

*A lovely dream, a vision fair,*
*Of some far-off forgotten land,*
*And of a girl with golden hair*
*And violets in her hand.*

———◆———

THAT time seems to me like a dream now; perhaps it may grow clearer again by-and-bye. There is the great sea in the background, running like solemn music through all the mean details of the day, and communicating to the people into whose life it insinuates itself a peculiar sobriety of thought and staidness of demeanour. These primitive people are nursed in the sad companionship of the Northern Ocean—that Mare Tenebrosum of mists, and icebergs, and snowy storms, out of which to the antique imagination issued the wintry gods of Walhalla. There, too, the yellow curly-pated children sport upon the rippled shore, and, used to the water from earliest infancy, speedily become the cherished and dauntless nurslings of the waves. Among the others, two are specially noticeable to us—one a grave, dreamy, large-eyed girl; the other a handsome, vivacious, mischievous boy, who gives the young nursemaid in charge of them a world of trouble. She has tried in vain for the last half-hour to catch the vagrant young gentleman, who, dodging round the sharp rocks, or splashing through the shallow pools with royal disregard of his nether garments, still continues to elude the chase. "Miles! Miles!" she exclaims at last, fairly out of breath, "see what her ladyship will say to you! No supper for you to-night, sir. O, Corry, get him to come."

"Miles, dear," says the little maiden, in her still way, "we must go home. Katie says mamma will be frightened."

The quiet voice seems to have a peculiar influence over Master Miles, who forthwith approaches within reach, looking very subdued and penitent about the unhappy shoes.

"Don't tell on me, Katie, darling," he says, looking into her face with a sort of comic entreaty, as she stoops down to set him to rights.

Katie is a good-natured little soul, who cannot remain angry for more than five minutes at most; and long before they reach the old manor-house above the bay, the two are chattering like "pyets," the closest allies in the world.

"Katie," says Miles, solemnly, as they enter the house, "you are the nicest, dearest, prettiest; and, dear Katie—let me have a dry pair of stockings."

Ay, Katie, nicest, dearest, prettiest! Miles was not so far wrong in his boyish estimate of the black eyes, the black hair, and the rosy bloom of health and happiness on the flushed cheeks. And you looked as solemn and prim withal, at times, as any little Puritan; while indeed you had the cheeriest heart, and the merriest laugh, of them all.

"Why do you weep, Katie? What makes you cry so? O, Katie! what is the matter?"

But Katie will not own that anything is wrong; she dries her eyes, and smiling mechanically on the child, bids her go sleep—it is late, and she must not waken again. Corry long remembered that hard, sad, woful smile; the smile of a heart bruised past recovery, and which no future summer will quite heal. When Corry woke next morning, Katie had gone; but how she had gone, or where and why she had gone, could only be vaguely surmised—in guesses that were not intelligible to a child's ear.

## CHAPTER II.

LA CRUCHE CASSÉE.

> And love
> Is something awful, which one dares not touch
> So early o' mornings.

HOW did it happen? I really cannot tell you; nay, it is perhaps better that I should not try. I think we are getting rather candid and out-spoken in this direction. The old writers were content with the simple tragedy of *The Fall;* they did not enter into a pathological examination of its consequences. Our story-tellers are more scientific. A modern novel or a modern poem resembles a lecture on midwifery more than anything else I know.

Katie is seated on the stile behind the laburnum shrubbery—as neat, trim, and dainty a little woman as ever bewildered the eye of man. A woman? no, barely; barely more than a girl yet; though the blush that plays upon her cheek is already womanly in its way. The pitcher she is carrying from the well —to ease old Jean, whose stiff joints are somewhat more difficult to move than the lithe limbs of this nimble nymph—rests on the wall beside her; her light summer dress is looped up to prevent its being wetted, and discloses the crimson petticoat, and the trimmest, daintiest foot and ankle in all the country-side,—ever so provokingly modest and coquettish. The plump arm is not very sinewy; so she has to rest on the stile here; yes, that of course is the cause of her delay; though, truth to tell, the rosy cheek does not look delicate, and the "pail" is one of the smallest. If a gentleman in shooting gear *will* pass this way can *she* help it, I should like to know? And if he will speak to her, somewhat too softly perhaps, and tell her how pretty and blooming she looks this summer evening—what of that? And if he will insist on "a drink" out of the pail, and if, as blushing and smiling she holds it up to him, he somehow slips his arm round her waist, and prints a kiss—

> Soft and warm
> As those the sun prints on the smiling cheek
> Of plums and mellow peaches,

not on the pitcher-mouth, but on her own rosy lips, how can she prevent him? She will spill all the water on her crimson petticoat if she let it drop; and to avoid such a mischance has she not expressly looped up her dress in this too charming *mode?* Nay, if it fall, may it not break?

Truth to tell, little Katie cares not how long those stolen summer nights may last. How clever, and handsome, and gentlemanlike he looks! How pleasant it is to feel the blush stealing across her face as he looks into her eyes—how the subtle shock goes through her as he takes her hand in his and traces her fortunes in its blue-veined lines! How small and delicately-fashioned that hand of his is, even when compared with her own, which is not so very large after all, she thinks! What clever things he can say when he wants her to laugh, and how caressingly murmur the tenderest words! How pleasant it is, too, to be able to teach *him;* to teach him to repeat the soft North country words which he affects not to know; and then how pleasantly the old words of rustic wooing come back from the smooth eloquent lips! And then she is such a child yet: so charmed with her new playmate, so ignorant of all evil or sin.

Beware, Katie darling! a snake lurks in the grass. *I* can see how insincere that dangerous and subtle homage is: how shallow and tawdry the hollow-hearted "love" which is already beginning to eat into your child-life, and hurt its innocent bloom. Oh, darling! did you know how cold and hard that smooth face can be when it chooses—how cold and hard the heart underneath always is—you would rather sit all night alone with old Janet by "the ingle-neuk," than listen to these false notes.

But the child does not perceive the *falsetto;* does not perceive that the words do not ring true, and are tipt with deadliest poison. To think of a smooth-tongued, cozening knave teaching this little maiden in the innocence of her heart to believe a lie, is bad enough; but to think of him ruthlessly, deliberately, spoiling her whole life, torturing every sensitive fibre of heart and soul,—it makes one's blood boil to think of it. Could no entreaty induce him to relent? None. Else how could he have disturbed the childish gleeful happiness that smiled up in his eyes when first he met her; how resist the silent appeal which the fair innocent face made to his mercy? But he had no mercy, and the cat-like claws held her fast in their smooth grip till she perished. There are some hearts that bleed to think of it even yet. Let each of us pray to be delivered from such evil; every man of us to be delivered from the hell of knowing that he has done a fellow-soul a hurt that eternity perhaps cannot repair; every woman among us to be delivered from that sense of startled convulsive shame which crimsoned Katie's neck, and made her flee—like a wild wounded animal, with the hunter's dart sticking in its bleeding side — to the homeless mountain coverts.

# II.

## AUTUMN DAYS.

# CHAPTER I.

### SÆVA PELOPIS DOMUS.

Knights,
Half-legend, half-historic, counts and kings,
Who laid about them at their wills and died.

AMBITION! Like the old Darian dynasty over all its satraps, king of kings, and lord of lords.

Rare fallacy of the young blood of nature. Can this pulse cease to beat? Can this warm being become as though it had not been? No,—its vigorous vitality projects itself into the future, and refuses to believe in the dust of the charnel-house. I may die and be buried; but my spirit shall walk abroad among the children of men. They will speak gently of the young poet who sang "so pitifully sweet;" the ringing sentences of the great statesman will still kindle patriot hearts, as when they fell, warm and lighted from the lips, "wet with Castalian dew."

One who has consented to settle down into the ordinary jog-trot of existence, who has never found time nor opportunity to make *the* great speech, to write *the* great book, and who looks forward indeed to the rest prepared for the people of God—" when at eventime it shall be light,"—as a heritage unspeakably more comforting than any uneasy fame, or vexed immortality, may yet regard with an indulgent eye these luxuries of the imagination. Who would break a child's wooden toy, because it is not the Apollo? Who would tear a boy's scrawl, because Raphael painted the Blessed Mother and the Transfigured God? Dear heart! believe and hope what you will; the clay and the wood are touched by the radiant glory that lies around thy heart; and to thee they also are transfigured. It would be cruel and sinful to break the illusion just now: the disenchantment will come at the appointed time, when new interests and new excitements have cast out the early ambition, and an unnoted hand has filled the vacant niche. And you will be a better merchant or mechanic, because you dreamed once that you were born to grow the Dryden or the Chatham of your age.

Honour—what is honour? "Detraction will not suffer it to live with the living," said Falstaff; but does the sepulchre shut it out? Fancy being dissected and anatomised for ever,—the unclean hands of critics wandering restlessly over the weary limbs that should rest in wait for the resurrection. "He was vain, pompous, superficial: his style is rugged, turgid, inelegant: he said foolish things, that have done much hurt to men." So the palaver goes on from one generation to another; you are spoken of as if you were a picture or a statue—not of marble, but of mud; and the shuttlecock is kept flying till the day of judgment. No wonder that men should stir in their coffins, and feel that they have defrauded their ashes of the respite that is bestowed on meaner dust. I cannot doubt that the Protector envies the quiet grave wherein rests " the Cromwell guiltless of his country's blood." There they lie side by side— the brother who conquered and cast down; the brother who was wisely silent and died. Mark the contrast. No sound disturbs *his* still repose ; his very name is forgotten among men—for on the tombstone which was meant, not unkindly, to perpetuate for a season his homely virtues, every letter (except only the numerals of some unknown event of birth, or marriage, or death) has been clean washed out. But even in his mutilated sepulchre the other may not rest; he is a renowned, a famous, an illustrious man ; one calls him a hero, another a liar and a knave ; of the writing of books about him there is no end. "Oh, that I had stayed at home!" exclaims the vexed and attenuated ghost, " and ploughed my father's acres! My eyes are heavy, but I cannot close them ; I am tired to death, and yet I cannot rest. See my brother,—he does not stir, nor moan, nor turn in his bed,—he sleeps as well as when we lay together on our mother's lap. Oh! dear brother, waken and speak to me but once; for the night is dark and tedious, and I am sick of the generations of fools that possess the earth so long."

But if, after this warning, you still desire to be remembered, do not despair. There are many forms in which a man may endure. Critics have kept many reputations alive by the supreme perfection of their hostility. The fool is preserved that we may be able to relish the sauce. The culprit is flayed into everlasting notoriety. You are not a man of genius yourself, but you may become the enemy of one, if you try hard enough; and some morning you will rise and find yourself among the Immortals,— scarified into fame. Fame, too, is capricious as fortune. "The iniquity of oblivion blindly scattereth her poppies. Herostratus lives that burnt the temple of Diana; he is almost lost that built it; time hath spared the epitaph of Adrian's horse, confounded that of himself." Age after age names drop out of the recorded calendar of time, and are never again reinserted. We cannot house above a certain number of great men; and so the world is forced to sift and winnow as it turns; and the reputation of the foremost is at the mercy of the most frivolous generation. The illustrious of the earth were as many in Homer's age as in our own; and when the destroying trumpet is heard the roll will not be longer than it is now. Who knows but that at the Last Day, by a wild freak, by an ungovernable caprice, by an immortal perversity, Dr. Martin Tupper may not be one of the celebrities?

Several great men besides Mr. De Quincey are rather apt to forget what they are writing about;

but as Miles Warrender was ambitious, I cannot suppose that the intelligent reader will deem these few observations on the last infirmity of noble minds out of place. Yes, Miles was ambitious, and he had a right to be ambitious. His race from time immemorial had borne no ungraceful nor undistinguished place in the national annals. It came straight down, so the history of the house asserted—a history compiled in the last century by a reverend cadet, who believed in his heart that the annals of the Warrenders were of more enduring interest than the annals of the Plantagenets—from fair-haired Vikings and bearded Jarls. One of these roving gentry, though everywhere else victorious, fell at length before the blue eyes of a Saxon maid. He wooed and won; and built himself a craggy keep above the Northern Sea, which stormed of winter nights a thousand feet below his bed-room window. His bride was descended from the younger shoot of a royal stem, and he himself traced his origin to a distinguished ornament of Walhalla. Well connected, therefore, on both sides of the house—on this with Charlemagne, on that with Odin—it was not surprising that the Earl should have enjoyed the protection and favour of his sovereign, who, on the principle of setting a thief to catch a thief, made him the Warden of the Northern Coasts. Thus the house was established, and with characteristic tenacity t had clung through good and evil fortune to the barren seaboard where it was planted. Dynasties might perish and empires decay, but the Warrenders sat unmoved in their hawk-like nest above the cliffs. But time was too potent even for the great house, and at last it began to give way. The Earl jealously watched the inroads of the reformed clergy, and after having, as a warning, hung one or two of the most active, gave peremptory orders that no more heretics should be admitted within the limits of his heritable jurisdiction. The edict would not work, however. Silently, the subtle miasma infected castle and cottage, and the Earl was forced sullenly to acquiesce in the change. The seventeenth century saw the family thrice attainted—twice for its politics and once for its religion. But the domestic influence at Court was so powerful that these were speedily reversed; and it was not until the beginning of the succeeding century that the Government of the day found it impossible to overlook the share which the Earl had taken in his cousin of Mar's rebellion. He was driven into exile, the estates were confiscated, and the title extinguished. One vain but romantic effort was made by the last scion of an unhappy house to recover "the likeness of a kingly crown," and the son of the old Earl accompanied his prince. Worn out with grief and hardship, the only heir of the elder branch of the Warrenders perished in some obscure continental brawl—that warfare of a hundred years ago which was entered into without provocation and ended without honour. Meantime the northern estates (which comprised but a moiety of their great possessions) were gifted by the Crown to an able commoner, who had married a pretty little niece of the Earl, and who thereupon assumed the family name and arms. He was one of the most noted House of Commons men of his day, and might have been made a peer had he liked. Since his time most of the gentlemen of the name had achieved parliamentary reputations; and at the moment when Miles entered public life, his cousin George Mowbray, wit, poet, and orator, occupied the foremost place on the Opposition benches.

Such was the blood which flowed in the Warrender veins, and which had been transmitted from the Norse Viking and his Saxon bride, through Royalist soldiers and Cavalier statesmen, to Miles Warrender, Esquire, of Grace Dieu and Carlyon, in the county of ——. But hold! no personalities, if you please. It was a keen, healthy, pungent *ichor*, smelling of the sea-breeze, smacking of its brine. The Warrenders were not a versatile race. Strong passions and strong convictions are not unfrequently monotonous; for their range is narrow; they always strike the same key-note, and keep at the same altitude. These races do not end in Shakespeares and Goethes, but Cromwells and Bluchers spring from them not unfrequently. They are too intense to be cheerful, too concentrated to be catholic. Yet the Warrenders could not be called monotonous; a certain humorous eccentricity prevented these grave men from becoming tedious. It was this also which enabled them to withstand as they did the levelling influences of modern organisation, and to retain a marked and not unpleasant angularity of their own. Men called it eccentricity—perhaps it was; it was either that, or the scent of the sea in the blood. And as the shell still murmurs of the wave, " though inland far it be," it was curious to note how, even when removed to the interior and planted at college or in the senate, a Warrender always recalled to the imagination the stormy seaboard where his fathers were bred. Even the great politician did not entirely fine down. He was by theory and practice as suave and courteous as a leader must be; but the ruthless mockery, the flashing scorn, the iron hardihood of heart and nerve, were inherited from his Norse kin and smelt of the brine. He sat there; his hat pulled across his brows, his arms crossed upon his chest—there at the head of the gentlemen of England, himself the most polished gentleman of them all. But how was it that when he rose, and the keen, clear words flashed from the curled lips and entered, like the noiseless steel, the hearts of his enemies—how was it that you dreamed of the stormy Walhallan ghosts, and the naked-legged Viking striding angrily through the surf?

## CHAPTER II.

### "THE TWELFTH."

Not in Ithaca broad glades or meads;
Yet dear the cliff whereon the wild goat feeds;
No sea-girt island's pasturing fields expand,
Yet most beloved of me, my rocky land.

A HEATH like that of which the poet sings—

a heath so dreary,
For ever mantled by the sad white snow.

Only there is no snow here during August, and the broad moors run down, purple with summer, to the sea.

Lying at the foot of one of the heathy knolls which relieve the monotonous level, the historian perceives, though they are nearly hidden by the luxuriant heather, a couple of sportsmen. It is the close of a summer afternoon, and the blue smoke of Manillas ascends gratefully—incense to appease the sad ghosts of the unburied moorcock.

From the top of the knoll you look down upon the sea—three, four, five miles away. Thalatta! Thalatta! Still it startles you, as it startled the

Greeks of old, with a glad surprise. Blue or grey or silvery, I know not which; but alive at least. Therefore it is that we who are gifted with a fatal immortality greet the sea. It, too, has inherited the unhappy prerogative of our house. The earth dies and is buried; the sea, which is its soul, endures for ever.

The blackened castle of Carlyon, rising from the white surf and the windy bents, is dimly visible. Carlyon stands on one side of the blue bay; the house of Hawkstone on the other. You get a bird's-eye view of the boats that beat out and in to the cove, or that lie with folded sails, like gannets, over the fishing ground outside. A green marginal border, such as the sportsman sees in summer round the moss-springs, skirts the shore. Then, north and south, far as the eye reaches—broad, barren, purple moorland,—here and there a squatter's hut, with turf roofing, and curling blue smoke of peat. A little community shut up by itself, like the aborigines in a Pacific island.

On the other side, it is still the muir, and the muir alone. But could you rise a furlong higher, you would learn how the muir terminates at length, and how rich woodlands, and rivers freighted with pleasure-boats and merchant craft, and the country-seats of county magnates, and the castle and demesne of My Lord of Otterburne, and a great city of labour and capital, lie beyond—not very many miles distant, indeed, by this smooth beaten road which slants athwart the moss.

Along which an elf-like carriage now approaches from the landward. It is drawn by two vigorous Highland ponies—the one pale as a star, the other black as coal. A dove-like flutter of ribbons and muslin dresses becomes plainly visible. Two girls —both pretty; one with Titian hair, and an exquisitely clear and child-like delicacy of complexion; the other dark and pensive, and doing her best to restrain the wild little Highlanders, while she listens to the merry badinage of her companion. She is still a girl, though on the hither verge of girlhood, and the shy fawn-like glance, which is sharply withdrawn the moment it meets your eye, contrasts charmingly with her mature and matronly carriage. That glance somehow arrests and startles you. I have called it shy, but it neither deprecated nor entreated; and though it reminded you somehow of the soft and dreamy lustre of the fawn's, it was keener, more penetrating and defined. So long as it knows that you are gazing on the face it belongs to, the dark lashes studiously veil it; but take a book, pretend to be occupied, or looking in a different direction, or at another face (as some can do), then on a sudden it will peep out in the stillness, like a mouse from its hole, and again retreat as suddenly whenever it *feels* that it is detected. The rest of the face remains perfectly quiescent; the eye only roams and investigates gravely, like the old vagabond conjurers, who left their bodies stark and untenanted, while they themselves wandered over the world.

The ponies had got very restive before the Titianesque face noticed that anything was wrong.

"Corry, Corry," she cried, as the ponies bursting into a gallop, brushed some large stones that lay on the road-side, "take care."

Corry looked very pale, but not distressed. "Don't touch the reins, Alice, you will frighten them. They only want a gallop. Pluto, good Pluto, wo-o-o."

But Pluto has got the bit between his teeth, and he and Proserpine are determined to "try a fall." The little wicker-work basket swings to and fro as the ponies, warming with the passion of the turf, gallop more recklessly along, and is sometimes almost concealed from sight in the cloud of dust which is raised by the hurrying hoofs. The mischievous prank is ending in a panic, under the influence of which they rush along as if pursued by the furies. Alice is already speechless with fright; but Corry, though her fingers are bruised and bleeding, holds to the reins like white death. Do what she can, however, the terrified brutes manage to get off the smooth road to the adjacent moor, and are apparently making straight for a deep and ugly-looking peat-hag, filled with greenish water, when—

Of course, at this crisis, the hero of the piece descends gracefully upon the stage amid a profusion

## "THE TWELFTH."

of fireworks, and cuts the traces. This being a story of real life, I was at first somewhat suspicious of an incident which bore so questionable a resemblance to the course of events in legendary history. It was much more probable, I said to myself, that that gentleman was at home, playing pool, writing poetry, or taking a glass of sherry as a whet for the salmon. Why should the ponies have halted purely, as it seemed, to give him an opportunity to stop them, to earn sweet thanks from the ladies' lips, and κυδος from the county paper? Had I reasoned thus, I should no doubt have produced an unanswerable argument; but I should have had to leave the ponies at the bottom of the bog, and only one white feather from that charming wide-awake floating on the surface of the mere; and this would never have done, for I have not yet come to the tragic part of my story. The argument, as an argument, is, I cheerfully admit, conclusive; and the only valid objection to it, as to modern historical theories in general, is that it chances to be entirely opposed to the facts. For this was the twelfth of August (*dies immemor*), and Miles Warrender and an old college chum were taking their pleasure on his moors (being in fact the sportsmen we have already incidentally noted), and were lunching and smoking as we have seen, at the precise spot where the accident threatened to occur. To a wiry sportsman like Miles, it was of course a matter of little difficulty to arrest the Highlanders, and his heavy hand quickly brought the little fellows, panting and perspiring, to a stand.

Alice rapidly recovered speech, and was profuse in her thanks. "In truth, Mr. Warrender, you have saved us. What a frightful scrape! How intolerable to have had that horrid green water splashed all over our new muslins! I should have died of it."

Corry said nothing. If the two girls had been quite alone, I believe they would have had recourse to what Mr. Tadpole calls "a good cry." As it was, Alice did not cry, but laughed and talked with her usual *esprit*, while Corry went up to Pluto's head, and reproached the impenitent miscreant.

"O, Pluto, I am ashamed of you; what *do* you mean, sir?" she inquired with childish gravity, stamping prettily on the ground with her tiny foot, and patting him not ungently on the nose, while the eye, like a startled sunbeam, shot through the thick cover of the lashes, and across Pluto's shaggy mane, to light on Miles's face.

## CHAPTER III.

SOLUTIS GRATIÆ ZONIS.

In all she did
Some figure of the golden time was hid.

IT is a great mistake to be specific. Half the "heresy" in the world is the result of trying to define. So the events already narrated, or about to be narrated, were transacted—no matter where. They were transacted in the year of grace—no matter which. Let it suffice that they *were* transacted; they will remain humanly significant, though I do not condescend to the where and when. There are obvious reasons why the present historian should not become prudishly circumstantial. An acute critic would then experience no difficulty in detecting the incessant anachronisms, in which, as a countryman of Shakespeare, he is pleased to indulge. Why should he heedlessly expose himself to the risk of capture by the detective police?

There is an after-piece to the incident narrated in the last chapter, which I had almost omitted to chronicle.

It was the first night of the full moon, and the moonlight rested whitely on the water, and on the bold promontory of rocks, and on the bleached towers of Carlyon, and on the fishing-boats withdrawn from the tide, and on the white muslin curtains of Alice's bedroom in Hawkstone. Her eyes are half closed; she is not yet quite asleep, but "the glamour is cuisten ower her." A pale statue-like figure moves noiselessly through the room. It is draped in simple antique white, but the black hair has been unloosed, and falls down dishevelled to the unzoned waist. It passes to the window, and gazes across the bay to Carlyon, amid whose grey towers red lights still burn. A priestess of Diana? No, she does not belong to the austere sisterhood; it is only a pretty innocent girl, who cannot rest for the new, unquiet pain at her heart.

"Is that you, Corry?" asks Alice. "Why are you up so late? You will get your death of cold, child."

The girl comes and seats herself by the bedside.

"Alice, dear, I can't sleep. I am so hot and restless; feel my hand. How thankful we should be that we got safe home to-day! I cannot tell you how terrified I was; it was dreadful." And she clasped her hands over her eyes. Then, looking into her friend's face, she whispered, "And dear Miles, how can I show him I am not ungrateful? I couldn't thank him; I was afraid I would cry if I tried; and I am now so sorry. What will he think?"

"You poor child, you have lost your heart to that dear Miles. That is the matter, is it? Well, write him a pretty, dutiful little epistle, and seal it with a *forget-me-not.*"

"Tush, Alice, you are unfeeling, silly. But I do love my cousin dearly, and I don't mind who knows it,—not a bit," she added, with a charming childish petulance that was graceful as a Greek jest.

"Why should you, you romantic chit? Miles is a king of men, just as you are a real little angel, with wings that you hide under your night-gown, I believe. But I rather prefer, for my own part, that huge friend of his, who rolls about like the Indian god on the mantelpiece downstairs. I'm sure he's quite as clever, and twenty times funnier."

"Miles does not care to be funny to—to—" said the child, loftily, and with great dignity.

"To a silly good-for-nothing like me," interrupted Alice. "But go to bed now, dear. You are shivering all over. Good night. Good night."

# CHAPTER IV.

### THE MOONLIGHT.

> Tasting the air this spicy night which turns
> The unaccustomed head like Chianti wine.

THE lights were still burning in the comfortable smoking-room at Carlyon, and Miles and Darcy, seated in two ample easy-chairs, were taking their pleasure on either side of the open window, through which came the soft breezes of the summer night, and "the voice of the long sea wave as it swell'd!" Darcy was reading the *Times;* Miles's whole soul was absorbed in his meerschaum—the reign of clay had not been inaugurated as yet.

"You will be glad to hear," quoth Darcy, "that His Grace is in perfect health, that Lady Manning gave the last assembly of the season on Tuesday night, that it was attended by the *élite* of the aristocracy who remain in town, among whom we noticed the Princess of Oxbridge, the Earl of Bedlam—"

"Hold, Darcy, there's a good fellow. You will make the room as hot as Lady Manning's temper, if you conjure up these visions of Pandemonium. Find something cool and unexciting."

"The coolest thing I ever heard of is young Porcupine standing for Middleton. Who could have put him up to it? Why, the man was at Codlington with us, you recollect, and he was a born idiot, if ever there was one. He was meant for the diplomatic service then—even his friends said he wasn't fit for anything better. It's just like those Nevils—they never had the slightest respect for public decency—they'll put up the family parrot or the family *cuddy* some day. I've a great mind to go and lead a revolt."

"I would, if I were you; the Earl will give you a shove."

"I would if I were a Crœsus, like you; I will when I am. Hang the Earl. I can fancy how he would take it.—' No doubt the country is—aw—aw—going to the bad, and the Nevils are the deuce and all that, but our family—aw—aw—has given up politics, and—aw—aw—in fact, Mr. Darcy Langton, I wash my hands of the whole concern.' No, no, the bar for ten years; but if I don't have a shy at the county the day I'm Solicitor, may I be blessed."

"Is the House up?"

"I don't know; haven't come to that yet. I always take the police reports first, they are so much more instructive than what is done in the other place. If it wasn't for the look of the thing I'd go and practise before Sir Peter. Let me see—'House of Lords.—Fifty bills were read a third time and passed, but there was no business of any public interest.' Think of that—fifty bills passed and no public interest! I can tell you it is a good deal for my interest though; I look upon each of these bills as so much clear profit. It's very considerate of these Parliament lawyers; but they are coming it a *leetle* too strong. Things will get into such an eternal mess presently, that Cobham will sweep us away like cobwebs some fine morning, and bring the *Code Napoléon* across the water."

"Too precious a blessing to be prayed for. The nation wouldn't consider itself safe for a day, if it understood its laws or its religion."

"Like old Widow Murphy. 'Unerstan' his reverence's sermon, sir? Na, na, I wudna presume.' But don't be profane. I hate the superficial way in which you laymen sneer at the most lucrative system of jurisprudence in the world." And Darcy relapsed into the newspaper. "Hullo! Here's the Great Man been at it again. 'Mr. Mowbray's motion on the Partington disabilities.' By Jove, how he walks into them! Listen to this. 'You may resist to-day and to-morrow, but the time will come when you must give way. Look at the noble lord! He has pledged himself to put down the movement. O devout imagination! The noble lord against the people of England! Let him try it.' And so your cousin sits down—his lip curled with that supreme scorn of his—and the House cheers him vociferously, and——"

"Divides clean against him, as of old?"

"Not a bit. 200 for, 225 against—majority against, 25, in prodigious capitals, and great cheering from the minority thereat."

"Things are coming to a crisis. A dissolution, I suppose. Mowbray will be minister next year."

"And Miles Warrender an Under-Secretary, or something better."

"No, thank you. I am not a politician, and don't mean to be one. I saw a good deal of the farce last year, and didn't like it."

"Tush,—'tis a good play, and I want you to make me Solicitor. Let us have All the Talents."

"Be Solicitor, O my friend, but I will sit under my own vines, if you please."

"Your own cabbages, you mean."

"Very well. But a Secretary of State—what a destiny! The man ceases to be a man, and becomes an abstraction—War, Justice, the Colonies. And an Under-Secretary is the shadow of a shade—an Under-Secretary can't smoke—an Under-Secretary isn't allowed a latch-key—an Under-Secretary must keep regular hours, and have no inconvenient convictions. And so—and so—what a glorious night!"

The moonlight lies on the water, which heaves like molten silver. Lights are moving among the cottages in the village—'tis the fishers preparing to catch the morning tide. Already the first boat has left, and crosses the lane of light that lies athwart the bay; its brown sail is set, but the warm night wind is soft and fickle; so the rowers pull, and the ear catches distinctly the regular beat of the heavy oars.

"Hawkstone is still as the dead," said Darcy, looking across the bay. "Very sweet pretty creatures these girls are. Corry is an old friend of mine, but she is as wild and shy as one of her own ponies. My dear Miles, I caught an expression in those eyes to-day, which I tried to keep to myself, only I fear it was meant for some one else. However, that yellow-haired, blue-eyed friend of hers, with her infectious laugh, is more to my taste. A simple man like myself would be afraid of the other; he would be perpetually hurting her, without knowing it; and then she would break away like a wounded fawn, and bleed to death in the woodland quite alone,—too shy to seek for help. A pretty figure, is it not? I sometimes fancy Providence designed to make a poet of me. Chance has given the world a Chancellor."

"Corry is a good child, and wouldn't do anything so absurd. But Alice would make an excellent help-meet for Mr. Darcy Langton, and we'll go and call to-morrow at Hawkstone."

"Heaven forbid! I am an anchorite, a pilgrim,

—the scallop-shell and green bag are my only possessions. No income under a thousand a-year should have leave to visit the drawing-room. I don't enter Paradise till I quit my garret. Then,—but then I will be crowned with age, if not with wisdom, and some of the blue will have melted out of these blue eyes. Alack! alack! Vanity of vanities! I wonder if the Chancellor sleeps as well as plain Darcy does. And so, my lord, good-night, or rather good-morrow, for 'the Lady of the Light, the rosy-finger'd Morn,' stirs over yonder,—an I mistake not."

# CHAPTER V.

### THE COMMONWEALTH.

*Who breaks his birth's invidious bar,*
   *And grasps the skirts of happy chance,*
   *And breasts the blows of circumstance,*
*And grapples with his evil star;*

*Who makes by force his merit known,*
   *And lives to clutch the golden keys,*
   *To mould a mighty state's decrees,*
*And shape the whisper of the throne.*

THE COMMONWEALTH was in commotion.

The COMMONWEALTH was the popular club with the younger men. It was not Whig, and it was not Conservative. Frequented by those who were not tied to the Ministry, nor bound to the Opposition, who had little sympathy with the obsolete traditions of the Tory, and none with the doctrinaire antidotes of modern Liberalism, it was a club of good birth and good breeding—a club of parts, culture, and ability, but at the same time a club better suited for the critic than for the worker, for the wit and the satirist than for the practical politician.

Yet the Commonwealth was moved. The Ministry had been virtually defeated the previous evening; and even the still waters of the Commonwealth rippled.

"Have you heard the news? His Grace has been at Windsor."

"But the King won't let him resign."

"I beg your pardon—I have it on the best authority—his resignation has been accepted. The Ministry is out."

"Well, I suppose the world will wag on. Who comes in?"

"Don't know. Mowbray's the man; but they don't like him up there. Easyhavers threatens to tell the Emperor."

"Yes, Mowbray's the man," was unanimously echoed from the bay window. Wherever else he might be disliked, the surpassing merits of the English Cicero were frankly admitted by that critical and fastidious assembly.

Mowbray, indeed, was very popular at the Commonwealth. He had taken a first-class at Oxford, and his prize poem was better than the Laureate's. He had written epigrams once—he spoke them now—and they were terse, brilliant, and sparkling with wit and scholarly point. He came of an old race, and the bar-sinister which crossed his coat did him little harm with critics who were better up in their horses' than in their statesmen's pedigrees.

For many years he was the petted Benjamin of his party. But at length he freed himself from the traditions in which he had been nursed, and assumed a higher position. At home he was now regarded as the most dangerous enemy of antique wrongs; from abroad, as the most sagacious advocate of an intelligent foreign policy, and "the last sighs of nations, perishing with their gods," were carried to the patriot politician. Only by the fools and bigots of political life was he hated. That party, however, is always a large one—one not unfrequently in the majority—holding office with peculiar tenacity, difficult to resist, and dangerous to assail. The triple brass of an English fool furnishes invincible armour.

As the evening fell, members gathered in to learn the rumours. The chances of the competitors were discussed, and the odds against the favourite, or in favour of the field, taken and given. At length a well-known figure, compact as a lady's glove, wiry as a Skye terrier, saunters along the pavement towards the club-door.

"Here's Maurice—Maurice will know."

"What's up, Maurice; what's the news?"

The gentleman addressed slowly raises his eyes to the eager inquirers, composedly glances along the line, and answers—

"Nothing I know of; there never is any news now. It was different when I was a boy. Then we had a new prince every six months or so—six months to a day, upon my honour. Now it takes twice the time, it seems, and we don't care about it when it does come. By the way, what kind of fellow is this Mowbray I hear people begin to talk about?"

"Begin to talk! Why, they have been at it for thirty years. But what of Mowbray?"

"Let me see, what was it? Yes, I recollect. He has been with the King, who shed tears—good old soul!—when he found Mowbray didn't mind being scolded, and ended by making him Minister. He is now forming a government; and I do trust you may be in the Cabinet, my dear Ashby! if you like that kind of thing."

Lord Maurice's voice was drowned. The Commonwealth was fairly beside itself. Mowbray was its favourite son, its peculiar pupil; and Mowbray was Minister. If the members of that critical and cynical, if not Christian, society ever embraced each other, it was upon this occasion. Many of them, no doubt, expected official pickings; but on the whole I am inclined to believe that unselfish satisfaction at the elevation of a wit, a scholar, and a gentleman, was the motive of the rejoicing.

This is not the place nor the time to attempt to discriminate with exactness the elements that concurred to create the admiration entertained for Mr. Mowbray by a large body of the public: but, generally speaking, they could be detected on the surface. There undoubtedly existed then, in many quarters, a reaction against the mechanical materialism of the century, and to this, in Mr. Mowbray, there was something congenial,—something which might be true or false in other respects, but which at least was,—whatever else it might be,—a sturdy protest against the principle of red tape. His earlier works were distinguished by a spirit of serene extravagance, which, even when most curiously inconsistent, was not wanting in a certain reckless fidelity. *Vaughan*, *Marvel*, and *Wharton*, are the polished and artistic elaborations of a mature intellect: but the same critical and fearless genius animates their most practical speculations. His opponents turned from his literary to his political life, and dwelt upon the contrast between the perfervid enthusiasm of the closet, and the interested intrigues of the Senate. But Mr. Mowbray, the leader of His Majesty's Opposition, and Mr. Mowbray, the Chancellor of His Majesty's Exchequer, were quite as popular characters with *his* friends, as Mr. Mowbray, the sarcastic assailant of a corrupt conservatism, and Mr. Mowbray, the author of *Wharton*. They admired the subtle and courageous thinker: they admired the subtle and courageous politician. In either capacity he manifested the virtues which secure the respect and fealty of men, who, practically taught to believe that all speculations and opinions are equally worthless in themselves, naturally attach exclusive importance to the *manner* in which a man acquits himself, and to the *personal* qualities or abilities he may display. Here, then, they found one, who, though conversant with abstract systems, and with the artificial speculations of a literary life, had yet displayed an unrivalled capacity for the management of public affairs, and manifested incomparable energy, daring, and resolution, alike in the conception and in the achievement of a career. Especially felicitous in this light did that connection appear, which once called forth so much violent animadversion,—a connection which was originally formed by Mr. Mowbray that he might more effectively gratify his hostility against Lord Stafford,—(and which he did gratify in a famous and protracted conflict, in which genius and audacity assailed with scornful success the conventional authority of place,)—a connection between the most subtle and brilliant intellect of these times, and a feeble and mercenary combination, without a creed, and without a principle. We all remember how, under his masterly dictatorship, this dispirited remnant gradually acquired reputation and importance,—how it became, by degrees, associated with a traditionary policy, and an historical confession,—how the confidence of democratic England was boldly demanded for an aristocratic connection, because it represented, forsooth, the party whose interests had been immemorially identified with those of the English people,

—how it ultimately acquired the authority of English power, and its author assumed the responsibilities of English government!

Associated with the genius which Mr. Mowbray manifested in the conduct of practical politics, two features were very noticeable,—especially in that intensely conscious and imitative age. Of all its public men, in the first place, he was the only one who relied implicitly upon himself. With cold precision he struck the blow that was, perhaps, to prove the turning point of a difficult and protracted conflict, and, when he had done so, he was immediately content to hold his peace. Unlike our representative "delegates," he manifested no desire to "explain his conduct,"—to "vindicate his position,"—to justify himself to his friends,—to avert the censure of his enemies. He had estimated the exact value of what he had achieved, and he was content in silence to abide the issue. It was from this characteristic that to many he seemed, as it were, to exert a direct and conscious control over his career,—as though he were not so much the creature of circumstances as other men, and had more thoroughly recognised and mastered the necessities of his position. He had *rehearsed* his career, and, consequently, he played his part with infinite accuracy and precision. And it was from this, moreover, that he never publicly manifested irritation, or annoyance, or vented his anger in the infelicitous language of passion. He was not moved, because he was thoroughly prepared. When he was indeed touched,—when it did seem as though the insult had reached him, through the cold and haughty reserve of his nature,—he never allowed himself to forget that he represented an important historical character. Even his passion was made subservient to his art. There was nothing impulsive or spontaneous in its expression. It had been anxiously adapted to serve a particular purpose,— perhaps to cover a bitter retort, which could not be tolerated except from a very angry and conscientious man. Consequently, in this light, Mr. Mowbray never appeared more severely artistical or artificial than when he was utterly in earnest. Nor, in the next place, was it possible to mistake the *impersonal* nature of the man. There was no part of his career which did not bear a direct and intimate connection with the rest; but, whenever it had answered the purpose it was immediately designed to serve, it became detached and separated from him,—whenever it ceased to engage the active energies of his mind, he was able to criticise it with passionless historical impartiality, as an object out and apart from him, for which he was not in any wise solicitous, nor responsible.

Such were the character and career of the great Tory chief. It was the same story throughout. Desperately against desperate odds, he kept his place in the perilous arena; but he never lost temper once. So his good things have not perished. The bitter repartees have crystallised into immortal gems. The diamond is curiously polished, and without flaw. I do not wonder that the Commonwealth loved him, especially when it came to know that *the politician* was as wise as he was witty; that *the man* was a sure friend and a magnanimous foe, never selfish and never base.

"Blessed be the man," says the wise Sancho Panza, "who first invented sleep. It covers one all over like a cloak!" Let us dry the ink and put the pen aside, Ponto. That is Saint Kilda, rising up sheer from the ocean's bottom, which, far to the south'ard, cuts the evening sky.

# III.

## THE SNOW.

# CHAPTER I.

### THE LEGITIMATE DRAMA.

This life of mine
Must be lived out, and a grave thoroughly earned.

THE Theatre Royal had arrived at Ashton: but—in the meantime—two years have elapsed since we left our friends in the COMMONWEALTH.

Two years,—passed into darkness on their noiseless wings. The roses have died out of the cheeks, and the garlands have been plucked from the hair. Only the vacant effigy of them survives,—"as in a glass darkly." Can these passionate moments, touched with sacred fire, thus perish utterly, leaving only a barren monument to the memory? Some people are content with the reminiscence, and flatter its mocking counterfeit of life. But let *us*, at least, be frank. A single throb of the pulse, a single glance from the blue eyes, a single pressure of the tender hand, is worth a dead Cæsar's victories, or the storied glories of an empire that has perished. *Carpe diem.*

During these two years, however, few visible

changes had affected our society. Mowbray was in office when they began, and notwithstanding the bitterly personal hostility of a portion of the aristocracy, still continued Minister. But it was a hard fight, a hand-to-hand struggle; and the next election was looked forward to with intense interest as likely to prove decisive, either for or against him. Warrender had not yet entered Parliament; for though Mowbray had lately offered his young kinsman a seat— one of the Government close boroughs—Miles had, for certain reasons of his own, seen fit to decline. With the exception of a couple of months in the metropolis during the spring east winds, he continued to reside exclusively at Carlyon. Nor was Hawkstone deserted. Mrs. Menteith and Corry were little addicted to wandering, and old Sir Maxwell never quitted the library where he sharpened the edge of his wit on Descartes and Hegel. Alice always spent the summer-tide with them, and she had just received leave from " home" (somewhere among the orchards and hedgerows of sunny Devon) to pass the incoming winter beside the frosty seas. Darcy was making his way, slowly but sturdily, at the bar; not permitting its dry lore and tedious mummeries to deform his intellect, or warp his common sense; and still retaining unimpaired the buoyant vivacity of temperament and the keen direct insight which had made him the popular favourite at school, at college, and in his profession.

To return. The "Theatre Royal" had arrived at Ashton, and a village group was discussing the play-bill displayed in front of the *Warrender Arms*, where the company performed.

It stated that, in obedience to the wishes of the nobility and gentry of the county of ——, Mr. O'Rook had visited Ashton, and would perform there during the week. The manager remarked that the well-known ability of his company had realized the ambition of a life spent in the service of his country— the production, namely, of the great national Drama, in a manner never witnessed hitherto off the metropolitan boards. On the present occasion (as a mark of respect to that August Personage who had deigned to mark in a way Mr. O'R., without violating the most Sacred Confidence, could not more precisely allude to, but which would never be forgotten, His appreciation of Mr. O'R.'s humble services to the Legitimate Drama), the performances would commence with "The National Anthem, by the whole strength of the company," would include the celebrated Dramatic Tragedy, "The Exciseman; a Tale of the Sea;" a comic song on Ashton, by Mr. Smiles; and the popular Comic Extravaganza entitled "Tibbie and the Bo'sun." Children in arms could not be admitted; whistling, riotous, or improper noises were not allowed under any circumstances whatever; smoking in any part of the house was strictly prohibited; and every person disregarding these regulations would be immediately turned out, and—"no money returned." Mr. O'R. was a resolute supporter (in large capitals) of *S*ocial *O*rder and *M*unicipal *I*nstitutions; and he trusted that the public would second his efforts "to elevate the *T*one, and purify the *A*tmosphere of the *S*tage."

The villagers were properly impressed by the views thus oracularly promulgated; and on entering the house, Miles and Darcy found the pit (6*d*.) and the gallery (3*d*.) well filled—chiefly by seamen and their "sweethearts." In the foremost row, by courtesy denominated the "boxes," there were, besides themselves, half-a-dozen of the *soi-disant* gentry of Ashton; grocers' lads with a passion for the legitimate drama, and an aspect of general seediness; a large family of little children, under the wings of a particularly pretty nurse, to whom Darcy, *more suo*, found occasion to make himself incidentally agreeable; an old marine captain on half-pay, and a member of the local bar, rather addicted to the use of stimulants, and who smelt indifferently of snuff, brandy, and coal-tar.

Though the programme might have been inspired by Mr. Charles Kean, the most cynical critic could not affirm that Mr. O'R.'s success depended on the employment of scenic effects. "Our great Shakespearian interpreter," as the *Ashton Tomahawk* put it, "is independent of the upholsterer. It is the *man*, not the tailor, that we recognise in Mr. O'R."

The stage-machinery, indeed, was of the simplest kind, and *spectacle* was as studiously avoided as if the manager had been a Præ-Raphaelite. The orchestra, the whole strength of which was exhausted on the National Anthem, consisted of a blind fiddler, and a cracked drum, which was occasionally beaten in an independent and incidental way by any member of the company who chanced to be disengaged. The company, however, was the strong point. There was Mr. O'R. himself, the ubiquitous smuggler, who defied the officials of His Majesty's Revenue, and declared unhesitatingly that death was preferable to dishonour. There was the elderly gentlewoman who enacted the heroine, and who walked about in the rain in an evening dress and a plume of ostrich feathers; and the young lady who, with other odds and ends, had lost her character, and a good many of her front teeth. There was a diminutive imp of darkness in livery, who "made his first appearance on any stage," and who succeeded in removing certain pieces of furniture from the scene, without producing any striking casualty; and who shortly afterwards re-appeared, with a basket of eatables, in front of the curtain, trying to look as honest and mortal as he could, while he disposed of gingerbread and gingerbeer to the occupants of the pit. There was a gloomy individual with a tragic squint, who represented His Majesty's Revenue, and belonged—it was generally rumoured about the room—to a noble family not unknown in the neighbourhood. Finally, there was Samuel Smiles, Esquire, to whom Providence was provokingly unkind, but who encountered all the mischances of life in a cheerful spirit, and conquered them with a comic song.

The Great National Drama represented the career of an adventurous smuggler, and the various shifts to which he was put while engaged in defrauding the Revenue. He had (as occasionally happens in the Legitimate Drama) ruined his sweetheart, who ultimately, however, rescued him from the prison where he was lodged preparatory to his execution, and whom, in a mingled transport of gratitude, remorse, and *drink*, he made "an honest woman" upon the spot. To do Mr. O'R. justice, he went through his part with infinite gusto, and defended himself from the charge of murder (on the ground that the deceased was only a "gauger") in a style that would have brought down the Old Bailey. So that when the curtain fell upon 'Justice Vindicated and Virtue Rewarded,' in the form of the murderer marrying his mistress, the plaudits were loud and unanimous. Mr. O'R. was sensibly moved, and when he appeared before the curtain, with his bride at his side, and his hand on his heart, his emotion almost prevented him from acknowledging (as in oblivion of his obligations to royalty, he succeeded in doing), that it was "the proudest incadent of me loife."

Miles had sat, not very deeply interested, laughing

a little at the performances, and a good deal at
Darcy's commentaries, until the heroine appeared
on the stage; but there was something about her
which at once arrested the attention. Once she
might have been really pretty; but the face was now
haggard and attenuated, the cheek-bones seemed as
if they would cut through the tightly-drawn skin,
which barely covered them; and the cheeks had been
coarsely and carelessly smeared with red paint. Her
black hair, however (and by the imperfect lamp-
light Miles could not see that it was streaked with
iron grey), was still thick and abundant. She began
her part mechanically, repeating each syllable with
perfect precision, but in a tired, fagged, inanimate
voice, as if she had failed to catch the sense of the
words, or were speaking an unfamiliar tongue. But
she warmed as the plot thickened; and at last, when
her lover was about to die, the impending catastrophe
seemed to nerve her, and to quicken all her faculties
into a painful life. She awoke; the hard, dry,
parched look left her eyes; she was struggling with
an imminent peril, and the glance grew moist, and
warm with dramatic life. "Oh God! and must he
die, and to-morrow? He who has lain on this heart;
whom these arms have clasped. No. If mortal aid
can save him, he shall not die!" And she does save
him; and there is one glad moment of victory (when
her face bore a wonderful expression of triumph and
ecstacy), and then the brief illusion passes, and the

hard, dry, sad smile settles down again on the parched lips, and the thirsty eyes.

Miles felt, in spite of the rouge and the tawdriness, that there was something genuine here—a natural refinement inconsistent with the coarse setting. Darcy, too, had been arrested.

"That woman is a real actress," he said. "For the moment she forgot all the world—except the instant peril of her lover. That is the true artist instinct. There is something fine about the wreck. What is it? Is it her hair, I wonder?"

And so they sat out the first part of the entertainment; but a comic song proved rather too serious for them, and they rose to go.

"Here, you young imp," said Darcy, taking the rose from his button-hole, and addressing the youth who had that evening made his *début*, and who was now actively employed in vending and consuming his wares, "take that to Miss Julia Stanley, or whatever the lady's name may be, and tell her Mr. Darcy Langton asks a real actress to accept of it with his respects. Do you hear, sir?" as the imp looked up in his face with an impish leer, "do what I tell you."

## CHAPTER II.

#### VENUS ANADYOMENE.

> Aut quis
> Simpuvium ridere Numæ, nigrumque catinum
> Ausus erat?

AT high water the waves wash within a few feet of the fisher's cottage. When the wind blows from the east the windows are sometimes darkened, as by snow, with the white drifted foam.

This winter afternoon, however, the tide is out, and there is a long space of black tangled rock between the sea and the cottage door. 'Tis a hard black frost, and the steep braes down to the beach are white with snow. The day has been sullen, and heavy and lustreless, and the shade of the winter twilight (though it is little more than three o'clock) already gathers into the sky.

Upon the beach a lithe figure moves stealthily from rock to rock, or lies and watches silently in their wake. Over the bay, scattered parties of wild ducks are feeding busily,—making the most of the few minutes that are left them before the dark closes in. A pair of huge "annets," that look very white and stately on the tawny water, have been gradually nearing the spot where the watcher is concealed, when suddenly a sharp report is heard, and a light puff of blue smoke rises overhead. The grey eider splashes away seaward, but the drake lies still and motionless, and in a few minutes the east wind and the incoming tide lay him at the feet of the fowler.

He has taken up his prize, and is regarding curiously the beautiful dyes of the rich eider-down—so charmingly warm and cozy for this bleak winter-tide —when he hears his name called from behind.

"Peter, Peter!—come hame to your supper."

"I'm just coming, Elsie," replies the fisherman, picking up his gun.

"What's that you've gotten?" the girl asks, pointing to the duck, when he reaches the place where she waits for him.

"A bonnie bird—ane of the muckle annets. Ye'll get ane o' the tail feathers for your mutch, only the Souter will be seeking it to skin."

"Gae it him, if ye like, Peter; I wudna' wear't."

"Ye'd like a red ribbon better. The neist time I gang to the Brough I'm to fetch ane, ye ken, Elsie?"

"I thocht ye were to gi'e it to Kirsty Davidson, when I last heerd tell o't," retorts Elsie, looking a little wicked. "But ye may gi'e it her for what I care, Peter."

"Wha tell't you that?" asks the straightforward son of the sea. "I'll teach them to lee, the cutties."

They had reached by this time the little brook that babbles o'summer nights through the village. Masses of ice were floating about on its pools, and the stepping-stone was away. Elsie paused.

"How am I to get over?" she exclaimed.

"Tak aff your hose and sheen," says Peter, becoming mischievous in turn. "It'll warm you, my lass."

"O Peter!" she replied, with the least little bit of a quiver in her voice; "it's no kind o' you."

Elsie looked really very nice. Her thick woollen shawl was thrown over her head, and the bright little face, all rosy with the cold, peeped from under the coarse cloth hood. Her fisher's petticoat was not too lengthy, and the clean cut ankle, even in its grey worsted stocking, was a study in its way. The little foot was not over-delicate, but quick, decisive, and *prononcé*.

"I'll carry you over," Peter says, relenting, and putting his gun down.

Elsie, however, wouldn't hear of that, and tripped down the bank to make the trial herself. But when she had put her foot on one of the nearest pieces of ice, and felt it give way under her weight, her heart failed her, and she jumped back.

"How *am* I to get over?"

Peter quickly solved the difficulty. Coming behind unperceived, the young giant put his arms round her waist, and fairly lifted her off her feet, as he would have lifted a child. Skilfully taking advantage of the broken ice, he was across in a second.

"Noo, Elsie, I maun ha'e a kiss for luck," he said, before putting her down.

But Elsie would by no means agree to any such overture, and buried her face in her hands. A brief struggle ensued, and then Elsie, her cheeks even rosier than before, recovered her feet, and ran off, like a scared fawn, to the cottage, smoothing her shawl and hair as she went, while Peter returned for his gun.

The inside of the cottage was sufficiently plain and rude, but it looked comfortable—homely, yet home-like. A bright fire of peat burned on the floor and played upon the whitewashed walls, and the earthenware plates and saucers which were suspended in a "haik" along them. A bed, sunk in the wall, a substantial-looking "dresser," a seaman's chest, a few three-legged stools, and some wicker baskets filled with lines, formed the whole of the furniture. A "kettle of tea" hung over the fire, and simmered with cheerful composure.

In this little cabin old Peter Stephen and his wife had lived for five-and-thirty years. They were, if not perfectly happy, at least perfectly contented. The idea of "raising himself in the world" had never entered into Peter's head. His forefathers had lived in this village, and fished in this bay, all their days, and he was ordained and appointed to do the same. So it would be with his sons, and his sons' sons. To them there was no world beyond the limits of their little sea-bound settlement. In this century of hurry-skurry ("progress" they call it), it is pleasant to meet with such people. Their placid peace, their supreme repose, their perfect content, soothes the chafed spirit as a Greek statue does.

"Whar are my glasses, lassie?" old Peter inquires, when they are all disposed about the hearth. "Here's a letter frae your brither, Peter."

Elsie finds the spectacles, and the old man spells away patiently through his son's letter. Then she takes her knitting and sits down quietly beside old Hester, who is "shelling" mussels to bait the lines for to-morrow's fishing. Peter, stretched at full length along the chest, glances occasionally over Elsie's shoulder to see how the "netting" gets forward. Unhappy boy!—it is clear as day that the little witch has bound the good-humoured lazy giant fast in her meshes.

And Elsie? She is the niece of the gudewife; daughter of a brother who was lost long ago in these fickle Northern seas. Father and mother are both dead, and she has lived ever since she was a child in her aunt's house. Is she pretty? Pretty, certainly, though you can't tell why exactly: for no one feature is quite perfect. But there is a light, and gleeful, and saucy grace about her which makes her presence felt like a sunbeam. Her bright red hair, in its untutored waves and ripples—

> Like a clue of golden thread
> Most excellently ravelléd,—

is quite in keeping with the careless and dishevelled charm of her face. Red, fair reader, the hair undoubtedly is; that hated colour in its fiercest intensity; but only a reckless and unprincipled critic could assert that in this instance it is unbecoming. In that homely interior, and amid these stolid and weather-beaten figures, Elsie moves like an antique grace, like a line of Horace in the Digest, like this radiant sonnet by Edgar Poe:

> Helen, thy beauty is to me
>   Like those Nicéan barks of yore,
> That gently o'er a perfumed sea,
>   The weary, way-worn wanderer bore
>   To his own native shore.
>
> On desperate seas long wont to roam,
>   Thy hyacinth hair, thy classic face,
> Thy Naiad airs have brought me home
>   To the glory that was Greece,
> And the grandeur that was Rome.
>
> Lo! in yon brilliant window-niche
>   How statue-like I see thee stand,
>   The agate-lamp within thy hand!
> Ah Psyche, from the regions which
>   Are Holy-land!

in the midst of a load of rubbish by M. T. or J. S. B.

"Bill's in the Ingies," the father says, looking over his horn spectacles. "A gran' place belike; sic floors and wud. There's ae tree, he says, like the muckle kirk—wi' doors a' roun', and a great ha' inside that huds a thousan' folk, and the licht glintin' thro' the green leaves. 'Deed it's surprisin'. The Injun wives are nae bonnie, though—brown as peat divets, and deil a coat saving a bit dud roun' their wames. But they soom like fush."

"D'ye mind the Yak wives, feyther?" asks Peter. "When I gaed wi' Captain Brown to the sealghing last spring, ane swam on boord five mile aff the shore. Her skin canoe had been crunched by the ice. We thocht her a marmaid when she cam' bobbing up first, wi' her lang hair hangin' doun till her middle."

"Ay, they're surprisin' bodies, the Yaks. Troth, they mak' their bit boaties skite thro' the water uncommin! I've seen them dancin' through the jabble, when we were beatin' wi' reefed topsails, as skeely as a loom or a deuk. They're skeely craturs."

"Hardie says they dinna believe in heaven or hell," interposed old Hester. "They're dounricht misbelievers."

"I dinna ken," answered her husband, reflectively. "Some are better and some are waur; they are a' thieves, the haill crew of them, nae doobt; yet the craturs are no that bad either. I mind a harpooneer we left ahint ae summer, and they were unca guid till him—gaed him a wife, and bits of sealgh blubber to eat in the winter-time, and biggit him a snaw house. It was desperate dark, though; and he was like to gang daft when we cam' back. His wife, puir bit bodie, was loth to leave him, and grat like Elsie when she tined her sweetheart."

Elsie tossed her head contemptuously.

"I ne'er had a sweetheart to tine," quoth Elsie, "and I'm no seeking ony." Peter gave a tug at one of the stray curls that had escaped from her cap. "Dinna, Peter!—ye're makin' me miss the stich. Did ye no bring her back, uncle?"

"Na; that couldna be, though she was fain to come. He had tocht her a wheen things, and she was mair *ceeveeleesed* nor the rest. She swam oot to the ship when we were leaving, but we wouldna' lat her on boord. She griped at the ropes and swung roun' and roun' like a monkey; but some of the lads pushed her back, and then she fairly gaed in, and lay on the water just like a dead finnock. We let doun a boat and took her to the shore, and left her there—quiet eneuch, but greetin' like to burst."

Elsie's bright eyes moistened and flashed.

"That was cruel o' you, uncle."

"What could we dee, lassie?" answered the old man, composedly, in reply to the reproachful glance. "They're nae like ither folk, ye ken, and the minister says he disna' believe that they've sowls o' their ain. But I'm no sure o' that—I've aye thocht better o' the varmint sin syne. Were ye at the Ha' the day, Hester?"

"Aye; they've company wi' them, and they were needin' fush. Sae I had up the cod and ling ye got yestreen. The young Laird and him they ca' Maister Darcy are bidin' at the Ha', over auld Eele. He's a fine spruce lad, that Maister Darcy,—he was speerin' for you. They're for you to gang oot wi' them, Peter, to try the new boat the laird's gat frae Lunnon."

A loud rap at the door.

"Well, Peter," said a short, strong, wiry little fellow, who entered, "are you for the sea the morn? Whan's the tide?"

"Four, or thereby,—but we'd better be aff earlier, to catch the ebb. There's cod aff the Gutterbank, I'm jalousin', John."

"Phelim got a heavy shot roun' the Boroughhead," interposed Peter Junior.

"We'll try thereawa' on Mononday," said his father. "It's ower far to gang the morn. Hoo's the guid wife, John?"

"'Deed she's but poorly hersel', and wee Ailie's very sair wi' the hoast. Jean's no like hersel' ava,—it's her sairest time sin' she had Ailie; and I dinna understand it a'thegither—she's dreadful doun and disjaskit like."

"I'll gae doon and sit wi' her a bit," Elsie offers.

"Na, na—no the nicht, Elsie. It's bitter caul',

and the snaw's driftin' thick. But come doon and read her a chapter the morn; Jean likes your readin' better nor the lave, — she aye says — savin' Miss Corry."

So John stuffs a "live peat"—*vivum cespitem*, as a punning Horatian would say,—into his pipe, and trudges out into the snowy darkness. Then the rushlight is extinguished; Elsie says her prayers on her knees, unlooses the coarse grey woollen petticoat, and slips in to her cosy nest at the "butt" end of the dwelling; and deep sleep falls upon the cottage, thickly and silently as the falling snow.

# CHAPTER III.

### THE VILLAGE WELL.

> Gelidos inficiet tibi
> Rubro sanguine rivos
> Lascivi suboles gregis.

IT snowed heavily all night; but with the turn of the tide the white passion of the dark abated, and the waning moon waded knee-deep out of the storm-spent clouds. The pale apparition was looking back, through the sad wintry silence, upon the muffled earth, when the fishers' boats moved out to sea. That would be about four; and then in the little village the lights were again extinguished, and until the first cold streaks of morning seamed the horizon, all was still—still as the polar winter or the grave.

The village well is nearly half-a-mile from the village, on the ridge of the picturesque little ravine through which the Norburn winds. On the opposite bank, and still further inland, stands Hawkstone. The gentle slopes of the glen are there covered with sheltered plantations and the flower-beds of Corry's garden. Now the wreathed snow bends the branches, and *pallida mors* has been among the flowers.

Corry had erected a pretty simple fountain over the well. No unfit combination,—*mens sana in corpore sano*. It was a favourite *rendezvous* for gossips and sweethearts; and the granite slab at the side—where the matron, out of breath with the pull up the hill, might rest her limbs while the limpid water filled her pitcher — was seldom quite unoccupied. Even this morning, in the dim winter twilight, a solitary figure might be discerned—a form simply draped, that paced uneasily to and fro, and leant for a moment once and again upon the cold stone, not to rest, but like Lady Anne in the bitterness of her pain.

> She leaned her back unto a thorn,
>   Ah, well-a-day!
> And there she has her twa babes born;
>   The wind gaes by and will not stay.

An inner anguish, that rent her heart, as the pitiless knife rent the sacrificial kid's whose life-blood stained thy murmuring stream—*loquaces lymphæ tuæ*—O famed Bandusian well!

The morning was now fairly risen,—risen, we say, in obedience to ancient law and custom, though the word is not the right word to describe the dawn. No. The whole atmosphere had gradually *filled* with light; a grey, austere, uncertain light, which is properly the dawn-light, and to which the daylight is as the living face to the hushed and vacant *Death* of the Vatican. Every object on a sudden grew wondrously distinct; the black tangled rocks, the stones upon the beach, the white-gabled red-tiled cottages, with grey masses of peat-smoke hanging overhead, which the wind was too light to lift. A solitary fisher, in a blue-striped shirt, and with a wicker basket slung on his arm, came trudging across the sands on his way to the rocks, to gather bait— mussels and limpets—for the day's fishing. Then along the uneven ocean ridge wavered a pearly flush, the *tremola della marina* of the paradisal pilgrim; and one little cloud, just hanging on the verge of the horizon, suddenly burned into gold.

I don't know that the black veiled form spoke aloud; but the anguish of the pained spirit spoke in the abrupt gait and uneasy gesture; and it was not difficult to construe aright that silent but expressive speech.

"Ay! I mind the place like yesterday, and its near twenty year. There's the very stane Miss Corry would aye sit on, as quiet and bonnie as a queen, just because it was the place, she said, Master Miles liked best. He was a keen-spirited lad, and aye happy wi' little Katie, as he caed me. I wonder wha are in the servants' ha' now; auld Jean must be dead lang syne, she was an auld-farand body when I first kent her. They're no up yet; they wouldna mind an' I gaed roun'. Na, na, I couldna, it would kill me. O God!" she exclaimed, as if struck sorely by sudden pain, " surely thou wilt remember me in thy mercy!"

Unmindful of the thick snow, she fell upon her knees and prayed passionately. The agony at length wore itself away in tears and prayers, and she rose and seated herself on the slab. Though still white with the violence of the pain, she strove hard to regain her composure; and by the time a fisherwoman, she had observed climbing the hill, approached, the strong will had triumphed, and the white face behind the black veil had grown hard and impassive again.

"It's a caul mornin'," observed old Hester, in a friendly way, as she placed one of her pitchers below the thin jet of water. "Ye'll be bidin' at the ha', mem?" she added, after she had "got hold of her breath." Hester was by no means an old woman; she must have been ten or fifteen years younger than her husband, and though known as "Old Peter," to distinguish him from his son, the fisherman was still hale, and hearty, and vigorous. But Hester had grown stout as she grew in years, and her "breath" was now rather apt to play her false.

"Yes—no—I mean, I have been there," answered the stranger (whom Miles, had he been present, might possibly have recognised as the heroine of the Legitimate Drama) greatly embarrassed.

"Have been there!" repeated Hester, arrested by something in the voice.

"Oh, Hester!" the other burst out, unable to restrain herself any longer, "do you no mind me? I'm Katie, little Katie, your ain sister Katie."

Hester uttered a suppressed cry, opened her arms a little, as if she would have taken the wanderer into them, and then drew them back rigidly to her side.

"Na, na," she muttered, "I hae vowed a vow, and maun keep it."

Katie had sunk upon the seat, and with beseeching eyes and outstretched arms bent towards her sister. But when she saw that sister draw back, and the averted face grow cold and rigid, her manner altered, the shrinking, appealing timidity of her address departed, and she stood up and faced the other, quietly but resolutely.

"I ken what you mean," she said; "but I trow, Hester, you might ha' said ae kind word to your mother's daughter; God knows she disna hear ower mony."

"Katie Armstrong," said the other, "I made a vow to God, and keep it I wull. Your feyther's folk hae been in Norburn for a hunner' year, and a' that time nane but yoursel' has brought disgrace upon her folk. Katie, Katie, it was an ill time when we kent what you had deen. It killed the feyther: he was never himself after he heard that you were aff. And then I vowed that I would not tak your hand, nor look upon your face again. Ay, I have prayed," she continued bitterly, "that you might dee; that she wha had been our pride, our sinfu' pride, might never come back to be our shame. Depart, and trouble us not."

A quiver passed across the pale face at the mention of her father's name; but the bitter invective passed by, and did not touch her.

"And so the old man is dead," she said, quietly. "God rest his soul; it wunna be lang till we meet. You wished me dead, Hester," she continued, with the same impassive calmness; "weel, sometimes I ha'e wished it mysel'. But God did not take me away, and I thocht it best to bide His time. I ken that I ha'e sinned, sinned sairly; but He saw how I was tried, and may be He will pardon the sin. I ha'e fallen," she went on, "but no so bad as I micht. I was blinded and the wily tempter owercam', but I sinned not again. Eh! that was an awfu' wak'ning. But I couldna lie doon and dee, and so I ha'e worked on for twenty year—work as hard and honest as your ain—to keep body and soul thegither. Perhaps God has heard my prayers—perhaps He may; I think sometimes He has, but I canna tell; whiles the foul sin comes back on me, and drives me into the blackness o' darkness. I didna' come back to shame you: I meant not to ha'e seen ony o' you; but I was fain to look once mair on the auld place. Ay, ay!" she murmured to herself as her eye wandered over sea and land, and fastened on each well-remembered spot, "it's the same as ever,—just as it was when we made snawbas at the schule, and Alick wudna' tell the maister wha broke the window. Puir Alick! puir Alick! Alick wudna ha'e been sae hard on little Katie. But he was *awa* afore I gaed. Fare ye weel, Hester, and may ye never fin' the sair, sair heart I have whiles." And she turned away.

No contrast could be more marked than that between the two sisters. The one was rude and homely as any rustic: a life-long sorrow had refined the ore and purified the dross of the other. Intense pain has this effect. " I believe that by suffering," Heine says, in one of his far-reaching lines, "animals could be made human." But it is a fatal school in which to learn the usages of polite society. Poor Katie! not only had her body wasted, but one could see as she spoke that the mind too had wasted—had grown over keen, and sharp, and luminous. She was not exactly mad, perhaps; but her eyes flashed out at times the acute glances of mental disorder.

Katie turned away. Hester had listened with averted face to her sister's rapid words. She was moved; the woman's heart was touched—she did not like to own how deeply. Even her vow might have given way under the pressure; but when she looked up, Katie was already at a distance, beyond reach of speech.

"Dinna gang, Katie," she exclaimed involuntarily; but Katie heard her not, and she did not follow her.

"It's better no," she said, as she watched her disappear along the high road that led to Ashton. "I couldna ha'e ta'en her hame wi' me. What wud the neebors ha'e said? And little Elsie—na, na; it's best as it is."

She turned to lift her pitcher; the interview did not seem to her to have occupied more than a few seconds; but the pail had long been full, and the water was running over, and wearing a black channel through the snow. She lifted it, looked again in the direction Katie had gone, and then wended slowly down the brae to the cottage. A cheery voice was singing within, and a blithe nursery stave greeted her ears as she approached:—

> Now in there came My Lady Wren,
>   Wi' mony a sigh and groan,
> "O what care I for a' the lads
>   If my wee lad be gane?"
>
> Then Robin turned him round about,
>   E'en like a little king;
> "Gae pack ye out at my chamber door,
>   Ye little cutty quean!"

"Na, it couldna' be," repeated the old woman, "but I micht ha'e been cannier wi' her."

So Hester, according to her own judgment, had acted very prudently—too prudently, perhaps, in the judgment of the Immortals. For prudence is sometimes a most reckless spendthrift. I believe Hester came ultimately to feel that her prudence on this occasion had been very costly. The retribution which

> the powers that tend the soul
> To help it from the death that cannot die,
> And save it even in extremes,

exacted from her, as atonement to the God of Sacrifice, palsied her hand, and bent her head. Her own people, indeed, saw no connexion between the selfish act, and the sentence which the Unseen Judge pronounced upon it. But I believe, on my honour, that it broke the cherished idol of the mother's heart; that it quenched the fires on the hearth; that it left her old age homeless, desolate, and unloved.

# CHAPTER IV.

#### WHAT IS TRUTH?

*Thus we play the fools with the time, and the spirits of the wise sit in the clouds and mock us.*

DINNER is the great political institution of our beloved land. I do not speak of public dinners: I was never able to endure the solemn weariness of a public dinner—its speeches, smacking of the unctuous oil that adheres to oratorical lips, its songs redolent of brandy-and-water; and therefore that is a phase of social life that I am not qualified to discuss. But the daily dinner of the Englishman is what makes him an Englishman. A Frenchman never dines; he goes to a *café*, and trifles with trifles. So he grows fickle, capricious, feverish, and is never at rest except in a revolution. But Dinner (with a big D, please) is the sheet-anchor which holds the English gentleman and the English ploughman fast to his moorings. It is a great periodical fact, which brings him back every day to first principles, and in which, amid all the moral difficulties of his age, he can steadily believe. Theologians may snarl over the dry bones of creeds; politicians may wrangle over the dead bodies of constitutions; but when the Englishman comes home at six from his club or his counting-house to the solid reality of dinner, he feels that he has entered once more upon the grand "veracities" of life.

An historic tenderness for this palladium of English liberty is justifiable in an English writer; and the only controversies I have ever entertained have related to the subordinate inquiry, Under what conditions is it best to dine? It is at its best, probably, when you have partaken of nothing since breakfast; but "liability to lunch" is one of the weaknesses of a corrupt humanity. It is good when you have pulled six miles on end against a head wind, with a strong flood tide running dead in your teeth; it is good after a plunge in salt-water, after a speech which has gained your cause, after a neck-and-neck tussle with "the Eleven;" specially good when, like Achilles, you have dragged your slain adversary three times around the immortal links of St. Mungo. Each of these is good; but dinner after a hard day's December shooting, the ground covered with snow and the mere with wild-duck, eclipses them all. The assimilative apparatus is then in unrivalled working order; then undoubtedly, if ever, we approximate most closely to the ideal of digestive humanity.

Well—the December dinner is over at Hawkstone; the womankind have retired, and the gentlemen and the claret have drawn round the fire. Four gentlemen in all—the host, Miles Warrender, Darcy Langton, and the Reverend T. P. Jones,—Tudor Plantagenet Jones, as he was named at the baptismal font, and who must now be introduced to the reader.

Tudor Plantagenet was a scion of the Prince of Wales' Principality. His ancestry on the Tudor Plantagenet side (it was his mother, dear good soul! who got him named so) wandered into a mythical antiquity; but the Joneses at least were by no means fabulous, and carried on with great practical ability a lucrative retail business at the foot of Snowdon. Tudor Plantagenet, however, quitted the distilling line, entered the ministry, and had recently been entrusted with the superintendence of the Episcopal " souls " in the neighbourhood of Norburn.

Why he took to the Church it was difficult to determine. The responsibility of his position did not seem to oppress him severely. That he was commissioned to teach truth and righteousness to sinful mortals, and that the duty he had undertaken was one more perilous and weighty than any other, in no way disturbed his mind or affected his tranquillity. Nature had not cast him in one of her finer moulds. He was not compactly put together. His limbs were long and lanky, and rambled about in an irregular independent way, uncontrolled by any general principle. That part of the head "which gave itself out for a face" was curiously like an otter's, and was marked by the same wistful, restless, and inquiring expression. Otherwise Tudor was good-humoured, susceptible, and carnivorous,—often in love, and always hungry. The chronic famine of his Welsh mountains had descended and settled upon his stomach.

"Mr. Jones," said the old gentleman, "help yourself, and pass the bottles." (Both of which Mr. Jones did cheerfully, especially the first.) "Sport good to-day, Miles?"

"Not particularly; a couple of cocks down in the birch copse—a right and left to Darcy."

"Lucky fellow. I never had the chance. But sport is not now what it used to be. The birds get scarce and shy; you don't see any of the rare divers now, Miles? They were splendid fellows. My bag used to be worth looking at then; but that was before either of you lads was born."

"Please, don't make me worse than I am," said Darcy. "It's bad for a man at the bar. They don't believe in you there till you are going down hill. In other professions, when a man loses his wits, they put him in the asylum. In ours they put him on the Bench.'"

"Do you shoot, Jones?" asked Miles.

"No. Murder is not seemly in a minister;

besides, I can't," replied Jones, who was often nervously honest in his admissions.

"Murder," said Darcy, looking him full in the face ; "you don't mean to tell me, Jones, that you disapprove of murder?"

Jones was taken aback at this unexpected inquiry, and could only murmur some inarticulate observations about "limitations of the general principle."

"Yes," said Darcy, "as a general principle, I admit that it may be carried too far. De Quincey was scarcely guarded enough. As one of the fine arts, it *is* calculated to demoralize. Still there are many cases in which, as a moral duty, it becomes imperative. Were I a Calvinist, I should, like Saturn, devour my offspring in infancy—the boys at least. It is inconceivable that these little children of the devil can ever belong to the elect. So I would take care to make things snug in time. What do you think of suicide, Sir Maxwell?"

Sir Maxwell was as gentle and artless-hearted a man as ever lived; but in the metaphysical world, where he spent most of his time, he grew more venturous than Spinoza. All the questions which are practically tabooed by our social sensitiveness he thought out clearly and discussed fearlessly. His childlike simplicity could never appreciate the barriers and fences which we have raised up between us and these questions. He saw no impiety in free

## WHAT IS TRUTH?

thought, no blasphemy in philosophic denial, and there was an indescribable charm in the naïve and piquant fearlessness of his mind. Darcy liked to get him on these proscribed topics. To the man of the world it was like exercising a new sense.

"Why, as to suicide, it's a very nice question. I don't quite see my way out of it; but I cannot say that I think it expedient, at least. It won't do for a man to try the next world, just because he has got into a mess in this. Depend upon it he will find the difficulties there quite as intricate as those he has tried to shirk here. He has a certain drill to learn, and if he doesn't go through his training here, he will elsewhere—if not now, *afterwards;* that is all. The child is more teachable than the man, and it will probably be better for him in every respect to take his schooling in time."

"Suicide is the act of a coward," said Jones.

"I'm not so sure of that," answered Darcy. "It needs some courage to take *that* plunge, I can tell you. It's very easy to talk about suicide; but it is a different thing when you have got the cup of hemlock between your teeth, and contemplate in a practical way the infinite possibilities it contains. No; it is indolence, not cowardice, that drives a man to self-destruction. He is too lazy to set himself seriously to unravel the skein, and so he cuts the knot."

"Jones means, I take it," interposed Miles, "that

there would be more courage in stoutly resisting the enemy, than in turning your back upon him. Does not Sir Thomas Browne say that 'where life is more terrible than death, it is the truest valour to dare to live?' It is never courageous to retreat, unless it be necessary."

"But it may be necessary sometimes?" asked Sir Maxwell, musingly. "I can fancy such a case. You are struck down by a lingering, incurable, torturing disease, which must kill you sooner or later, and in the mean time deprive you of reason, incapacitate you for work or thought. Are you not then entitled to die—to take the matter into your own hands? I don't say that you are; but I don't exactly see why you should not be."

"An interference with the laws of nature," said Miles.

"Yes; but we continually interfere with her laws. If I break my leg and it mortifies, I cut it off—*that* is an interference. But if I did not cut it off, I should die by a law of nature. This incurable disease is another law—the law is, that in the course of a certain number of weeks or months the disease will kill me. Now, may I not assist nature a little—give her an impulse forward, so to speak? In fact, there is less interference in the one case than in the other: *there* I artificially evade the law, *here* I aid and abet it."

"Exactly," said Darcy; "rapidly secure the result

to which Nature blunders by inches. My dear sir, you would make an admirable lawyer. I should like you for a leader."

"Very ingenious talk," replied the matter-of-fact Miles, "but it wants substance. You don't either of you believe what you say. 'Thou shalt do no murder' is an old commandment, graven not only on the Tables of the Law, but on the heart, the reason, the affections of man. Life is fenced in by our strongest fears and our most cherished instincts. No one has a right to touch with his rude hands its delicate and mysterious chords."

"The soldier and the hangman," answered Darcy, "have rough hands, and yet you pay them both. Why? Merely because, as Jones observed, the sacredness of life has certain limits, and when these are transgressed—when, for instance, life becomes an intolerable hindrance—the natural respect which we owe can no longer be enforced."

Jones was horrified at the idea of being the author of such a theory, and vigorously disclaimed the sentiment.

"Well, if you didn't," said Darcy, "I beg your pardon. But the idea is quite true, notwithstanding. I was talking," he continued, "with one of your brethren the other day about a matter upon which a good deal has been written lately. The proposition I maintained was, that when a man thinks and speaks sincerely, no matter what, you have no right to condemn him for his opinions. They are, in relation to himself, true, real, the logical development of his inner man."

"Doubtless," said the philosopher; "but you rather evade the point. There is, I suppose, such a thing in this world as absolute truth,—wherever it is to be found, at the bottom of the well, or elsewhere: the *where* being, I grant, not as yet perfectly settled. Either the Hindoo, or the Mahometan, or the Englishman, or some one else, has got hold of it. But if one, why not all? If you see it, why should I not see it? And if I don't see it, but see something quite other in its place—something else which is not truth at all, but pestilent error, is not that proof in itself that I do not choose to see the truth; and loving the darkness rather than the light, am responsible for my perversity of vision? You assume in your argument that a man may sin honestly. I don't say that he may not; but the assumption needs to be examined."

"True," said Miles; "yet I agree with Darcy. Some men in this world are not responsible for their perversity; goodness is a thing which early associations, imperfect culture, social injustice, the world's hardness, has made impossible to them. They cannot see otherwise than they do: their minds have been set in a certain rut; and their errors in consequence are perfectly honest. If such men, obeying selfish or prudential motives, were to profess absolutely true opinions, they would profess opinions which, in so far as they are concerned, would be positively false."

"The argument, I own, looks a little startling on the outside. It seems, as my reverend friend said, to deny the existence of absolute truth altogether."

"Not at all," replied Miles. "When I say to a man, 'Be true, be sincere; tell the truth and shame the Devil, who is the father of lies,' I am giving him the very best advice. Perhaps it would be well to say to him at the same time, 'See that your nature is true; see that you have not allowed prejudice and custom to warp your intellect, to bias your judgment. Search out and cast away from you whatever will not stand the most searching scrutiny.' Perhaps some of our teachers who preach voluminously on the former text, neglect the latter a little. Still, we may be sure that, after the most thorough scrutiny, a residue of involuntary and transmitted error must be left in every man's constitution; and for the diseased opinions and judgments which are the logical *outcome* of this plague-spot, it is impossible to hold him responsible."

"And of course," added Sir Maxwell, "we don't assert that it is a matter of no moment what a man believes, whether it be true or whether it be false. It *is* a matter of moment to him if he knock his head perpetually against the Universe. Believe me, the Universe will bring him sooner or later to his senses.

'This is not a precipice,' he says, 'I believe it to be a turnip-field,'—and he walks over it and breaks his neck. When in the next world he recovers from the effects of the fall, be sure that for the future he will admit that a precipice is a precipice, and not a turnip-field. So that in one respect his fall will have done him good; it will have knocked one false notion, at least, out of his head. And thus, perhaps, it may be with all the material and spiritual falseness in our nature: experience will winnow it by degrees: the fire will purge the dross. But come," he added, " I hear the lassies singing: we shall have coffee in the drawing-room to-night."

So ended a conversation which I have thought proper to record, and which the reader may consider at his leisure, if he is so minded. I do not write it down as being specially characteristic of the different speakers; I write it down because I think that it is, as to the subjects discussed, not altogether without value of its own. I am acquainted with critics who believe that such topics should not be treated except in books avowedly devoted to philosophy or theology. A drama should be a drama; a romance a romance; a moral essay a moral essay. The literary artist is quite entitled to reason in this way, and perhaps no book is entitled to *live* which neglects the condition. But the social, political, or religious reformer is entitled to reason differently. He uses the poem, the romance, and the essay to serve his own purpose; to enforce the cause which he has at heart, and to which he devotes his life. If the people read a drama with avidity, while they altogether refuse to read a sermon or a political treatise, the politician or the theologian loses an invaluable weapon when he declines to employ the dramatic form. The novel is the great literary vehicle of the present day; reformers of every class have in turn made use of it; and that it has popularized and familiarized many abstract forms of thought, many admirable philosophical speculations, which might otherwise have failed to obtain a hearing, cannot be denied. This consideration must be allowed to modify the criticism we pass on such books. "Compare Sir Walter Scott and Mr. Disraeli!" the critic exclaims, "you will find more flesh and blood in one of the Waverley novels than in all the Chancellor's put together."[*] But Disraeli wrote *Coningsby*, and *Sybil*, and *Tancred*, not to limn a character, but to ventilate a creed, and create a party. We must not, therefore, judge his novels as we judge those of our ordinary novel writers. We do not ask, Is this a first-rate romance?—but, Has it served the cause it was written to serve? When that cause has triumphed, it may be put away. When the enemy is wounded to the death, the weapon may

[*] At the same time I am not prepared to adopt the critic's conclusion,—the life and conversation of the young "swells," for instance, in Mr. Disraeli's novels, being, I think, truer to nature than anything that we have—out of Mr. Leech's "portraits."

be hung up in the banquet hall. "A thing of beauty is a joy for ever." A perfect piece of art—an Apollo or a Cymbeline—has a right to endure upon the earth while time endures. It draws its life from a perennial spring. Unlike fashion, it never grows old. The coat, the cloak, the ruffles of this year are out of date next year. Founded on no large principles, drawing their nourishment from the fancy of the saloon and the caprice of the boudoir only, they perish with the fancy and the caprice. Thus it is with the logic of the lawyer and the eloquence of the statesman; and thus it is also with the poem, the drama, and the picture, when these are used as instruments to enforce the politics of the hour. Immortal forms rush into the battle, and are stricken and perish like mortals. But the contest at least becomes exciting when the gods mingle with men; when wit, and wine, and storied song, and the fire of genius, are used for the common purposes of life,— to plant a party in power, to hurl a demagogue into the dirt out of which he sprang, to scathe a political charlatan. True, genius so employed must quickly die: but let no vain moan be made over its ashes. The fleeting satire serves its end, and rounds its orb, as well as the severe and lofty epic. The politician who writes a poem to bespatter his rival does not care that it should survive the fall of the Minister. *Coningsby* is dead, but Mr. Disraeli is Chancellor of the Exchequer. Sometimes, indeed, the ephemeræ do not die with the day; sometimes the brightest sparks are struck out in that sharp and angry collision; sometimes a trifle, lighted by the electric fire, outlives the annals of an empire. The Attic salt preserves them fresh and green; and the nicknames of Aristophanes survive when the Phidian Zeus has perished.

## CHAPTER V.

#### PRINCE CHARLIE.

Singing of men that in battle array,
Ready in heart and ready in hand,
March with the banner, and bugle, and fife,
To the death, for their native land.

THE lassies were "lilting" in the drawing-room; both Alice and Corry sang Norland songs sweetly enough, though neither was perhaps a very consummate performer. Sir Maxwell got hold of a philosophical treatise, which proved that everything was true because everything was a contradiction in terms, and settled himself in an easy chair by the fire; the young men gathered round the singers. Jones, whose tongue the "sunny south" had unloosed, confided his mischances to Mrs. Menteith, who listened placidly to their recital as she hemmed a handkerchief.

"We will be Jacobites for one night," said Darcy. "Down with the Hanover rats, and let the White Rose flourish! What say you, Miss Evelyn?"

"O yes,—I am a vicious Jacobite. Corry, who is

a Whig, and false to the good cause, says that I am a renegade. But it is not true; *she* is the traitor."

"As Montrose remarked, ' *Thou* traitorous and untrue!' But I don't believe it. The heiress of the Menteiths untrue to her religion!"

"Thank you, Mr. Darcy," replied the fawn-eyed; "Alice likes to appropriate all the heroism to herself. But she is a wretched coward at heart, and would have run away, I believe, at the first shot."

"Now, don't be abusive, Corry; you know I have the heart of a lion."

"You do look rather fierce at times, I admit," said Miles. "Do you recollect how you shook your mane the other day when you found little Tony Lumpkin (the *wee devilikee*, as they call the little villain) walloping his sister? You rushed into the fray most valorously; but when the imp unexpectedly showed fight, and doubled his chubby fists——"

"Stop," exclaimed Alice. "Do not believe him. It is a story altogether;" and then she retreated to the piano, and dashed into the middle of a stirring Jacobite fray—

> Wha wudna' fight for Charlie?
> Wha wudna' draw the sword?
> Wha wudna' up and rally
> At the royal Prince's word?

"Yes, dear Charlie! we would have loved you, and bled and died for you, better than that high-cheeked Miss Flora the story-books make such a fuss about, let them say what they like."

"Leave Flora alone, please; we have not come to her yet. The clans are gathering, and the Royal standard streams o'er Lochaber. Let us have a battle-piece—cloudy and brilliant."

"Help me, Corry,—no, we will keep you for the sad finale," and Alice sung with infinite spirit—

> Cam' ye by Athol, lad wi' the philabeg,
> Down by the Tummel or banks o' the Garry?
> Saw ye the lads, wi' their bonnets and white cockades,
> Leaving their mountains to follow Prince Charlie?

Alice was nearly naturalized; and the foreign accent barely touched the song, and did not hurt its Doric.

"Now, Corry, the clans are broken, and poor Prince Charlie is hunted across the muir. It is your turn now." Corry sat down and played with a pretty, child-like simpleness a sad coronach over the beaten array,—

> "O no, no, no!" the wee bird sang,
> "I've flown sin' mornin' early;
> But sic a day o' wind and rain—
> Oh, wae's me for Prince Charlie!"

"And so, goodbye to Prince Charlie," said Miles, after a pause.

"Do the common people here," asked Darcy, "still recollect him? In England our country-people know nothing of their history."

"This was a keen Jacobite district, and we all spilt our blood for the good cause. So the Prince is better kept in mind here than elsewhere. Some of the best of these old songs were written within a few miles of this, and the people still sing them at the Harvest Home, and talk to you of 'Charlie' as of an old friend. But we are all growing by degrees too wise for this. The associations which a district shut up within itself could not help preserving, stand no chance when the *Times* makes its appearance every morning. People find other things to think about—things not very much worth thinking about, perhaps, and that make no permanent impression on the heart—and so the old names, and the old stirring histories, that mixed with the life-blood, and silently enriched the imagination of a whole people, are carried away, and nothing is got to replace them. Thus, at certain points our modern life grows poor and deteriorated,—though perhaps it gains at others."

"Your cousin is a fine old Tory, Miss Menteith, and should be put in a glass case as a curiosity." The fawn-eyed looked indignantly at the mocker; mockery of this sublime cousin of hers seemed to her little short of impiety. But Darcy did not heed. "I'll tell you what he did at Rome. Of course we went to the Vatican, and the Capitol, and other places where there are Apollos, and Laocoons, and

Raphaels, and Michael Angelos and such trifles. Sublimely indifferent, Mr. Warrender walked after the crazy lawyer, whose raptures he would not understand, and thought it altogether a bore. 'I don't care about these imperfectly dressed people,' he said. 'I would rather have a beggar-boy by Wilkie or a clump of pines by Turner.' However, this impassive gentleman always disappeared at an untimely and unrighteous hour—before I was out of bed, in fact—and as he could give no authentic tidings of himself, I set Massimo to watch him."

"That wasn't fair," broke in the fawn. "I am surprised at you, Mr. Darcy."

"Oh! I was set to look after him, you know. Besides, a lawyer sometimes does evil that good (in the shape of promotion or otherwise) may come. Now, where do you think he went?"

"To breakfast," exclaimed Jones, abruptly (he and Mrs. Menteith were listening to the narrative), as if he had fallen upon a fine nest-egg, and wished to keep it all to himself.

"Well, not exactly; indeed, he always came back with a remarkably keen appetite, I noticed. However, Massimo followed him one morning and saw him cross the bridge of St. Angelo, and enter St. Peter's. When Massimo arrived, his master was prostrate on his knees, worshipping a graven image——"

"Of the Virgin!" exclaimed Alice, in a tone of constrained horror. "Mr. Warrender an idolator! How could you?"

"No, not the Virgin—he hadn't the taste for that; many is the Virgin I have prayed to in my time, especially these Raphael ones, with their rapt eyes and heavenly lips. No, not the Virgin—that might be forgiven—but a starched, wizened, eighteenth-century-looking old scarecrow, in yellow marble. Massimo couldn't make it out at all, and thought his lord had gone crazy, as English lords are in the habit of doing—an opinion, perhaps, not very wide of the mark. However, I went off forthwith to examine this queer saint, and then I found that he had been saying his prayers to a fallen royalty,—'King of England' the inscription called him. There's something catching in mental disorder. Do you know, I felt half inclined to do likewise."

"Delightful!" said Alice. "It is so pleasant to know that the age of chivalry is not quite past."

"Darcy has heightened the colouring a little," said Miles, laughing; "not to mention his having substantially altered the facts. It was a boyish whim. I believe I went there to see *that* tomb more than anything else. I used to dream about it when I was a boy; my old nurse had a melancholy rhyme in which Prince Charlie complains that his dust cannot rest out of Scotland, and prays any kindly clansman to carry it back to the old land. I believe it was some association with this ditty that stirred my piety."

Alice and Darcy sat down to a rapid game at chess; Corry continued at the piano, and ran her fingers idly over the chords,—Miles at her feet in a low sofa-like chair, which overflowed with cushions, listening indolently to the careless music which the instrument discoursed.

"Miles," a soft voice whispered under cover of the music, "I think you were quite right. How I should like to go to Rome!"

"We will go one day," said Miles, trying to look into the eyes;—but the music faltered and ceased.

Jones, having finished the narrative of his mishaps—his landlady, it appeared, had lost all feeling for the beautiful and good, and charged him fifty per cent. on his sugar—rose to go, and Miles saw him to his nag. The night was clear, cold and frosty—a winter night cresseted with stars, and dazzling you as Lady Emmeline dazzles you with her diamonds.

"Tell the Dean," said Miles, as they parted, "that I want to see him. I will ride over to Otterburne during the week.".

# CHAPTER VI.

### THE NORTH MAIL.

> Not one except the Attorney was amused,—
> He, like Achilles, faithful to the tomb,
> So there were quarrels, cared not for the cause,
> Knowing they must be settled by the laws.

DURING the night the frost broke up, and Darcy left in the morning. Alice was not in general a very early riser; but this morning she was up before breakfast. But these untimely hours did not agree with her, seemingly; at least she was subdued and quiet, not by any means so bright and saucy as she could be. Early rising, in fact, under any circumstances, is a mistake, and ought to be discouraged. You feel dirty and disagreeable the whole after day,—obnoxious to your acquaintance, and a burden to yourself.

The groom drove Darcy to Ashton, and Miles drove himself to Carlyon. Two or three days thereafter the following letter arrived:—

DEAR MILES,—I am once again settled in the old ace. It looked sadly shabby and disreputable when I opened the door. Who could have believed in the rosy evenings it has witnessed,—*noctes cœnæque Deûm?* "O the mad days that I have spent! and to see how many of mine old acquaintance are dead!" It needs a soft hand to set it right; and my Abigail's are as hard as horn.

I was five minutes too late—as usual—for the coach at Ashton. Jim, who is a plucky lad, offered to "catch it" in half an hour, but I had more respect for the laird's horse-flesh, and so deposited my baggage at the *Warrender Arms* (whence our theatrical friends have flitted), and determined to make myself easy for the day. After an incidental flirtation with the rather prettyish barmaid, I went down to the harbour, and had a crack with certain sailors just returned from warring with Polar bears, and finally fell in with Tudor Plantagenet, who asked me to dine with him at his lodgings, and go to Lady Gardiner's tea and cookies afterwards. As I had my own views about his larder and landlady, we compromised matters. He came and dined with me—a more satisfactory arrangement, as he subsequently allowed. In justice to mine host of the Warrender, I must not omit to notice a bottle of Lafitte, which he produced with a strong show of feeling; and which, if I may judge from his nods, becks, and wreathed smiles, has not materially contributed to the increase of the Imperial revenue. Pity *that* trade is all up,—we never see such claret now as we used to get from your grandfather when we were boys. Our youth, alas! is dead; but amid its faded roses the bouquet of that divine Mouton is ever fragrant.

Poor Jones,—he is a good-natured cub, after all. The rosy nectar quite warmed his heart (I dare say it would be more exact to say his midriff); and he made me the custodian of a great many valueless little schemes and secrets which he hugs in private. It appears that he is always looking out for something to turn up,—a chaplaincy at Hong-Kong, or the Gold-coast, or the penal settlements. He makes incessant applications, which are never answered; and at the present moment is quite confident that he will be appointed to Christchurch, because he asked for it last week. He must have carried sad havoc into the hearts of his fair hearers,—wherever he has come and *been* seen, he has conquered. He has never, however, been positively "hooked," as he calls it, till now. Miss MacGroggy, his intended, is the daughter of MacGroggy the corn-dealer, a nice, blooming, red-cheeked little thing, who positively seems to like him. We met her in the street, and he introduced me, and was on the point of proposing to bring me to dine with them. Indeed, this engagement is a first-rate thing for Jones—capital feeds at Mac's, and unlimited kissing of Minny; and then he is so poor that there is no chance of his being brought to book. So, in effect, he gets the eating and the rest, *gratis*.

Lady Gardiner's *fête* was rather a trial,—the sort of thing the early Christians went through. The six gawky daughters, two evangelical parsons, and the cracked piano, nearly drove me frantic. She spoke about you in a dubious way: you are not of the elect, but you belong to a decent family. I should not wonder, were you to make up to one of the unmarried, that she might be induced to overlook the defects in your religious training. Think of this, my dear Miles, and luck be with you.

Well,—next morning I mounted the mail, and dashed away South,—past cities, and churches, and farm-houses, and quiet lanes, and then across the estuary of a mighty river hushed by the tide and the frost, and so on in the darkness to the Northern Capital. At the last stage but one, our old friend, the Farintosh, entered the coach with a huge bundle of papers, tied with red tape, under his arm. He was delighted to see me, but *atra cura* sat above his eyebrows.

"This is a teind business," he said, with a sigh, squinting at the bundle of papers (which he had placed as far from him as the circumstances admitted), as Christian squinted at the bundle on his back, or Sinbad at the hairy old chap whose knees were knuckled into his ribs. "The minister of Cladach-clough wants an augmentation of stipend, that is to say, an addition to his income. A very natural feeling you suppose; but unluckily, certain unprincipled heritors start up and exclaim, Bless the fellow, what does he mean? Where does he expect to go? We haven't got a halfpenny to give him. To which my client replies (he's a prodigiously learned old dog, and drinks like the fish in his own lochs), "That though the infeudation of teinds to laymen was forbidden by Innocent III. under the heavy penalty of the want of Christian burial, and the yet heavier one of eternal damnation, yet that by the Act, 1567, cap. 10, commonly known as the Assumption of Thirds, the lords of erection, or titulars of the teinds, were required to surrender such a proportion as the Commissioners of Plat might determine; that the lands of Towie, not being held *cum decimis inclusis*, were liable *pari passu;* that if the thirlage of the lands of Macorkindale imported an astriction of the tithes to the Laird of Drumwhalloch, that could only be because the servitude had been created prior to the Act of Charles, which was not the case, and was at least no business of the minister, nor of the titular, who might allocate any teinds that he chose, seeing that there was no locality, and that though the leases had expired, the tenants continued to hold on tacit relocation." By Jove, isn't it awful? I have wakened every night for the past week in a cold perspiration, dreaming of the *Purgatorio,*—a straitjacket, and a shaved head. However, it will be over to-morrow. Will you come and hear us at it?

Eleven, sharp." And as I got into a cab at the *Royal*, I promised to attend.

Having a spare hour next morning before the train started, I kept my engagement. The court was sitting, and I took my place on a side bench to watch the proceedings. "That's the President, you know," said my friend, coming to where I sat, "looking as fresh as a lark,—he don't seem a year older since you left us; and that is the Vice on his right. The two cleverest men in England at this moment, I take it."

True enough, Miles,—able men both. The President, serene, luminous, equitable; never swayed by passion, never bent by prejudice; an orderly and abstemious intellect, disinclined, though not unfitted, to deal with principles and abstract propositions, and clinging to fact with characteristic tenacity. Orderly —for the manner in which he marshals the leading facts of a case, groups them into relation, and keeps them in subordination to the end to which he is cautiously working, is often quite admirable; so that when the end does come, it seems to you, without further demonstration, that no other is possible, and that any argument would be superfluous: abstemious—never throwing away a word, or a scrap of logic, or a grain of sense; always equal to the argument, never below it, and (an infirmity almost as common with men of great powers) never *above* it; never expending force when it is not demanded, and never feeble, even when combating a truism, or extinguishing a bore. This abstemiousness is not timid carefulness or an artificial restraint; it is the natural fruit of a supreme sense of order. When he has arranged, analyzed, and sifted, with untiring patience, all the facts of the case, it is wonderful, in many instances, how little remains to be done. The "logic of fact" is "inexorable" when we can get at it; but it needs an intellect like the President's to disengage the fact from what is accidental or superfluous,—to sweep away the rubbish, and make the true reading visible. This is a very fine and a very peculiar faculty. For an indolent and speculative mind dislikes facts, slurs them over, commonly mistakes their application and value, and then retreats, from the chaos which it cannot shape into order, on metaphysical subtleties or a general principle. The judge who retires majestically upon "the eternal principles of justice," and leaves the Judicature Act to take care of itself, possesses, as a rule, reasoning faculties that are either slothful, feeble, or helplessly inaccurate.

The Vice-President was, as you know, a great advocate: his speech in a *cause celèbre*, of which all the world has heard, is one of the finest of these times, —symmetrical in arrangement, and executed with a consummate knowledge of strategy and effect. When he was opposed to you, however good your cause might be, you felt that you were doomed. He convinced you that you were a rogue. No innocence could resist the weight of that immaculate indignation; it could as well resist the Ten Commandments. He was neither witty nor sarcastic; but the haughty scorn of his virtue, the intense bitterness of his integrity, crushed its victim to pieces. His presence was imposing, and he knew how to use it to perfection. He folded his black stuff-gown about him with the offended dignity of a Chatham. The contemptuous curl of his nether lip was deadly. His manner was singularly still and impassive, until the victim was fairly in his toils, when he came down upon him like a thunder-clap. As a judge, he is powerful, intrepid; a profound civilian, a great logician. If it be possible to rescue our jurisprudence from the meanness and empiricism of modern practice, the Vice-President is the man to do it.

The Farintosh made an impressive appeal. His client's parish was extensive and important; Mr. Malthus's arguments had had no effect upon the nursing mothers of the flock, and the population had increased outrageously; the necessaries of life were not to be purchased for love or money; the heritors were as rich as Crœsus, and the minister as poor as Job. It was a cheerful picture, but his adversary disposed very summarily of the Farintosh's statistics. The parish was a large one, no doubt, but it consisted entirely of fresh-water lochs, and sand-banks covered by the sea at high water; snuff, tobacco, and whisky, on which life was exclusively maintained in the district, could be had for an old song; nobody lived within ten miles of the church, except seals, otters, and rock-cod. What augmentation the minister succeeded in getting I did not stay to learn: the argument on Drumwhalloch's thirlage was not concluded when I departed; it is possible that they are talking on at this very minute.

The town is as empty and dull as heaven (according to the Calvinistic theology); and the only jest afloat is one that Mowbray made last week. Some one asked him to give your sapient neighbour Lord M—— the vacant *Thistle*. Mowbray pondered — hesitated — declined. "He would—*eat it!*" he urged gravely. Neat and incisive, is it not? *Vale, iterumque vale!*

# IV.

## CONFESSION.

# CHAPTER I.

### EFFIE ON THE ESK.

> Three years she grew in sun and shower;
> Then Nature said—" A lovelier flower
>   On earth was never sown;
> The child I to myself will take:
> She shall be mine, and I will make
>   A lady of my own."

It was a sultry afternoon in June,—twenty years ago, let us say. Though the thunder was muttering among the higher hills, the sun shone brightly enough on the blue valley of the Esk. And among the pines of Otterburne shafts of golden mist came down all day through their shattered branches, and rested upon the white lilies and the wood anemones at their feet.

At one point, near a sharp bend in the river, the rocks rise abruptly from its bed. The precipice there cannot be less than a thousand feet in height. It is covered with spruce, except at intervals where the light soil, unable to sustain the weight of vegetation, has given way, leaving channels for the floods of red clay which the rain brings down. On the summit a small space is cleared of wood, and a flock of goats with twisted horns and pointed Vandyke beards graze eagerly on the short sweet mountain grass. The southern slope is very gentle, and the vegetation, protected from the biting "Nor'easters," belongs to a kindlier and more delicate fauna. The deep green and the ragged masses of the pine are exchanged for the quivering leaves of the birch and the white spray of the hawthorn. In spring the wood burns with the golden fire of the laburnum.

Among the cover on this southern slope a picturesque wood-lodge had been built many years previously. It lay among the hawthorns and the laburnums, as the mossy nest of the field-lark lies in the grass. You could not in your dreams imagine a more perfect seclusion. Except for the light blue smoke which rested upon the tree-tops, and rose up and died in the deeper blue of the sky, no stranger could have suspected the existence of a human dwelling-place. Hidden from prying eyes with anxious jealousy, and lined with green lichens and purple mosses, it inevitably recalled the nest of some shy, jealous, and solitary bird—a wild-duck or a cushat.

From the top of the ridge, where the goats are browsing, the prospect is noble and commanding. A thousand feet below, the rapid river frets its rocky bed. Turner-like vignettes of the white perturbed waters are visible through the encrusted green of the pines. On the opposite bank lie the wide lawns and woods of Otterburne, and the old Keep itself looking as cheerful in the sunshine as such a musty piece of antiquity can do. A stone could easily be dropped from this among its angular pepper-boxes; but were the rock itself to fall it would disturb no living creature, except perhaps the round-eyed owl who keeps a drowsy ward over the ivied gateway. The New Place is a mile down the river, at a turn where the river, escaping from its pent-up passage through the rocks, breathes a moment, ere it resumes its stormy march upon the sea.

On either side of the river, here, and down to the sandy sea-bents, stretches a narrow stripe of level land—peculiarly fertile, growing the finest pasture in the north, and feeding the finest sheep in the world. Inland, however, the hills rise rapidly, through their green mantle of pines, to the bleached and naked granite, among whose " quarries " the snow often lies through the summer. The Graic guard the western entrance to the Pass, but on the east it widens into a noble amphitheatre, through which the eye follows the stormy onset of the river, till the smoke of battle is lost among the lowlands of Moravia. On a clear morning before sunrise, a white sharp line cuts the eastern horizon; but during the day a luminous reflection upon the distant sky alone indicates that the sea lies *there*.

Among the heather on the summit of the ledge, a

rosy-cheeked child was lying fast asleep. The lassie had tired herself clambering after the mountain blaeberries, a small wicker basket of which, covered with lime-leaves, was placed beside her. She had thrown her brown broad-brimmed gipsy hat, with its bright pink sash, carelessly aside; and through the dark cloud of curls the prettiest little mouth in the world peeped out, like a bunch of cherries. Such dainty little red lips! The blaeberry juice had stained them, perhaps, or a bee had stung them as it passed to the foxglove; but Titian had never a richer red on his palette. The mouth, too, possessed a certain defined character of its own, which you could not miss—the upper lip, though very delicately cut, was quite firm and decided, and the under one protruded slightly, indicating a composed, perhaps even haughty temperament. It is not often that a smile plays about a mouth of this stamp, but when it does it is the sweetest and rarest of any. It comes direct from the soul. One can guess the eyes that must belong to such lips, but they are not visible just now—the white lids are closed upon them, and the long dark lash is folded along the brown rosy cheek. She makes a charming picture, this comely little maiden in her white dress; if you were a poet you might fancy that among the rough pines and the dark hills you had come upon an angel unawares. Indeed I once noticed her, I am sure, in the disguise of a red-cheeked cherub, looking down with grave welcome on the Virgin, in a picture by Murillo at Seville.

This little lady has grown since to be a very beautiful and famous woman. As such, indeed, she will not appear in our story, nor does she in any way greatly concern us. But I have tried to sketch her because she often reminded me in her childish way of Corry. She was Corry in miniature—a tinted, fairy-like edition of the indolent grace, the grave self-possession, and the shy but sedate girlhood of the other.

Meantime she sleeps. The goats browse quietly on—sometimes resting from the labour of eating to contemplate their long beards with evident satisfaction. An old billy-goat takes as much pride in his beard as a Jew in the Ghetto or an Englishman in the East. A white kid, with a red ribbon fastened round its neck, frisks towards the child, and looks curiously into the sleeping face. Then it snuffs at the gipsy-hat, and turns it round and round with its nose; and having finished the inspection assumes a pretty air of affected timidity, and rushes away to the shelter of its mother, who regards her vivacious offspring with maternal wonder and admiration. Then the whole flock gather together, and on the very verge of the precipice, their beards dangling over the rock, look down into the valley. A hawk hangs suspended before the face of the cliff, its wings quivering in the quivering sunlight. From the gray distant hills comes the sharp rattle of a rifle, which tells that a stag has died among its corries. A cushat, dreaming upon a tree-top, suddenly wakens, and, with a startled flutter which shakes the branches, rises up out of the wood.

The scene charmed Miles, who gazed at it in silence. Then he came forward and raised the child in his arms. She awoke, not a bit alarmed; threw her tiny arm round his neck, and looked smilingly into his face with her round blue eyes.

"You thought to frighten me, Miles, but I don't mind you. Now, you shall carry me home all the way. But stop; let me get my bonnet and my berries." And the little maiden insisted on being "put down;" and having gathered her chattels together, returned and asked gravely to be "taken up," which Miles accordingly did, and carried her off towards the wood-lodge.

"Is papa at home?" asks Miles.

"Yes; he told me that you were coming to-day, and I went out ever so early to get you berries; and Minnie there," (the white kid was following them), "came with me."

"You dear little fairy," said Miles, "how good you are!"

"But you know I am your wee wife," she responded gravely; "you told me so!"

The two chatted away merrily. Miles was never reserved with children. There was a sort of sympathetic understanding between them,—children, like dogs, knowing by instinct who are fond of them.

The Wood Lodge was the residence of Dean Leighton,—Tudor Plantagenet's Dean. The widower with his little daughter, Effie, to bear him company, clung to the moss-grown retreat where his wife had died. The Wood Lodge was ten or twelve miles inland from the Episcopal church near Ashton; but at the little chapel attached to Otterburne the Dean ministered on the alternate Sundays.

How shall I describe the Dean? I speak the simple truth; but it sounds like flattery. I cannot help it. He was simply the most perfect man I ever met. When I try to fancy what the old martyrs and truth-seekers were like, I cannot help thinking of Leighton. Heroic love, and valour, and charity, waited upon that worn and attenuated frame.

The Dean was one of Miles's oldest friends. Miles was more indebted to Frederick Leighton than to any other man in England. I must try in a sentence or two to show how this was.

Miles's father and mother died when he was very young (they had led a wandering, straggling, rather vagabond life); his grandfather, however, the old laird, and one of Consul Plancus's men, liked the boy, and his haughty, domineering ways. The pleasant heathen (Plancus and his associates were rather addicted to Paganism) relished the daily bickerings between his grandson and the Oxford tutor; and had it not been for Mrs. Menteith—a cousin of his mother's—the lad would have been permanently spoiled. Mrs. Menteith, a woman of considerable tact, had learned the boy by heart, and knew the motives that would most effectually appeal to him. He was passionate, high-tempered, obstinate as any Warrender of the race; scrupulously honest and honourable, and severely truthful. From the accidents of his early life, he had been forced to rely very much on his own judgment, even in matters that were too weighty for a child's judgment. This made the boy grave, taciturn, self-reliant; and spite of the pretty subduing ways of his cousin Corry, had given a somewhat austere cast to his mind. He wanted flexibility. There was a certain hardness in his manner. His mind moved ponderously. When he once got into the rut, he stayed in it. Obstinate men are generally the men who are least independent. They don't think so, indeed. But that very immobility out of which obstinacy springs, forces them to retain a dominant impression better than other people. The mark cleaves to them longer.

Miles went to Codlington. The life there did him good. It did not altogether subdue the obstinacy of his understanding; but it quickened its life—it made it work more pliantly.

Codlington, for those who love the country which God has made, is the queen of cities. Even Rome in her widowed beauty cannot be spoken of in the same breath. A canter across the Campagna is tame in comparison with Mary's drive. And they want the sea at Rome; from the very summit of the Dome there is nothing save the thin radiant line over Ostia; while in the Northern City you lie in its lap all day. These are the waves of the Northern Sea itself that break against the pier. Such an opening out of the town life is perfect redemption. It gives a man room to breathe. It washes the dust out of his lungs—the eau de Cologne out of his hair—the cobwebs out of his brain. In short, it *cleans* him, externally and internally.

Codlington, at that time, had not ceased to be a city of great men. The Whig faction, a brilliant brigade of sharpshooters, still scorned and defied. Opposed to it were the veterans who had fought the rude battles of an earlier world,—Jove himself in the van, giving and taking such blows as were dealt long ago, when the immortals came down and warred together before Ilium. But the fierce ambrosial nights were now well-nigh ended. Pan was finally planted among the knowes of the forest. And the great master no longer recalled the light-haired and bright-eyed god who carried fire and sword into the camp of the Titans. A splendid old man still; but the passion of battle and the glow of victory were past, and the Thunderer rested serenely from his labour.

The University of Codlington was a favourite and famous seat of the Muses. It was the best school in Christendom,—so, at least, the men who had been there alleged. All its geese were swans. If a Professor wrote a Commentary on the Epistles, he was the successor of St. Paul; the head of the aspiring undergraduate who composed a third-rate volume of poetry touched the stars. The *Codlington Review* took its stand on Codlington. Every good thing came from Codlington. Out of Codlington was no salvation; the barbarous peoples beyond the gates— the poets, and wits, and statesmen, who had not been bred at Codlington,—lay in thick darkness. The Codlington Reviewers were the Puritans of literature. If an author relished the country, and said so, he was "a word-painter;" if he was ever warmed by the heroic, or touched by the pathetic aspects of life, he was guilty of "fine writing." They aspired to become perfectly dry and colourless; and they succeeded. In their books at least; for this harmless affectation—understood to denote classical culture, as a listless manner indicates aristocratic blood—did not go farther. Otherwise these Codlington men were good fellows, — rather heretical, perhaps, on matters of faith (about which they talked largely towards the close of the evening), but,—on slow bowling, Badminton, short-whist, and the long odds,— sound to the core.

At College Miles and Darcy had come together.

Miles was a year or two younger than his friend, and threw himself eagerly into the moral and metaphysical mist which then and there was reckoned solid land; while Darcy peaceably smoked his pipe, and would not listen to the charmer. He did not believe in that deceptive shore, "whose margin fades for ever and for ever as we move;" and consequently made no attempt to reach it. When the first hope and excitement were past, Miles came back to his friend's side, and smoked his pipe likewise. God and man, heaven and earth, this mortal and that immortality, were put aside with philosophic composure.

Leighton held at that time a metropolitan rectory, and so came to know the young men. The contests in which they engaged were keen and earnest; but the noble enthusiasm of the Christian pastor stirred them from their lethargy, and his still nobler temperance made the victory permanent. Miles was thus sincerely attached and deeply grateful to Leighton; and when, under the pressure of town work, the Rector's health gave way, got him, through his influence with Mowbray, appointed to the Deanery of Otterburne.

The Dean was a perfect gentleman, and was popular among the gentlemen of the county. But it was to the working classes that he chiefly devoted himself. Their elevation was the one ambition of his life. He longed to see them better fed, better housed, better taught; and he worked at the work with all his might. Already he had earned his reward. Not only had much positive progress been made; not only were his reformatory schemes bearing fruit; but the polished and cultivated scholar had won the entire confidence of his uncourtly friends. He never flattered them; never employed the rhetoric of the demagogue. On the contrary, he spoke to them with resolute boldness, and denounced without hesitation their peculiar weaknesses. But he loved them from the bottom of his heart; and they felt it, and loved him in return.

The Dean was not a voluminous writer: during his long life, indeed, he published only one brief pamphlet. "For we trust we have a good conscience," said the Apostle. "For we trust we have a good conscience," was the text from which Parson Yorick preached a famous discourse. "For we trust we have a good conscience," was the motto which the Dean of Otterburne prefixed to his contribution to the theological literature of the age. It is a sentiment which at one period of the Church's history would not have been held to indicate any special religious partisanship. But times had changed. Protestant as well as Papist controversialists, had been content to renounce the hope of the ardent Apostle. Conscience had few, if any, friends left in either camp. " 'Tis wrote upon neither side," quoth Trim, " for 'tis only upon *conscience*, an' please your honour."

The Dean loved fair-play, and so he lifted the glove. An athletic theological "pet,"—"the Brompton Chicken,"—had been hitting out heavily right and left, and had left a number of ugly marks behind him. The Righteous were in raptures. Their champion had finally "smashed" the Conscience, and planted Christianity upon an impregnable basis. A bull in a china-shop could not work greater havoc than this logical sledge-hammer worked among the delicate tissues and sensitive fibres of the moral life. It was a famous victory,—yet one or two impracticable and uncourtly divines, little beloved by their brethren, who did not relish their grim humour, and who did not know that at heart they were true and tender as children, stood aloof, and declined to join in the *Te Deum*. They were supremely unreasonable; it was whispered that they could not distinguish a synthetic from an analytic syllogism: but they said, in a few sharp and ringing words, that Victory was sometimes more damaging than Defeat: and I have now and then fancied that they had not the worst of the tussle. And my dear Dean, who was always on such points alarmingly honest, simple, and chivalrous, cast in his lot with the wicked. The good gallant Quixote!—I came across the poor, yellow, musty pamphlet the other day, and as I glanced over its queer old-fashioned pages (it was printed in the country, and its type is the type in which remote colonial newspapers are printed), it brought to my eyes a vision of that deserted battle-field, where the drum ecclesiastic once beat so loudly, and where so many latitudinarian heroes,—" the gleanings of hostile spears," — went down before the Calvinistic Achilles.

I distinctly remember the immediate provocation which drove him into print. He had been discussing in the College Hall one day, with the celebrated Professor of Faith and Fiction at Codlington, a central position of the Calvinistic theology. The Dean remarked that he considered the doctrine immoral. The Professor retorted that the conscience was fallible: that we must believe what we are taught: and that it was as easy for the Almighty to work a moral, as a physical, miracle. "A moral miracle!" exclaimed the Dean, turning round contemptuously on his antagonist,—for he could be scornful at times, especially in his younger days, and he saw at a glance the profound scepticism involved in the plea,—" A *moral muddle*, you mean!"

"Papa! papa!" exclaimed Effie, as they entered the Wood Lodge, "here's Miles!" She lay in his arms as a bird lies in its nest, or a bee in the bell of the foxglove.

Dear little Effie! my brilliant Queen of Fashion, is the heart as glad as when it beat under the child's pinafore? I hope so; but I know at least that it is pure and dovelike as ever—as true as *his* who is now at rest with God.

## CHAPTER II.

#### THE DEAN.

How best to help the slender store,
How mend the dwellings of the poor;
  How gain in life as life advances
Valour and charity more and more.

"I ACTED as Mowbray's private secretary last summer, you know," said Miles, "and I think he liked it. He is badgered and worried by his House of Commons' work. There is no one on his side that he is entirely at ease with, and he wants me to come in. Now what do you think?"

"Does he offer you a seat?" asked the Dean.

"He *has*, frequently; but I don't care about a Minister's borough. My own wish is to try Ashton. We have some influence there, and I think the people rather like me upon the whole. And there is another temptation."

"And that is?"

"To oust Sir Jasper. He hates Mowbray with his whole soul; has attacked him virulently more than once; and to such a man I am disposed to offer no quarter. Mowbray made a jest on him once, and somehow he has never forgiven it."

"I wish your kinsman would give up making epigrams. It spoils a Minister. He might have been Premier years ago had he not been a wit."

"He has little enough time now, poor fellow, for that sort of pleasantry. War with the Empire, and national taxation, are decidedly serious subjects. Yet it is curious to see how the old spirit survives. I went down to the House with him one night last session. He was fagged and harassed—intensely anxious about a negotiation going on then, which a blundering diplomate threatened to spoil. But Barton got up, and made one of his fierce ungainly onslaughts. Something he said tickled Mowbray; I saw his eyes kindle as they do when he is going to say a good thing; and then he rose and quizzed Barton in his light humorous way till the House laughed and cheered him to the echo. I believe he shook the black care off his back for the moment, and enjoyed the fun as he would have done when a boy. It is a mystery how any man can hate him— as Sir Jasper does."

"Sir Jasper is no favourite of mine. I see a good deal of him at Otterburne. The Duke likes him; I don't. He is clever, good-humoured, I daresay, but wretchedly insincere. I would not have thought that he could either love or hate very heartily. His bitter animosity to Mowbray surprises me; it is something

K

unique in his character. A man of no principles, I should have fancied he had no resentments. Do you know the provocation?"

"I don't know—though I guess sometimes. But to return to what I wanted to say to you. I have really no political convictions, as people call them. As far as the welfare of the nation is involved, it does not seem to me to make much difference whether Whig or Tory be in power. Neither party is governed by any very unselfish or lofty motives. I scarcely know a man in the House—among the smaller men, at least—who would not sell his opinions for a good place. Now I think this tone hurts. A few days among them always makes me feel that what looks like clear duty down here, is in practice Utopian and sentimental. One loses sight of large aims and unselfish ends, or comes to ridicule them as the dreams of well-intentioned impracticable Christians."

The Dean assented. "Parliament, certainly, has little Christianity except the transmitted and hereditary. It has its chaplain, and its public prayers—that is about the whole. From such a body it is in vain to look for any practical acknowledgment of the Christian scheme of government. A speech which enforced the doctrines which Paul taught—obedience, self-sacrifice, humility—would be looked on as the speech of a jester. Like the rest of us, Peers and Commons, I fear, think too much of their 'rights'— the divine right to be as selfish, exclusive, and unmerciful as we choose—too seldom of their 'duties.' But it is hard to say whether the Parliament be worse than the society it represents. Try the lives of any of us by that standard, and how miserably do we fall short! Even we—the ministers of the Church—consider our petty controversies and animosities of more moment than the message of the Master. It is hard work to be honest anywhere—I don't think it is more difficult in the senate than it is here."

"I am not certain of that," Miles replied; "but I should like to be near Mowbray. He is my political creed in the mean time; and I really think he represents all that is freest and worthiest in our political life. But don't you feel—I do more and more every day—how difficult earnest work is in this country at present?"

"I do,—often intensely. It is no mere cant to say that our life everywhere and in every direction has become painfully dishonest. How many men among us, even when alone, dare to be sincere? A certain dramatic untruthfulness sticks to us all; so that we never think or speak out quite plainly even to ourselves. You say it is hard to be an earnest politician; think how much harder it is to be an earnest pastor. The nation believes thoroughly in the importance of your function; it reads every syllable of your speeches; Mowbray and Barton are the names in all men's mouths. It must be your own fault, surely, if you make this vocation, believed in by the people as it is, the wretched farce it has become. But we—what is our position? Our people come to listen to us, not because they care for the Gospel we declare, but because it is considered becoming to attend public worship once a week. I never wonder when I see one of us fail in the race; my wonder oftener is, how any of us should be able to persevere to the end. Some one said the other day that it was impossible for a bishop in the modern Christian Church to be a Christian; and he was not very far wrong perhaps. A colonial bishop with a hundred and fifty pounds a year may be sometimes. *There*, the Apostolic life is in a sense still practicable. A great college chum of mine—the best Greek of his day—has gone out to the Antipodes, and in his last letter he writes me that he begins to see that Christianity is, as matter of fact, a boon to men. 'Here,' he says, 'as in the early Church, they hear the word *gladly*.'"

"Perhaps earnest politicians are possible there too. Shall we try?" said Miles. "As for myself, were it not for Mowbray, I would prefer to stay where I am. It seems to me that now-a-days we work too much in the general. We centralize everything—destroying the provincial life, and all the good that is associated with it. We pass Poor-laws, and we subscribe to societies that undertake to convert the heathen abroad, and at home, in the abstract; but we never get close enough to elicit sympathy. Society puts a man in the workhouse, and keeps him from starving;

but does he love society for its official alms? How different is it with the poor around us, where our personal charity is twice blessed—to him who gives and to him who takes! The giver does not grumble, as he does when he finds the rate which is to support that political burden, 'the poor,' increasing year after year; the taker is thankful and grateful to the friendly hand which relieves his want. It stirs quite a different sentiment in his heart—a sentiment which it is well, for the sake of his own and of every other class should be there—than the statutory relief by the parish inspector. The landlord who stays at home will effect more for the elevation of the people than the landlord who reforms them through a corporation. Corporations have neither conscience nor heart; and both conscience and heart are needed to work any effective scheme of political amelioration."

"There is doubtless much to be done in private," replied the Dean,—" more, probably, than in public. When Mowbray gets these religious disabilities repealed—and the next session may see an end of them—the last rag of intolerance will be torn down. But though we banish bigotry from the Constitution, we do not banish it from society. Men will remain as narrow, as pitiless, as vindictively selfish as ever. Persecution must then be met, not in Parliament, but in the household. Public and private life, however, always influence each other; and the statesman who strives most earnestly to abate the selfishness of caste, and the violence of sect, will deserve best of his country. Let *that* be the new crusade, and even to-day a politician may find a worthy creed for which to work."

"Miles, Miles," exclaimed Effie, looking in at the open window, "I want you to come out. Such a nice evening, and I am going with Jean, to milk the cows; so let Miles come, papa."

"We will all come, Effie, and see your miraculous cows. Will Jean let us, think you?"

"Oh, yes. Jean is very good to-day. She has had a letter from Aus-tra-alia (it came out syllable by syllable), from her sweetheart—"

And the little maiden paused and hesitated and stammered, and ran off to the pet kid which was feeding in the middle of the lawn.

# CHAPTER III.

### THE OLD STORY.

O wind of strife—to us a wedding wind
O cover me with kisses of her mouth,
Blow thou our souls together, heart and mind;
To narrowing northern lines blow from the south.

MILES, Corry, and Alice were standing on the village pier, waiting for Peter, who was trimming the *Lapwing* for a run. It was a lovely September day; a light cool breeze blew from the hills, but barely rippled the water, and did not shake the shadow of the castle that rested upon the bay.

"You need not come, Peter," said Miles, "I know you are busy, and there's no chance of a blow."

"Varra gude, sir," answered the sailor. "We're for the Dodder Bank the nicht, and the lang lines are no baited yet."

"I don't think I can go either," said Alice, who did not particularly love the sea, except from the shore.

"That's too bad of you," exclaimed Miles, "Corry's quite right, I fear."

"I *am* a dreadful coward sometimes, and I never go to sea except with people who know a little about it," Alice retorted.

"Oh, Miles is a capital sailor—isn't he, Peter?" asked Corry.

"Never mind that," said Miles; "Alice is bent on staying, and there's no good trying to move her; she is inflexible as fate. You will come, Corry?"

"Yes, Miles, of course," said Corry. "I like a sail so much. But, Alice, you will have to go home by yourself; tell them we shall be back in an hour."

So it was settled; and ruffling her snow-white plumes, the clean little craft slipped gently from the pier. It looked so pretty and swan-like, and the sea was so transparently calm, that Alice began to repent that she had not gone. She waved an adieu with her handkerchief, and then slowly sauntered homewards, chatting gaily with Peter till they reached the village.

"Give my love to Elsie," she said, as they parted.

The cousins were famous sailors, and Corry guided the boat with the skill of a blue-jacket. She looked very pretty under her wide-awake, as the salt breeze gathered the roses into her cheek and played with the tangled curls. A sweet innocent girlish face, but with a depth of grave repose in the soft April eyes that took away the sense of girlishness.

Miles had brought a volume of poems by Heine with him, and Corry never tired of hearing Miles read.

## THE OLD STORY.

They were strange poems—the utterances of one who had lived upon the stern North Sea, and learned to interpret what the Norse gods said to each other while the North wind blew.

"What do you think of this, Corry?" said Miles. and he read the poem until he came to these wonderful lines :—

> A wondrous tumult, a whistling and whispering,
> A laughing and murmuring, sighing and washing,
> And 'mid them a lullaby known to me only.

"I have heard it at night often," said Corry. "Alice and I lifted the window late last night—it was so lovely; and we heard the sea talking to itself just so."

"A little more to the left, or we'll graze the Scrath rock. And what said the sea, fair cousin mine?"

"Oh, we couldn't make it out, though it talked away without minding us in the least. There was something going on clearly; each wave was chattering so eagerly, and not minding a bit what the rest said."

"You didn't notice the scent of a cigar, did you? I went down about midnight, and sat on the stones at the Raven's crag, and heard the white ripples chime like a row of silver bells on the beach, and the herring-fishers heaving at their nets outside the bay. But I was luckier than you; I learned what the sea said."

"And what did it say, Miles?" Corry demanded. " Though I don't quite believe you, all the same."

"It said," responded Miles, gravely, "that she was deep as death, and endless as eternity; that at night she was warmed by the moonlight that lay upon her breast; that the light breeze that wandered among her tresses cooled her by day; that I was to be member of parliament for the borough of Ashton, and that the electors might rest assured I would take a warm interest in the cod-fishing; that she did not wish to indulge in any personal reflections, but that to the best of her judgment it was time certain young ladies she would not more particularly mention were in bed; that——"

"Nonsense, Miles; you are as bad as Darcy. Read on, please."

And Miles read of

> The ever-quivering, grey, and silvery-world sea;

and then Corry looked ever and again across the water, to make sure that the German poet spoke true; and she found that the words were as true as Gospel words.

"I think," said Miles, "that greeting of the sea— ' Be thou greeted, thou infinite sea!'—shows how he loved it. That's the one I like best."

" I like the first you read better—about the god who came one night to the fisher's cottage, where the pretty daughter,"—

("The wondrous lovely fisher's daughter," broke in Miles).

—" is waiting alone by the ruddy hearth for her father and brother, who are out on the dark sea. Only another, Miles," she added, coaxingly.

So Miles had to read another, and he read one which the maiden beside him loved better than any, and which is indeed the most perfect and exquisite of ballads. It tells how the poet came to the miner's cottage in the lone Hartz Mountains, and how, like brother and sister, he and the grave innocent child-daughter of the host talked together long into the night; and how she fears from his mocking lip that he is not a true follower of the good Jesus; and how he tells her that he believes in the Father, the Son, and the Holy Ghost. Yea, in the Holy Ghost —who breaks the bonds of the oppressed, who frees the captive from his chains, who pours God's truth and God's light through the dark places of the heart, and who has erst chosen a thousand knights to do his bidding.

> Lo! their precious swords are gleaming,
>  And their banners wave in fight.
> What, thou fain wouldst see, my darling,
>  Such a proud and noble knight!
> Well, then, gaze upon me, dearest,
>  I am of that lordly host.
> Kiss me; I am an elected
>  True knight of the Holy Ghost!

And Corry looked shyly, but proudly, at the

reader, and thought in her heart of hearts that he too belonged to that elected band, and was as good and true a knight as any in the chosen company.

"A knight of the Holy Ghost," quoth Miles; "a teacher of the truth that maketh free. I wish some of our great friends would throw away their dirty ribbons and garters, and join the order. What device shall we bear on our banner?"

"Alice and I will work your colours," said Corry, smiling, "only tell us what they are."

"Let me think; yes," continued Miles, half in play and half in earnest, "the cross and the bleeding heart—the bleeding heart of Menteith."

The breeze had been gradually freshening, and the light craft now sped swiftly along, taking a firmer grasp of the water; no longer toying voluptuously on the sunny bosom of the sea, but in good earnest buckling on its armour for the fray. The scornful little beauty brushes away the spray that would fain kiss her brow, opens her white wings like a cygnet, and speeds toward the Happy Isles that lie just beyond the horizon—

>Where beats not hail, nor rain, nor any snow,
>Nor ever wind blows loudly, but they lie
>Deep-meadow'd, happy, fair, with orchard-lawns
>And bowery hollows crown'd with summer sea,
>Where I will heal me of my grievous wound.

Ay, they are nearing the Happy Isles, and their wounds are not very grievous. The heartache, like the toothache, "though it be not mortal, it is very troublesome;" but Corry's serene devotion did not sting as the mosquito stings. The tyrant might kill her, no doubt, if so inclined, but could not make her pettily miserable.

While the cousins thus read and talked over their book, the *Lapwing* had left the land far behind on its lee; and when Miles looked up (he was lying at the helmsman's feet), he found that they had quitted the bay and reached the open sea. Though the water was comparatively smooth, yet in the rapid tideways of the North it is never quite at rest, and into one of these they had now passed. The boat began to rock uneasily to and fro; the breeze died away for a moment, letting the sail flap unpleasantly against the mast; when it returned it came down sharp and cold. A threatening mass of white cloud was rising over the nearer hills. Miles prepared to tack.

"Look, Miles," said Corry, suddenly, "how black the water in the bay has grown."

"There is wind there, but only a capful. It will die away before it reaches us."

But even as he spoke he let go the sail, hurriedly gathered it into the boat, and getting out the oars, turned the bow toward the coming squall—for a squall it was. The bay grew darker and darker, little flakes of white foam were dashed across it, and in a couple of minutes the gale was upon them.

"I will keep her head to the wind," said Miles. "It can't last. Wrap your cloak about you, Corry, or you will catch cold. There is no fear."

"I am not frightened, Miles," said Corry, quietly, though there was a brighter flush upon her cheek now than the wind had brought; "but I don't think that it gets better."

The wind whistled shrilly through the rigging, and the waves began to beat unpleasantly against the sides of the boat. The white bank of clouds had suddenly descended from the hills, and lashed the bay with sleet. The sun was no longer visible, and even the shore grew indistinct, as the thick rush of rain descended between it and the boat. Miles and Corry were both drenched with spray ere the rain came.

The situation was alarming, as any one might see—as Corry did see from Miles's face, when he turned round and looked through the driving sleet for any glimpse of a break in the clouds. But there was none such; the rain came down close, thick, and drenching; the wind blew coldly and shrilly; worse than all, he felt the damp water rising about him, and knew that the boat was beginning to fill.

"We must run for Ashton," he said, in a tone of unconcern. "We shall get our deaths of cold if we stay in this pelt. Corry, do you think you can manage to steer us through this bit of a blow?"

"Yes; I will try."

## THE OLD STORY.

So Miles drew his oars on board, double-reefed his sail, and then raised it cautiously. The moment the wind touched it the boat yawed suddenly to leeward, and Miles fancied that they were over. But it recovered in time, after having shipped a few gallons of salt water, and then set itself stoutly to work, rushing along straight as an arrow, except when a heavier blast came down, and Corry involuntarily turned its head still closer into the wind. Miles meanwhile baled, doing his best to keep the water down, but with indifferent success. "If we can only make Ashton!" he muttered. Ay! if they can only make Ashton.

The wind blew dead from the land, and Ashton lay to the north—five miles to the north-west from where they were. Even in its present "airt" the wind blew so nearly from the point on which they tried to keep, that they had to "hug" it as closely as the sail would lie. It seemed, however, that they would succeed; Miles could dimly discern the church steeple,—a wild disordered gleam of stormy sunshine touched it once when he looked; and they were then apparently sailing on a point considerably to windward of the town. He drew a deep breath of relief, and turned to Corry with a smile.

"The fishes won't get us yet," he said; "but keep close to the wind, Corry, keep close."

Corry returned the smile: if Miles was confident, then they were safe. There could be no real danger;

and she did his bidding cheerfully and in perfect trust. There and then, at that very moment—suddenly, convincingly, and impetuously—Miles learned the truth. Yes, it was more than a cousin's fancy, a school-girl's romance; he felt instinctively that the perfect sacrifice of a woman's life had been offered up to him. Hitherto he had never dared to ask, for it had seemed to him almost like sacrilege to stir the innocent child-heart with the story of a love stronger and more vehement than the boy's. But now the soft fawn eyes had mutely told their tale, and Miles knew that he loved, and that he was loved.

Upon my word, had you seen her then, you would not have wondered at *his* love. The braided hair was unloosed and dishevelled, and floated freely behind—like Io's when she fled from Jove. The pitiless rain and wind beat against the beautiful pale face — very pale now, though composed and undaunted as ever. Very pale; but the sweet grave smile—so soft and yet so winning, so girlish and yet so mature—played about the eyes, and touched the finely-chiselled and decisive lips. Corry's grave sedateness and quiet self-possession had given to the child a piquant and contrasted interest; but now Miles felt that the child was gone, and that the woman had come to possess the shrine which waited for her. Who has not witnessed this transformation? Some of us, perhaps, can recal the day and the hour when it took place—when the eyes which were only blue and sunny with the clear child happiness in the morning, darkened and deepened into a richer and softer life ere night. Ay, and some of us have witnessed that grander yet stiller dawn, when a strange and awful light gathers into the familiar eyes, which will not dwell upon us with kindness any more, but pass us by unheeded, to rest upon the Light beyond.

It was a great joy, but it was a joy dashed with bitterness. He had found the treasure, but only to have it taken from him again. For Miles had indeed begun to lose hope. He undid another scrap of sail to aid the boat in closing with the wind; he even left the indispensable "baling," to try if his strong hand could not make the rudder work better. No, it would not do; the ebb-tide was running strong to the north, and it became evident that they could not reach Ashton. They must be driven past. And beyond Ashton, what was beyond? Norway and the Northern Sea. Nothing between.

For one moment Miles was stunned, and in that moment Corry learned the truth. But it did not alarm her: it only made her anxious to comfort her cousin.

"Oh, it's not myself!" exclaimed Miles, passionately, as she spoke; "but you, Corry—you, Corry!"

"Miles," she said, very quietly and solemnly, "I

would rather die with you than learn that you were dead." And she looked into his eyes with eyes so full of faith, that Miles could not but believe.

Do not let us intrude into the sanctuaries of the soul. I believe that there, on the brink of death, confession was made. But why try to describe this solemn consecration of love? We may be sure that in that moment of awful suspense there was no false prudery or reserve. Frankly and bravely, if not with a profounder and holier tenderness, the love would be told; frankly and bravely the love would be returned.

I do not know if there are such things as "special" providences in this world. Certainly, in the sense of the religious public, who exclude Providence on all other occasions from any participation in public affairs, I am inclined to believe that there is not. And for my own part, holding that there cannot be anything very exceptional in the Maker guiding and governing the creatures who in Him alone "live, move, and have their being," I cannot say that I love the word. However (as Mr. Ruskin observes), "I hate dogmatism;" and I know that Lady Gardiner described what followed as such; nay, as a *very* particular special providence indeed; seeing that, according to her theory of the universe, Providence commonly interferes not to save but to destroy.

The wind still blew bitterly, and the sleet poured down in torrents; Miles could indistinctly perceive

Ashton, a mile, or a mile and a half, distant. Was there any chance that they might be seen?—that assistance might reach them? If it is to come, it had best come quickly, for the ebb tide is bearing them away. No; there is no help from man.

But even while they strain their eyes towards Ashton, an invisible Helper approaches. Not the angel Michael, with whom Lucifer wrestled of old on the battlements of heaven? Oh no!—there are no angels now; the angels, like the devils, are abolished, except in Mr. Coningsby's novels, and then they talk politics only. Who then? It happened simply thus:—

The wind, which had been hitherto blowing dead from the land, went round a point to the south. Miles felt that it no longer struck against his cheek; he drew the sail "taut," and saw with unspeakable thankfulness that if it held so they might yet gain the harbour. It did not hold only: it changed more and more into the south; until when they reached the pier they were rushing along—water-logged and nearly sinking though they were—before a fair wind. The wind, which "bloweth where it listeth," went round a point, and two living souls were saved from death. A special providence, no doubt, but probably only one—the last—in a chain, which reached back into the Beginning.

I should not wish, were I an artist, to be required to paint the expression on Corry's face as they passed the pier-head, and heard the eager greetings of a crowd who, pale with excitement, had watched for the last mile the perilous passage of the boat through the reefs. I doubt if mortal art could do much to secure and convey it. I think some of the emotions —some of the pride, gratitude, triumph, love—are portrayed in the wife's face in Mr. Millais' "Order of Release;" only that face is harsh, and worn, and livid, as if its owner had been long abandoned to sorrow or drink; *here*, it is a maiden with rosy lips, and soft auburn eyes, and rich masses of dark hair, and who has only learned to-day that the man she loves is her lover.

## CHAPTER IV.

THE FADING POLITICS OF MORTAL ROME.

And when he raised his lance,
Up Hesperus rose among the evening stars.

WARRENDER, on his return home, found a bundle of letters awaiting him. I am not going to copy the whole of them; but two of them were important; and, as they aid the progress of the narrative, I make no apology for inserting them. The first was from Darcy, and ran thus:—

"DEAR MILES,—That cousin of yours is a trump. Let us drink his health in a bumper of Glendronach—fit libation to the silver-tongued Apollo. By the way, accept my thanks for the ten gallon cask I found waiting me; all the Dorians of my acquaintance have tasted it, and declare it genuine and unique. Ten to one he goes down to posterity (Mowbray I mean, not the Glendronach), as "the Great Minister." He is the Chatham of the age, only a Chatham with finer ear and more attuned temperament. I believe in a politician at last, and am quite prepared to become Solicitor.

"'But why this excitement?' you inquire, in your icy way. Has the silk gown been offered already? Not yet; but perpend, and I will tell you. Last night (after having listened solemnly all day to Sir Richard havering over a pyramid of papers at the bar of the Lords), I went across to the Commons, and having dined and drank with a senator, was conveyed to the Speaker's gallery. I tell you honestly that I was as sober as a judge. The Burgundy was no doubt very fair, and I took my lawful share; but I had merely arrived at that state of mild elation which, like charity, thinketh no evil. The House was very full; a great debate on the Soap-Bubble question was coming on. All the swells were present—the heavy swells on the Opposition benches; Mowbray in the van of the free-lances he has trained. What a splendid gentleman he looked! Graceful and manly, gallant as an antique paladin,—the representative of whatever is refined and noble in English life,—I do not wonder that he is such a prodigious favourite with the women, or that the 'bright *eyes* which sparkled through the lawn' should have hailed the haughty and victorious chief. His opening speech was calm, lucid, statesmanlike; it showed a profound acquaintance with the internal politics of foreign governments, and their relation to the liberal national policy he was carrying out. Only towards the close, only when he declared that the English Government had prepared for the threatened war, and that that very day English troops had embarked for the Mediterranean, did he warm himself and his hearers. Then for a few seconds, though his voice never lost its clear bell-like tone, he spoke vehemently and rapidly. The House was all with him, and cheered him till the old walls rang again. But the triumph came later. One or two third-rate men tried a little feeble abuse—your friend, Sir Jasper, being, like himself, bitter and malignant; but even Josey hesitated to move any formal amendment, and contented himself with some very general remarks on the Minister's foreign policy and past administration. Then Mowbray rose once more, and what a speech he made! I shall hear nothing like it again while I live. Even a hardened sinner of a lawyer was carried away. The eye brightened, the form dilated; you saw Europe at the conqueror's feet,—you learned that the intrigues of cabinets, the ambition of kings, the passions of nations, had been directed by the master's hand, or foiled by the master's skill. But a higher altitude remained; it was no longer Europe alone—no longer a nation here or a nation there—but 'the whole round earth' obeyed the Minister's behest. The Emperor might disturb the balance of power in Europe if so minded—he might occupy the Peninsula if he chose—what did that matter? 'Did I attempt a petty retaliation? When he

crossed the Pyrenees, did I blockade Cadiz? No,—
I looked another way;—I sought compensation in
another hemisphere. Contemplating Spain such as
our ancestors had known it, I resolved that if the
Emperor had Spain, it should not be Spain with
the Indies. I called the New World into existence to redress the balance of the Old.'* My dear
fellow! had you heard these last words. They rang
like a trumpet-call. They electrified the House: for
a moment the members sat silent, spell-bound, unable
even to cheer,—and then what a shout! Every man
rose; a crowd gathered round Mowbray; business
for that night was at an end. And this in the
prosaic House of Commons, in this prosaic nineteenth
century, which we all abuse so heartily!

"You can have no idea how grand your cousin
looked when he spoke these words. People thought
of Chatham. I doubt if Chatham even was ever so
vehemently great. 'I called the New World into
existence to redress the balance of the Old.' Ay,
there stood the maker, the creator; the Atlas who
stayed the world; the Zeus who presided over its

---

* This passage bears so strong a likeness to one that occurs in
a speech delivered by a great statesman thirty years ago, that it
might have been interesting to ascertain which of the two was
spoken first. Though it is impossible in this imperfect and
transitory world to be sure about dates, I rather incline to believe that George Mowbray was indebted to George Canning.

destinies. And, after all, only a simple English gentleman in a black surtout and checked breeches! Great is the mystery of genius; for a time the most *blasé* of us ceased to believe in the eternal dominion of red tape.

"It does one no harm to go a little crazy now and again; so, pr'ythee, Miles, look with grave compassion upon your friend's insanity. Ere I write you again, I shall have regained my wits."

The next epistle had a semi-official air—the air of a great official when he unbends in private life. The note was very brief, but not hurried—Mowbray was never hurried; nothing could disturb that grave and sinewy repose. It ran—

"*Private and confidential.*

"DEAR MILES,—I am going to dissolve; the time is ripe; and I want you to come in. You *must*. I need a lad who can give me a friendly arm to the House, and chat with me cousin-wise. I put it on this score, because I know that you wont take the trouble on your own account, though it should make you a Minister—which it may. So, either get a seat, or I find you one. Which is it to be? I am told that you can hit Sir Jasper pretty hard at Ashton; should you do so, I shall not be inconsolable. The Whigs will strain every nerve against us; but I take the bull by the horns, and 'the Houses' shall be taught a lesson they wont forget. All this will be visible next week; in the mean time, not a word. "G. M."

"So," mused Miles, "the moment has come. To be, or not to be. Not the nominee of a Minister— even though the Minister is Mowbray. Ashton is the card. It will be stiff work though, and bitter as nightshade."

## CHAPTER V.

### THE SABBATH REST.

> This blessed hour is yours and eve's,
>   And this is why it seems so sweet,
> To lie as husht as fallen leaves
>   In autumn at your feet,
> And watch awhile, released from care,
>   The twilight in yon quiet skies,
> The twilight in your quiet hair,
>   The twilight in your eyes.

ONE other day of peace for Miles, and then—"the noise of battle hurtled in the air."

It is the Sabbath day; and the party from Hawkstone are on their way to attend evening service at "Our Lady's Chapel of the Cliff." Sir Maxwell has stayed at home—Corry always reads the Morning Service in the library; and, unless at Christmas or Easter, this suffices the old gentleman. "She reads as well as the Dean," he heretically avers.

It is a splendid autumn afternoon; and straggling parties of villagers and country-people dot the steep ascent which leads to the old chapel. They are all good churchmen here; the dissenting interest languishes, though it has built itself a brick conventicle among the rocks in front of the village; a building not remarkable for a nice adherence to any architectural canons — Greek or Gothic — where the Rev. Mr. Sturmup, a yellow and lanky methodist, officiates. The people, indeed, are not addicted to any form of Protestant dissent; on the contrary, it is asserted by religious agitators that the district is a nest of malignant prelatists; and certainly many old heathenish words and customs—grey and venerable like Our Lady's Chapel itself—are wrought into the daily life of the people, and recal the time when all the lands around belonged to the great Abbey of Otterburne.

Mrs. Menteith, Alice, and Corry, slowly wend up the steep path, resting ever and again to look down upon a scene of noble beauty, or to exchange a few kindly words with the country people they know. The round ocean lies at their feet; bright, and calm, and lustrous with autumn sunshine. The white ripples break gently on the sandy beach far below them; but the sense of sabbath rest lies upon the sea. There are no busy fishing craft darting across the bay; all are drawn up high upon the shore; only near the horizon the white sails of a great merchant ship from the Pacific sparkle against the blue. The place used to remind me of scenes I had often witnessed along the delicious skirts of Northern Italy—the blue seas, the snowy sands, the nestling villages; and far aloft, above the strife of men and the contention of the waves, the arched and moss-grown windows of the ancient church.

The interior was grey and sombre; two rows of simple massive pillars—massive as Roman masonry—ran from end to end. Entering from the brilliant sunshine and the laughing sea, the effect was cold and sepulchral—an effect which the rosy faces of the children, and the bright dresses of the women, did not tend to diminish. The pews of the Menteiths and the Warrenders occupied spaces on either side of the high pulpit; and Miles could see through the arched pillars of the screen the glow of grateful acknowledgment which flushed Corry's upturned cheek when the thanksgiving for those who have escaped great peril—a thanksgiving of the Early Church, elsewhere forgotten, which praises Him "who has redeemed our souls from the jaws of death"—was read with great solemnity by the Dean. Perhaps he also noted a look of softer tenderness in the violet eyes when at the close they rested upon himself.

The Dean was an admirable preacher, and his short, pithy sermons were listened to with that earnest attention which is so grateful to a speaker, and which shows him that his argument is intelligently followed. He was preaching on the obligation to observe the Sabbath, his text being taken from that noble chapter in which Saint Paul expounds to the Colossians the practice of Christian liberty. A fierce agitation had been going on against the attempt to open certain places of instruction and amusement upon the Sabbath, and the disturbance had even reached this remote district, and petitions against the proposal had been hawked round the parish. The Dean, though always moderate, never hesitated to announce and enforce his opinions with unhesitating straightforwardness.

"I cannot recommend you to sign these papers," he said. "I do not see that we have any right to interfere with others in this matter. Let each man satisfy his own conscience; that is the obligation which St. Paul requires us to observe. And I think we who lead what I may call the pastoral life—the life led by the patriarchs of old—are peculiarly unfitted to tell the great towns and cities of the empire how they are to observe the first day of the week. No one loves more than I do our beautiful and simple Sabbath, when man and nature alike rest from their labours. The work of the week is over; the ploughman leaves his plough in the furrow; the fisherman's nets are spread upon the beach; the horse and the ox are released from their harness. It is well that we, and such as we, should assemble in God's house to-day, to thank Him for His mercies during the week on which last night's twilight so softly and graciously closed. But during all that week *we* have been breathing the untainted air; we have been looking on the sea; God's serene heaven has never been shut out from us. How different it is with those who live in the cities—in their wretched garrets, in their filthy cellars, in the heated and poisoned atmosphere of their great workshops! The sight of a green field, of a hawthorn hedge, of a noble elm or oak, may fall upon these soiled and thirsty hearts like dew. When, therefore, I am asked to prevent our workmen from seeing the works of God, I answer—No. The Sabbath is given to us that we may regain mental vigour and moral freedom—may wash away the foul impurity of the week, and the truest homage we can offer to our Maker on this day is to put his Divine gift to the best use. And who except the dogmatist or the ascetic will venture to impose any inflexible and merciless law of observance? I believe that to some men—to the sick child or to the tired mechanic—the purple clouds and the wayside flowers convey a message of mercy which they cannot learn from any other teacher—which they cannot learn in their garrets, in their ginshops, in their churches. Yes, my friends, I say "their churches," without shrinking, because I hold that you must put physical stamina, human hope, and manly vigour into a man, before you can do much for him either morally or spiritually. Give him something—green fields or fresh air or innocent recreations, I care not which—that will make his pulse beat, and arouse the soul paralysed by incessant toil. So do not let us judge one another any more, but judge this rather, that no man put a stumbling-block, or an occasion to fall, in his brother's way."

Simple and manly words—words, however, which in that age and society few clergymen had the courage to utter.

They walked back to Hawkstone together, only Miles and Corry lingered a little behind. They had been engaged for nearly a week now, and she hung upon his arm with a winning and wistful confidence, very distracting to male onlookers, but no doubt very pleasant to its object.

"Stay, Corry, I want to speak to you about something that concerns us both," said Miles.

She stopped and looked into his eyes with a quick alarm.

"Let us rest a minute here. There's young Peter and Elsie just behind us."

"Well, Peter," said Miles, "have you been at the kirk?"

"No, sir, Elsie and I gaed down in the mornin' to see the auld grandmither at Langhaven: she's been sair hauden doun a' the winter wi' the rheumatics, and she's aye girnin' for some o' his to bide wi' her. But we're thinkin' to bring her up here in the fa', and Elsie was telling her she'd be less uncanny like among her ain freens than bidin' her lane in that eerie place."

"Will the old lady come?"

"She's hard to drive, sir; she likes the place, though it's cauld and weet in the winter. Puir Bob gaed doun a mile aff the pint; she saw the boat upset hersel, and she canna thole to leave it. It's my opinion she'll no come. But she likes Elsie, and mayhap she'll bring her."

"She's not singular there at least, I suppose, Peter? But where's your father—I haven't seen him to-day?"

"Deed, sir, he says he's growing deaf, and he disna care muckle, I jalouse, for the new-fangled preachings down by. Forby he was lookin' through a wheen papers that came for him yestreen."

"I dare say the packet I sent him. Tell him to let me know if he wants to speak to me about them."

"I'll dee that, sir; many thanks to you."

"Good day, Peter; good day, Elsie."

"Corry," said Miles, "could you bear to leave this place?"

"Why do you ask?"

"I fancy that by and bye we may not be able to live much here. Could you quit the old place for a noisy bustling town? I will tell you why I ask afterwards."

Her answer did not come at once. Her eye wandered over the familiar scene—the quiet sea crowned with the autumnal glory—across the shore, the green braes, the smoke curling quietly above the old hall.

"Yes, Miles," she said, very quietly and earnestly, as if casting her childhood behind her, "I think I could leave everything for you." And then, actuated by a sudden impulse, she turned her eyes full upon his face, and stooping down—for he lay along the bank at her feet—touched his cheek with her pure lips: "Oh, my love, my love!"

There was no reserve, or shame, or shrinking shyness about her love. It was her boy friend, her dear old cousin Miles, who was now her lover, and who was to be her husband; and she never fancied for a moment that she should not show him her whole heart. But that heart was so tremulous and dovelike—so like the eyes through which it looked—that Miles felt that the most clear and outspoken words left a whole mystery of unexplored tenderness behind. The love was visible and complete, and almost childlike in its clear simplicity and honesty of assertion; but its honesty did not make it common or commonplace. The single light that played upon her heart was as chequered and richly toned as the light that plays upon the sea.

Corry would have followed Miles over the world like a dog or a child; but this unquestioning worship did not destroy the delicacy of her love, or the womanly reserve of her character. It is indeed only through the perfect obedience of the heart that the full strength and self-reliance of which a woman is capable can be ascertained. Without this plummet she cannot sound her deepest powers. It is the woman whose whole soul has been lavished upon her lover, who for a time has seemed incapable of any independent energy or volition, who in the end will prove the strongest—the sagacious wife of the statesman, the courageous mother of the hero. She must have felt with Corry, and said with Ruth,

"Thy people shall be my people, and thy God my God."

# V.

## THE ELECTION.

# CHAPTER I.

### A LESSON IN DANTE.

*Sweet girl-graduates in their golden hair.*

THEY were staying at the Duke's. The Duke was a keen politician, but a very gentlemanly man. The Duke—I am not positive that he occupied that position in the Peerage; but we all love to mingle with the great, and why should we not do so—on paper? It does not cost me a penny more to say that he was premier-peer of England; and a writer who

> Can mak a belted knight,
> A marquis, duke, and a' that,

is likelier to come to a better understanding with his publisher, I believe, than if he deals only in " honest men "—a somewhat unsaleable article.

Lofty moralists, with an air of general dilapidation, are to be found here and there, no doubt, who denounce what they call " the silver-fork school " of literature. If you chaff them a little, and assure them that your friend De Morvil, or Jack the Giant-killer, or St. George of Cappadocia, or the Dragon, had Norman blood in his veins, or if you happen to know a man whose name is not basely plebeian, you are assaulted by a vicious whelp like Brown, by a mangy cur like Jones, or an unlicked cub like Robinson. But these stern mentors, happily, remain in the minority, and their professional slang has not yet come into fashion. For my part I own that I prefer a silver fork any day to one formed of the baser metals. "The silver-fork school?" Snobs repeat the phrase, but an authentic "flunkey,"—a "flunkey" morally and socially—must have been its inventor. "A 'aughty haristocrat," Plush observes contemplatively, as he washes up the silver, "uses this ere fork, and a Man,—a man of iligant 'abits, and even superior calves,—is condemned to polish it.

> O cursèd spite
> That ever I was born to set it right."

There was a large party at the Duke's; for September was well advanced, and the partridge-shooting had commenced. There were a lot of embryo diplomatists and members of parliament; one or two full-fledged specimens of the same; Lady Gardiner and her five daughters—

> Morning doves
> That sun their milky bosoms on the thatch;

Mrs. Graham and her husband; Sir Jasper Trelawney,

the member for Ashton; an Italian refugee, and a Polish Count.

The drawing-room at Otterburne was a very pleasant room. A certain air of artistic confusion and dishabille always characterized it of a morning. None of its features were stiff or angular. It stretched along the whole front of the castle, its bow-windows bending over the noble river that foamed below.

Kate Gardiner is busily employed this morning on a mysterious piece of worsted-work, which, like Penelope's web, never seems to advance beyond a given point. The design is chaste and impressive. It represents a scantily-coated shepherdess with a conspicuous patch of pink on either cheek, and a love-lorn swain, attired in light Arcadian peg-tops, who gazes blankly into her blue eyes. As far as one can judge from the intense vacancy of his stare, and the fiery complexion of his countenance, this victim of an unrequited attachment has abandoned himself to the habitual use of intoxicating drinks. A pair of dyed sheep, as large as life, stand by in an easy idyllic attitude, and constitute a background which Giotto might have painted, and Mr. Ruskin glorified. Had she lived at present, Kate would have become no doubt, a distinguished Præ-Raphaelite Sister. Mrs. Graham, in that triumphant issue of our civilization—a really easy chair—sits beside her; a pretty, fashionable woman, with the clear, cold directness of manner which distinguishes our highest class. No emotion penetrates that icy affability—no tempest can ruffle that superb and insolent politeness. There is not a hint of hauteur, not a particle of pretension; but the queen-like courtesy, which listens and replies without constraint to your mortal talk, just because you are mortal, and cannot by possibility say anything that can hurt a Divine Olympian, freezes you like the sun shining through an east wind in winter.

Ah! Lady Beatrix, many is the heart you have broken, while all the while—though the world knew it not—your own was mortally hurt. Those who have only seen the haughty beauty of the London ballroom—very beautiful, no doubt, but still with certain hard lines about the mouth, and a sad weariness in the heavy violet eyes—cannot fancy how exquisitely lovely you were at seventeen, when I saw you first. The only daughter of the house of Kinkell and the Lord of Otterburne—you were haughty even as a child, the world fancied. Corry would say, indeed, that when you unbent at night, as you sat together over the dying fire, when all the household were a-bed, you would soften strangely; the confident voice would falter, the mocking eyes moisten with unusual tears. And especially if the storm roared outside among the pines and lashed the river into foam, that strange tenderness would grow more solemn and earnest, and a prayer for those who go down to the sea in ships would be repeated with sad seriousness by the pale lips. That "Charles Edward" was cruising in the *Pioneer* across the Pacific, Corry knew; but Lady Beatrix never whispered her penniless cousin's name. In those days the beautiful victim was only a pretty girl in her teens; not quite Olympianized, nor raised above mortal conflict. But even then she knew that she was destined for the altar; the daughter of a northern duke, the granddaughter of an English earl, could not fail to be a victim to her order; yet she sometimes dreamt vaguely, notwithstanding, that true love would win the day; and at these times—her cheek leaning on the white hand, a rapt smile flickering about the parted lips, grave happiness dwelling in the pensive eyes—how beautiful she looked!

In one of the bay windows—there were three of them, quaintly fitted up with elegant trifles, so that when the massive gold and crimson curtains were drawn, each formed a miniature boudoir — Lady Beatrix and the Hawkstone girls were engaged on their Italian lesson. Sir Jasper, half-buried among the drapery, vouchsafed occasionally the benefit of his advice, which, I fear, did not aid their progress much. The pleasant murmur of the water, as it lapped the crag underneath, came in with the rich September sunshine through the open window. A nice place for an Italian lesson; for Petrarch especially. But they were reading Dante.

"That vowel is short, you will observe, Lady

Beatrix. It is a matter of no consequence, of course; and I have no doubt your way is really the best. But the Tuscans are prejudiced."

"Sir Jasper," retorted Lady Beatrix, "I hate criticism; and critics likewise."

"They are an obnoxious race, certainly," he replied, "more especially when they are right. I quite agree with you: but that passage is really worth noticing."

"You mean," said Corry, "that the sound imitates or echoes the sense. I thought so when I read it."

"Yes," said Trelawney, repeating the line. "A man with any ear could tell what it meant, though he did not know a word of the language. How cold, hard, dead, every syllable is here!

> Ecaddi comè corpo morto cade.

It is the blank dull fall of a mass of lifeless matter; there is no rustle of life—not a single S—through it all. The dust has returned to the dust."

"Is it Pope?" asked Corry, a little tremulously, "who has that line about one breathing and panting up the hill?—

> Up the high hill he heaved a huge round stone."

"Ay, Pope, or Homer, or some of these great old swells. But I thought no one read Pope now—that ladies, at least, only kept Hannah More or Montgomery below their pillows——"

## A LESSON IN DANTE.

"Don't answer him, Corry. It is too bad."

They began resolutely to read again. Trelawney closed his eyes, and seemed to be in a fair way of going asleep. Perhaps he was only testing the doctrine that colour cannot be rightly apprehended by the unclosed eye. And certainly, not to speak of the purple hills, and the bloody carmine of the beaches, there was such a delicate flush of rosy light on the faces of the girls, that the experiment was worth making.

"I can't like Dante," exclaimed Alice, suddenly; "he is so pitiless."

"Oh, no," said Sir Jasper; "he is the kindest-hearted of poets. There is no tenderness anywhere like Francesca's. But he did not wear it on the outside—as your Anacreons and Petrarchs do—like a cross or a ribbon. He had family troubles, poor man! and his temper was somewhat soured. But there was a well of love underneath that would not dry up. You do not meet with it more than once or twice; but *then* his whole soul weeps. 'Tis the intensest language of passion; and so these brief words, winnowed of all dross as by fire, live for ever."

Corry's eyes acquiesced.

"I think you are right," she said. "Alice, after that you must repent."

"Very well. I have sinned," she answered. "But there is a wretched man who writes a dreadfully dry preface to our copy, and who says that Beatrice went away, and married somebody else. How could you, Lady Beatrix?"

Lady Beatrix looked up, and smiled somewhat drearily.

"Don't believe it, please," replied Sir Jasper; "your cousin knows better. On the contrary, Beatrice died when a mere child, and was buried in a garden of lilies in Vallombrosa. She went meekly enough to heaven, poor soul! but her little heart was very sad for her playfellow, notwithstanding. Just think of that, and then how grand the after-meeting, when forty years are past—when the boy's brown hair is grey, and his cheek furrowed. But the old love remains—fresh and vernal as at the beginning."

"It is very beautiful," said Lady Beatrix, gravely.

They went on with the reading, and there was another pause broken only by the voluptuous vowels of the Italian, and the sharp tones of Kate Gardiner's voice, who was discussing the Dean with Mrs. Graham. The girls were not particularly good scholars; but Trelawney had never understood Dante better, never understood better the strange theology which, with all its bitterness and uncouthness, is not wanting in a certain impassioned charity,—the wonderful vividness with which he daguerreotypes the most fantastic conceptions,—the intense force and energy of the thought which transfigures the meanest details, and touches the most puerile incidents with "authentic fire." Some such vague critical impressions, into which the Greek braids of Corry's brown hair somewhat inconsequentially entered, were floating through his brain when the door opened, and Lady Gardiner entered. The curtain under which Sir Jasper sat suddenly collapsed.

"Our Lady of Bitterness," he whispered to Corry, as he passed through the open window on to the terrace. In a few minutes *The Faerie Queen*, with her white sails set, emerged from among the rocks, and held away close-hauled towards the Salmon Pot.

"Trelawney is a most agreeable man," was the first impression which Sir Jasper's animated conversation and varied accomplishments excited; yet, curiously enough, the latter half of the criticism would run, after a pause, "but somehow he frightens me." He was intensely amusing; but the fireworks were artificial. He was exceedingly good-tempered; but one felt instinctively that those thin lips could say on occasion the cruellest words to man or woman without compunction. He spoke and wrote excellently; "the ever-cheerful man of sin," as a great satirist named him, was everywhere popular; he prided himself especially on his stock of those cold and clever *un*truths which vice mistakes for wisdom; and yet his tact was so exquisite that they were never used except where they were welcome. He had no warmth of heart, nor force of imagination; but his power of appreciation was so genuine and so consummately cultivated, that he was supposed to possess both,—the fire of the lover, and the fancy of the poet. I never, indeed, have known any man with finer tact. Like some marine animals, Sir Jasper had feelers all round him. The subtle voluptuary concealed his bad points admirably; only the grey merciless eyes, the thin merciless lips, sometimes betrayed him to the keen observer.

## CHAPTER II.

### THE UPLAND RIDE.

*This Egypt-plague of men.*

IS there any pleasanter place in the world than a country-house in autumn? I don't know of any —do you? And Otterburne, in September, was the pleasantest of country-houses.

Immediately after breakfast, most of the males started for the moors or the stubbles. They walked and shot till the light failed them, and then returned in time to read their letters and papers, and enjoy a warm-bath before the eight o'clock dinner. The Duke intrenched himself during the forenoon in what he called his "study;" while Sir Jasper, always gallant, rode with the womenkind, or thrashed assiduously a favourite pot, where the salmon lay, grim and sulky, watching his flies. The evenings, with their dash of billiards and music, and stately Lady Beatrix sailing serenely from guest to guest, though not immortal, were divine. That is to say, they were not so utterly wearisome as they might have been.

It was a fine frosty afternoon in the middle of September. Shots were heard among the distant covers, and the salmon leapt bravely in the black pot below the Linn. Two or three horses, with side-saddles and attendant grooms, waited in front of the castle. Lady Beatrix, Corry, and Alice, appeared in their riding-habits.

"We are to have your escort," said Lady Beatrix to Sir Jasper, who came up from the river.

"If you don't forbid me," he answered, with a glance at Corry, as if he meant to direct his appeal to her. Lady Beatrix, with her quick sympathy, detected the gesture; Corry did not, she only bowed and smiled and looked radiant, as she always did now. The light in her heart—"the light that never was on sea or shore," except to the lover and his mistress for about ten days or so —lighted the world.

Otterburne was deliciously situated. In front of the castle, a noble chase dotted with forest trees— magnificent limes and chestnuts—retreated slowly till it lost itself in a thicket of spruce and brushwood. The approach swept in a succession of fine curves along the brink of the river. There were no gates to shut in the face of the people; nothing to indicate exactly where the lawn terminated, and the outer world began. Cottages were scattered here and there among the cover; blue smoke curled in lazy wreaths over the tree-tops.

They rode through the castle grounds, till they came to the barren upland, where the plover and the muirfowl breed. It was a glorious ride—the road continually ascending from the rich banks of the river to the region of the heather and the pine, and disclosing a new "coigne of vantage" at every turn. The picturesque antiquity of the historic keep—the lordly sweep of the modern mansion—Lady Beatrix's rose-illumined flower-garden —the blue curves of the river gleaming through the golden autumnal woods—the birchen glades through which they passed, and whose witch-like leaves rustled in the breezeless afternoon—the white swans upon the lake ruffling their snowy plumage, or dipping their long necks into the clammy weeds; and each object transfigured and glorified by the mellow lustre of the declining day! A charming ride, in sooth—three pretty girls, one of them, at least, supremely beautiful, and Sir Jasper in his pleasantest mood.

"Did you see Lady Gardiner and her highland brigade arrive?" he asked, his eyes sparkling with fun and malice as he went on to describe their advent. "It was in one of those primeval conveyances which still survive in the regions of the Old Red Sandstone. This immortal vehicle—I have been taking an inventory of it—is elevated on wheels of enormous height, and swings about in the upper air like a gigantic meat-safe. A long ladder leads up to a hole in its side, through which the explorer precipitates himself into the abyss behind. Dante alone could describe that murky cavern. Many generations of bilious moths have pined and died within its faded linings. A few survivors yet remain who, incensed by the unwonted light, dash themselves blindly on any venturesome intruder. We know that her ladyship's tastes are peculiar, else I should venture to assert that she must look forward to the day when she will be permitted to exchange the family carriage for a commodious and well-aired hearse."

However clumsy it may look on paper, his grave and solemn quizzing—graced by the charm of voice and manner—was inimitable; even Mowbray, a master in the craft, admitted that Sir Jasper's good-humoured raillery was in its way unrivalled.

"A canter over the heather," pleaded Sir Jasper.

"Oh, yes," exclaimed Corry, her face flushed, and glowing with exercise and the keen autumn air.

"I am tired," said Lady Beatrix, bending indolently over her charger's neck. "Alice and I will wait for you here."

They stood on the sky-line of the valley, and the glorious river unwound itself like a silver snake far below their feet. Behind them stretched "the low backs of the bushless downs," crowned with a shining crest of purple heather.

The horses were fresh, and galloped gallantly

across the heath. Corry was a graceful and fearless rider. A single tress of the brown hair escaped from the meshes of the silken net, and floated, like an elf-lock, behind. Sir Jasper looked at the lissome girlish figure with visible admiration, which every moment became more marked and unrestrained. For indeed that brown twilight-touched hair, and those brown eyes, with their liquid, fawn-like pensiveness — that soft, silky, insinuating beauty — had touched a chord in the jaded heart which had long been silent; and Sir Jasper to-day felt younger than he had felt for years. For though the wiry figure still looked fresh and vigorous and almost boy-like, Trelawney, a lying world asserted, was already on the wrong side of fifty.

They drew up their panting horses in the middle of the encrimsoned downs, and turned their faces homeward. A gorcock crowed lustily, startling the lustrous silence of the autumn evening. There was no sound or trace of man; the wild Highland cattle that fed upon the scrubby herbage were the only denizens of these dreary flats. Obstinate, mouse-coloured, picturesque little brutes, with shaggy manes and shaggy heads crowned with long branching horns, who looked at the riders with brown, tranquil, meditative eyes, as they went past.

"The ox-eyed Juno," said Sir Jasper. "They have just such a breed of shaggy Highland caterans among their Greek hills."

I don't know how it happened; it even took the veteran experience of Trelawney by surprise; but somehow or other, possessed by some good or evil spirit, some malicious imp or guardian angel, he found himself then and there, upon these lonely uplands, making an offer of his hand, in due form, to Miss Menteith. Poor Corry, who had never dreamt of such a catastrophe, was too much taken aback at first to utter a word; at length she faltered forth an inarticulate refusal. For a moment Sir Jasper did not seem to comprehend that he had been rejected; but Corry's evident distress was too real and unaffected to admit of doubt; and then an ill light, such as Corry had never seen there before, came into his eyes. She recoiled before it, and Sir Jasper, with his practised instinct, felt that he had betrayed himself; but he asked, calmly,

"Is there no hope for me, Miss Menteith?" and he looked into her face with a calm, freezing smile upon his thin lips, as she answered hurriedly, and with a tremor in her voice she could not quite disguise,

"None; never!"

She hated that smile; it was, she felt, an insult to her womanhood—a mockery of the heart which she could not but resent; and she turned her head away and forced her steed into a gallop. Trelawney kept by her side, but did not speak until they had nearly reached the rest of the party, when he asked, in his old, frank, good-humoured way,

"And how is my ancient ally, your cousin, Miles Warrender, Miss Menteith?"

She winced as he spoke; she felt that he had divined her heart's secret.

"We have had a famous gallop, Lady Beatrix," he said, blandly; "what a capital horsewoman Miss Menteith is! She nearly left me in the lurch."

## CHAPTER III.

### THE KNIGHTS OF THE ROUND TABLE.

> Boy! False hound!
> If you have writ your annals true, 'tis there,
> That, like an eagle in a dove-cot, I
> Flutter'd your Volscians in Corioli.
> Alone I did it.

A LARGE oval table—so I am hardly entitled to address "the Knights of the *Round* Table "— sparkling with green and purple dies from Bohemian glassworks; heavy with gold, and antique porcelain, and Sèvres china; glowing with swarthy pears, and golden peaches, and yellow melons; a veiled Ariadne (the gift of an emperor to an ambassador) in the centre,—its chaste purity and pale perfection contrasting with the splendid glow of colour underneath. A party of twenty, men and women, the men, wealthy or clever, the women, all of them well dressed and distinguished-looking, one or two exquisitely beautiful. Corry and Alice—the twilight and the dawn—sit on either side and catch fugitive glimpses of each other through the leafy branches of an Etruscan vase which flowers between them. The wealth, the magnificence, and the beauty of England, are never seen in greater perfection than at one of its great dinner-parties.

"A clever fellow, Sir Jasper," said a lively young diplomate, who sat beside Alice. He looked little more than a boy, and you would have guessed that he was still at Christ Church, and yet you (the British nation, that is, of course) were surprised, the other day, that in a negotiation which he had virtually conducted, you had been, as usual, vexatiously put to shame. His *chef* happened to be writing a romance or an opera at the time; so the office-work was left to the sub. Otherwise a good lad, and a future Secretary of State. "A monstrously clever fellow. He has the best taste in sherry of any man I know," he rattled on. "Did you notice his drag the other day?"

"No," said Alice, absently.

"Well, let me advise you as a friend," he continued, confidentially, "to go and see it to-morrow. I'll manage it. It's perfect."

"What style is it?" his auditor inquired.

"O, quiet—decidedly quiet—so quiet that its owner must be proud as Lucifer. The dark green is a study in itself. That's an exclusive colour which belongs to your aristocratic coach-builder alone. To the trade in general it's a profound secret, like the purple in Tintoret's *Ariadne*."

"You excite my curiosity immensely," said Alice,

in her sarcastic way. "We are surrounded by mysteries."

"So we are," retorted the embryo secretary, cheerfully; "and your way of looking at them is far too flippant, let me tell you. There are more things in heaven and earth, Miss Evelyn, than are dreamt of in your philosophy. For instance, you see nothing striking in this table, I presume?"

"Nothing—at it, or on it," she said, with a meaning glance at her companion.

"Thank you. Just as I supposed. Now, the truth is, that it is constructed on the profoundest philosophical principles. I spoke to the Duke about it myself. A round table is not fitted for a refined society, though it might serve, no doubt, for a very primitive one, like King Arthur's at Camelot. A square one, on the other hand, is formal and freezing; it destroys wit and good-fellowship. Our square dining-tables are, I believe, Miss Evelyn, at the root of the national moroseness," he added, gravely, as if rising to the height of a large generalization.

The ladies retired.

"What a graceful creature Miss Menteith is!" said the Duke.

"And what a trump the other one is!" sighed Charley Latimer to himself. "I wish you would lend me a thousand a-year, my lord."

The letters and papers were brought in, and laid

on the side-table. It was customary to do so at Otterburne, and during times of keen political excitement they were opened forthwith. But this was the dead season, and nothing of interest was looked for. So they lay unnoticed for some time, until a sporting legislator said,

"Please, Charley, look at the racing news in the *Times*, and tell me who has won the cup.

Charley did as directed, lazily unfolded the paper, cast his eyes lazily over it, and then started up suddenly—

" By Jove, sir, a dissolution!"

" A dissolution!" was echoed on every side.

" Yes. Here is Mowbray's address to the university."

" Read it," was the unanimous demand.

It was not an address calculated to soothe the feelings of that assembly. It treated "the great families" with studied disrespect, and told the "proud combinations" which had intrigued against him, that the Adventurer was not afraid "to look them in the face." The good government of the people of England, not the aggrandizement of an aristocratic faction, was the purpose for which, it said, the present government had been formed. Because it had adhered scrupulously to that purpose, it had met with bitter and unscrupulous hostility; but that principle it was still determined to vindicate. The minister was prepared to submit the issue, as he now did—for parliament would be dissolved during the present week—to the judgment of the English people.

"Utterly revolutionary!" said the Duke, who had held a silver stick in the days when the Great Houses were dominant.

"A good cry," said Sir Jasper. "I don't like it much. What says the *Ashton Tomahawk?*"

The *Ashton Tomahawk*, published that afternoon, was clearly in a state of keen excitement. It was bespattered all over with huge capitals. Half of its leading article was printed in the most emphatic italics. And on the first page, the address of Miles Warrender, Esquire, "To the Electors of Ashton," though brief and terse, was *leaded* to such an extent that it occupied a column and a half.

Miles had long desired, he said, to represent Ashton in Parliament. Old memories and early ties bound him to a constituency with which the Parliamentary fame of more than one of the Warrenders was associated. Moreover, he knew them intimately —had known them since boyhood.

His political position was easily defined. He was the kinsman of Mowbray, one of the greatest ministers who had ever ruled the empire. To him he was attached alike by principle and affection. He did not hesitate to make this avowal, for after the violent hostility which had been shown to the minister by their present representative, he considered it only fair that a plain issue should be placed before the constituency—the great and single-minded minister, or a narrow and sectarian oligarchy.

"That's a dig at you, Trelawney," said Mr. Graham, yawning. Confident in the enlightened and steady patriotism of a close Whig borough, Mr. Graham was disposed to regard the dissolution with his usual serenity.

The principles of the minister, Miles went on, were, and always had been, his own. He was quite satisfied with the constitution. He saw no necessity for political reconstruction. He was utterly averse to theoretical change. But the wise efforts of the minister to secure religious freedom to his fellow-countrymen deserved the earnest aid of every man who truly valued liberty of conscience. "It is not merely these antique disabilities," were the concluding words, "which require to be removed. The subtle tyranny of opinion is now more to be dreaded than the active intolerance of the State."

"A very good discourse," said Sir Jasper, who had recovered his composure, at first a little ruffled. "The style of thing for a mechanics' institute. I understand his game; 'tis rather a fine one to play well, and will try the lad's metal."

"I give you five to one in fifties, Trelawney, that Warrender beats you," said Mr. Graham, who would have bet on the Resurrection.

"Done," replied Sir Jasper, with perfect sweetness.

They entered the bet in their books, and adjourned to the drawing-room.

Lady Beatrix and Corry were at the piano. Sir Jasper approached them, paper in hand.

"You will be glad to hear, Miss Menteith, that Mr. Warrender is wooing the affections of the Ashton electors. He is a dangerous rival, I know. But he sha'n't beat me again," he added, in a perfectly good-humoured and unembarrassed tone, which, to Corry, however, was perfectly intelligible.

"What an enemy that man will make!" she thought, with a sort of shudder, as she took the paper from his hand.

# CHAPTER IV.

### THE WAY OF THE WORLD.

Then, weary, go thou back with failing breath,
And in thy chamber make thy prayer and moan;
One day upon *His* bosom, all thine own,
Thou shalt lie still, embraced in holy death.

FROM Gilbert Burnet, M.D., in Codlington.

"MY DEAR WARRENDER,

"How the years roll on! It seems an age since I wrote you, ages since I heard from you. 'Tis our way, I suppose; and though we can't be bored to write and speak to one another, we don't forget. I am a wretched correspondent, but I keep my old friends somewhere near my heart, and I will be very happy to meet you in Hades or elsewhere Hereafter. Now, I want you to do a little piece of business for me. You know I work a good deal at the hospital here. Well, a month ago a poor woman was admitted; that she was dying of consumption was evident from the first. She was rather pretty, very patient and uncomplaining, and I chanced to take an interest in her, and got her a few luxuries that kept soul and body a little longer together, I daresay.

"I suppose she belonged to what politicians call the dangerous classes; at least, a girl who came to see her every second day, undoubtedly did, and she herself had been a strolling actress or something of the kind. Poor souls! it was touching to witness the sort of affection that existed between the two. To the sufferer, the bitterness of death was already past; calm, but wearied with the conflict, she waited for rest. The other clung to her passionately; there was a defiant gleam in the overbright eyes when the dying woman talked of death, a sore and vexed displeasure of the fair face, when a harder cough than common shook the wasted frame. The poor creature was angry, in her childish way, with the great enemy, and clenched her little hand defiantly in his face, and would fain have induced her wearied friend to brave him, as she did. But it was of no avail, and one morning I found the poor little animal sitting in a tearless, helpless way beside the cold body of the dead woman. When I spoke to her and tried to take her away, she started up with flashing, bright eyes, and said, fiercely, 'Ye're no' to touch Katie! I promised her to bury her mysel'.' Which she did; out of the wages of sin, no doubt,—honest wages have often been less honestly spent.

"The day before her death, the dying woman

gave me a small packet, which she asked me to keep for her. 'She didna' want it to be lying about in folks' way,' she said. 'When I dee,' she added, 'send it back to *him*—.' A fit of coughing came on, which prevented her finishing, and when I returned next day she was gone. I have accidentally discovered since then that she came from your part of the country, and that her family belong to the little fishing village beside you. I wish, therefore, you would find them out—Stephen is the name—and give them the enclosed packet, which is the one I received.

"Ah, my dear Warrender! how I envy your country life! Seeing, as I do here, day after day, the whole sin and misery of the city gathered into a single chamber, a weight oppresses me, which makes me wretched at times. Still the mind gets hardened (not, I hope, in the bad sense of the word), the nerves are braced, and one comes at last to believe that, even amid the foul defilement, a Great Physician is at work.

"Ever thine,

"GILBERT BURNET."

"What a complex machine a woman's nature is!" says a great modern sage. I think there is a time in the lives of most men when they are rather disposed to resent the aphorism. It seems such a simple matter, after all; the mystery is no mystery at all, or, at least, is so easily penetrated. The best and the worst of the sex are united by a monotonous uniformity. The lorette, as well as the titled gentlewoman or the untainted maiden, can do generous things with a free hand and a warm heart. It is not Traviata alone who takes a childish pleasure in the masquerade or the milliner. The opera-cloak that goes to the casino does not conceal very different feelings—in so far as positive value is concerned—from those hidden by the cloak that goes to the ball at the palace. Frail Sophie, day after day, sits beside the frailer Marie, who is coughing away her lungs in the hospital, and never fancies that her patient kindness will be recorded to her credit above. The Angel of Death hovers overhead; but she does not fear him; when the awe and majesty of love have departed out of life, death ceases to terrify. She puzzles her little head in considering how much the coffin will cost; how much Mr. Mould will charge for a decent burial; for she has promised the dying girl that the emaciated body will not be sent to the surgeons, and the forsaken sinner has no relative who will even consent to bury her out of sight. The steady undemonstrative sense of duty which actuates her, has nothing about it that is touched by any romance; she entertained no vehement attachment to the other during life; her death causes her no violent regret; the little interests of her dress and toilet have remained quite as attractive as ever; and perhaps the strongest emotion that she experienced was when she found that it would be necessary to send her new silk to the pawnbroker for a day or two, to enable her to discharge Mr. Mould's peremptory account. Looked at from one side, her conduct has been noble and sacrificial; looked at from the other, all the motives appear poor, meagre, unsentimental.

The Lady Clara is said to be generous and devout; she builds a church, she endows a charity; the Swiss Annette exhausts her genius on the plaited hair, or the sweep of the lordly silk,—which is twice as plain and twice as costly as poor Traviata's. 'Tis a magnificent piece of art; it dazzles the eye; you fall down and worship, and believe that the mystery is not so transparent as you had fancied. But subject the lady's motives to the same analysis; put her into the same crucible; use the same tests; and see how much more of eternal goodness there is in her soul than in the other's. "I protest to you," said a friend to me the other day, "let Lady Clara scorn Traviata if she will for the mighty gulf between them, in the face of eternity the saint is not distinguishable from the sinner. Both have given the cup of cold water —what then? Sophie, as we have seen, is not magnanimous: the critic, unblinded by accidents of place and circumstance will find as little magnanimity in her ladyship."

To all which there is only one reply,—" We are greater than we know." No man, and no woman, perhaps, is altogether aware of what his or her motives in any one case are. Those that lie on the surface are not the only ones involved. The cup of cold water has been given; and though, as you think, you have ticketed all the virtues it represents, you will be taught some time that the most subtle—those that partake most of the Divine beneficence—have eluded your coarse scrutiny. That homely sense of duty—on what does it rest? Whence does it derive its unfaltering constancy? On the side turned to you there is nothing very admirable, as you say; but to be even meanly and basely constant is not consistent with the only elements your analysis has recovered. The chivalry of the hero, and the charity of the saint, may not be very different from the unromantic devotion of the sinner; but this happens, perhaps,—not because the gold in every case is counterfeit,—but because it is tried in each. The deserted outcast rises to the level of a sacrificing charity, of a divine forgiveness, as well as the heroic and blameless king.

> And all is past; the sin is sinned, and I,
> Lo! I forgive thee, as Eternal God
> Forgives; do thou for thine own soul the rest.

Old Peter sat by the ingle-neuk alone, spelling through the bundle of old letters which Miles had sent him, his horn spectacles elevated in such a position on his nose that he might comfortably see *over* them. *She* had kept these letters carefully even when the old love that had made them memorable to her had been put away. Had she lived to see how hollow they were? I looked over them once: they did not ring *true*, I thought. They were gay, clever, insincere; and yet I read them with more interest than they merited. They were the miserable trophies of a sad tragedy: they had spoiled a woman's life.

"Puir lass! puir lass!" said the old man, wiping his eyes, "she was sair beguiled." And then he put them aside, and went out to the seat at the cottage-door to watch "the kirk scalin'."

So Katie sleeps among the roots and dews,—while the rival candidates canvass the electors of Ashton. The long grasses and the coarse sea-side weeds now nearly cover the unpretending slab we laid upon her grave. When last in the Northern City I could barely trace a single line of the brief prayer we inscribed upon it and which asks pardon for "one who has sinned." It is a prayer, however, that need not be forgotten by any of us, and that may bear, perhaps, to be repeated once more.

"Our Father in heaven, forgive us our sins, as we forgive them that sin against us."

One of us thought of a secular inscription,—two lines from *The Blot on the 'Scutcheon.*

> I was so young—I loved him so—I had
> No mother—God forgot me—and I fell.

But the holy quiet of Holy Writ suits the sepulchre better.

## CHAPTER V.

### THE GOLDEN SCALES.

> To be in heaven sure is a blessed thing;
> But, Atlas-like, to prop heaven on one's back,
> Cannot but be more labour than delight.

THE humours of an election have been frequently enlisted by fiction. It is only needful to say, therefore, that the election at Ashton presented all the usual features, and may be found fully described in the works of Mr. Dickens and Sir Edward Lytton. The ladies—the Devonshires and Crewes of Ashton—took a very keen interest in the fight, and, like the nymphs of Hawthornden, sported the colours of the candidate they espoused.

> For nymphs they seemed; about their heavenly faces
> In waves of gold did flow their curling tresses;
> About each arm, their arms more white than milk,
> Each bore a blushing armlet of silk,—

—Miles's colours. For Miles was, upon the whole, the popular favourite. He had youth on his side;

he had not been tried and found wanting; he came of a great house which the Ashton people had looked up to for generations. Sir Jasper, on the other hand, had offended many by his occasional hauteur, the scandal of a loose life, and his violent hostility to Mowbray, who had by this time taken everywhere a strong hold on the popular heart. But he had many personal adherents,—the exquisite charm of his manner, when he chose to be gracious, the familiar humour of his public talk, the airy boldness of his character, which enabled him to charge the Minister or the Leicestershire fences with equal ease and gaiety, had originally attached them to him, and still kept many true to their allegiance. So the fight was a well-balanced and a fair one, and it was fought out bitterly.

Trelawney spoke of his antagonist with an air of good-humoured toleration. The audacity of the boy was to be admired; these juvenile escapades were always rather amusing. But the farce had been played long enough; and it was now time Miles should go home, and leave the sober-minded and sound-thinking citizens of Ashton to their ordinary avocations. It was not a bad jest at first; but it had been protracted rather too long. "My uncle's nephew" was not the man for the independent electors of that ancient burgh.

But though Sir Jasper spoke confidently enough,

he was far from feeling so. He found that Miles was no contemptible antagonist. There was a gravity and a vigour in the young man which impressed even his adversaries. His convictions were clearly the convictions of one who had tried them for himself—the independent convictions of an independent thinker. Such a character impresses even the vulgar. A thoroughly earnest man is always powerful, however narrow and inflexible his intellect may be.

The Reverend Tudor Plantagenet was of course a warm ally, and he did Miles good service. For the slippery Plantagenet had been booked at last, and Minny was now The Reverend Mrs. Jones. Her father, old Bailie MacGroggy—a very jolly, rotund, red-faced corn-merchant—was a man of no mean authority among the Ashton worthies, and through Jones's persuasions he enlisted himself under the Warrender banner.

"He's no an ill lad," he whispered confidentially to his cronies on the Exchange; "and it's a guid thing to hae the Minister's lug, tak my word."

Sir Jasper fought to the last; but it would not do. Even his great card—Miles's alleged alliance with the scarlet lady—did not win a trick. He had reserved it to the end, and he played it on the hustings.

"After all, gentlemen," he concluded, in a low

and impressive voice, "right views on politics are not all that is necessary. A man must be a Christian, as well as a politician. What says my honourable opponent? Does he respect the venerable faith which the blood of our forefathers watered? Or does he not denounce your loftiest convictions as narrow and bigoted? Would he not substitute a superstitious ritual for the noble simplicity of our Protestant faith?"

Ingenious Sir Jasper! After this outbreak of devout invective, he did not surely deserve to be left in a minority of 29, as he was at 4 P.M. of the polling day.

After vainly endeavouring to address the electors, Trelawney, accompanied by two or three supporters, walked to his hotel. The exquisite urbanity was at length ruffled. Sir Jasper was in a thoroughly vicious temper. As he passed along the High-street, a group of men, clad in the blue jackets of fishermen, and talking eagerly together, blocked the way.

"What right have you to stop the road?" said Sir Jasper, in an irritated tone.

"As guid as your ain," answered one of the party.

"What, sirrah," exclaimed Sir Jasper, lifting the light cane he held in his hand, "you mean to be impertinent, do you?"

An old grey-haired fisherman interfered.

"Come awa, lads,—he's no worth fashin' aboot. I'd gae him a bit o' my mind an he were."

"You old rogue," said Sir Jasper, bitterly, "if it wasn't for your grey hairs, I would let you feel the weight of this stick."

"Better try it," exclaimed a young fellow, turning round savagely on Sir Jasper.

"In God's name, come away," one of his friends whispered to Trelawney. "These men are dangerous."

But Sir Jasper was obstinate.

"And wherefore not, fair sir, if I may presume to inquire of your worship?" he asked, in a taunting tone.

"Go your ways, Sir Jasper Trelawney," said the old man, coming between them; "ye hae done ruth eno' to me and mine already. Ye'll no mind little Katie, may be—na, na. Ye hae ruined mony a bit lass, that lippened to your fause tongue, sin syne. It was a braw job—to take her guid name, and syne leave her to dee at the dyke-side. Ay," he went on slowly and bitterly, "ye may forget, but God Almighty has pit it down to your reckonin'. Leave him alane, Peter."

"The deil will look after him hissel'," said one of the group.

Sir Jasper grew pale when Katie's name was

mentioned; then the old wicked light came into his eyes, and he lifted his cane over old Peter's head——

In a moment it was grasped by a powerful hand. Trelawney was on the alert, however, and freeing it by a sudden jerk, laid it sharply along young Peter's cheek. It left a bright livid line in its track.

For a second the two stood looking at each other. In another Sir Jasper was lying on the pavement, stunned by an ox-like blow delivered full in his face by the swarthy son of the sea.

"Serves him right," shouted the crowd who had gathered round.

Bailie MacGroggy sat in state, balancing the Golden Scales, and dispensing justice to the Ashton public. The Bailie was a portly man, with a good-humoured twinkle in his eyes, which, as inconsistent with the gravity of his judicial functions, he vainly endeavoured to suppress.

Sir Jasper, stung and exasperated, had charged Peter with assault; and that an assault had been committed, the ex-senator's black eye supplied unimpeachable testimony.

"My opinion is, Sir Jasper," said the worthy Bailie, after hearing a number of witnesses who voluntarily came forward, "that ye were baith to blame, and ye had best let by-ganes be by-ganes. The action is dismissed."

"Take care, Mr. MacGroggy," interrupted Sir Jasper, "how you allow your political feelings to bias your judgment on the bench."

"My conscience!" said the magistrate, loftily, "I've mair than a mind to commit ye, Sir Jasper, for contempt o' court. And if ye wull hae it, sir, troth had I been Peter, I suld hae gaen you as guid as ye gat."

The crowd laughed and cheered. Trelawney, with a parting threat, "that the Home Secretary should hear of the business," departed; and Peter was borne out of Court—the hero of a popular ovation.

A rumour had reached Norburn of the fray, and Elsie, who had been left to keep the house, waited the return of her "folk" with keen impatience. At length she heard the sound of a footstep outside, and, on unbarring the door, found herself in her lover's arms.

"What is't? Has onything orra happened, Peter?" she asked, anxiously.

Seating her on his knee beside the glowing hearth, Peter told his tale.

"Now, Elsie," he said, "just ae kiss, to finish wi', ye ken.'

Elsie's answer is not recorded; but (truth to tell)

she could not help looking with a kindly eye upon the stalwart giant; and Love is even now, though the world grows old, and its Mays are misty, as it was in the bright heroic days, when Perseus wooed Andromeda;

> Then lifting her neck, like a sea-bird
> Peering up over the wave, from the foam-white swells of her bosom,
> Blushing she kissed him: afar on the topmost Idalian summit
> Laughed in the joy of her heart, farseeing, the Queen Aphroditè.

## CHAPTER VI.

HESPERUS.

> Dame Life, though fiction out may trick her,
> And in paste gems and frippery deck her,
> Oh! flickering, feeble, and unsicker,
>    I've found her still;
> Aye, wavering like the willow wicker,
>    'Tween good and ill.

MY friend Miles used often to remind me of the association which gives a grotesque charm, a strange humorous power, to Mr. Carlyle's books. On *this* hand, the supreme law which nominally shapes our life; on *that*, the fantastic departures from it which in our practice we admit. Miles, in his grave way, was always thus contrasting practice with first principles. He tried the codes of Christendom by the precepts of Christ. The investigation undoubtedly produced some sufficiently startling contrasts. Is a system of universal selfishness the logical offshoot of a system of boundless beneficence? Christendom is a *civitas Dei* constructed by a Divine lawgiver,—does it at a single point conform itself to his law? Is there a single tribunal in Europe where the Sermon on the Mount is an authority?

Every bagman of that age saw in unlimited competition the great principle which was to renew society. "Give us free trade, and we will lick creation." Eighteen hundred years of Christian government had made this, and this only, clear to the British bagman. "To lick creation" was the ideal of human success at which he had arrived. The toil of apostles, the devotion of saints, the agony of martyrs, had not been expended in vain. The British bagman was the fruit of the soil which they had enriched by their lives, and watered with their blood.

The excitement of the election was over; and with infinite weariness and disgust Miles looked back upon his experience. "I would not do it again," he said, "for a ransom. It is filthy work." And he threw up the window impatiently, and let the evening seabreeze wander into the heated room. "Let us take a cigar and a stroll, Dean," he pleaded. "Darcy is fast asleep, *more suo*, in the big chair."

"What a selfish lot they are!" he continued, as they sauntered along the cliffs. "Everybody wants something, and something that will hurt some one else. Who will sacrifice a day's work to save his neighbour's soul? Are we to hate our enemies and our friends alike? It cannot be said now, surely, that we make any distinction between them."

"Hush," said the Dean; "you are fagged and

unstrung. No truth worth living for is to be got without work; and yet the reaction after work often leaves us too weak to profit by what we have gained. However, it fits in ultimately."

"No, no, I am sick of the whole thing. It is essentially bad and demoralizing. This unrestricted competition that they rave about is unchristianising society."

"It is certainly difficult at first sight," replied the Dean, "to believe that competition and a gospel of goodwill agree."

"At first sight!" exclaimed Miles. "Why, they are radically opposed. The principle of competition is—Every man for himself, and the devil take the hindmost; of the Gospel—Love your neighbour as yourself. To do so is to co-operate, not to compete."

There was no quality in Leighton's intellect more admirable than his consummate impartiality. He steered with brave moderation between fanaticism and infidelity—a most rare and difficult excellence. But on every subject he manifested the same calmness and justice of judgment. He would not suffer sympathy, or enthusiasm, or the *popularis aura*, to drive him in any direction where he did not clearly see his way, knowing that the unguarded impulses of the purest sympathy, or the most upright enthusiasm, are always to be dreaded.

"I trust they are not opposed," he answered. "For if co-operation is opposed to competition, and if competition be a true economical principle—as I believe it is—then co-operation cannot be sound. And if it is unsound in politics, it is not a precept of the Gospel."

"But is it not found there?"

"I think not—at least, as commonly understood. Socialism is false; it is the application of individual to political relations. It confounds the conscience of the man with the conscience of the nation. Apply it without qualification, and you arrive—logically and not remotely—at persecution. But competition is a true principle of government; it encourages healthy life; it secures the greatest average amount of good to the State."

"Hang the State!" exclaimed Miles, irreverently. "The State devours the individual."

"But we must take care," continued the Dean, "that we work the principle in a Christian spirit. To do this, we must intelligently and constantly recognise that competition is for the good, not of one only, but of all."

"But how many respect the imaginary barrier you would set up? How many, in the heat of the scramble, recognise it as the public good and not as the private benefit? A man competes because he believes that it is for his own advantage. The motive power of competition is selfishness."

"It is, no doubt; it ought not to be. The motive should be—will be some time, I hope—a wise and righteous recognition of its large national expediency. We will come right, not by changing the system, but by changing the spirit in which the system is worked."

"It comes pretty much to the same thing in the end."

"By no means. You want to abolish a true rule of policy; I want to keep it, but to clean and purify it, if I can."

"Well, I can't argue with you to-night: but I feel that such a principle is at least an inducement to selfishness."

"Alas! my dear Miles," said Leighton, with a quiet laugh, "that will not do, I am afraid. Why, life is at every point an inducement to selfishness. To be born is to receive an inducement, a very strong inducement, to selfishness. The only way to get out of the way of these inducements is to cease to be altogether. It is just because all the laws of life are inducements to selfishness, that there is any room for self-sacrifice. Because these inducements surround us on every side, we are able occasionally to turn out a really great man, who dares to disobey the clamant instincts of interest, and sacrifice himself that he may save his people."

They sat down on the sheltered bank of a deep ravine. A hawk or a raven, disturbed by their presence, swept silently along the cliffs. The white reflection of the harvest moon lay upon the water at their feet, and heaved in silvery ripples round the mouth of the Witches' Cave.

"This is refreshing," exclaimed Miles, as he lay down, and laved his hot hands in the cool green grass. "After life's fitful fever we return to thee, O venerable mother! and thou layest thy cold hands upon our hearts, and they are still."

After a pause, Leighton said—

"I am glad you denounced intolerance so strongly. It is really the greatest temptation in our way. How intolerant all of us are at heart!"

"You, my dear Dean, are the only man I know who shouldn't say so."

"Nay, I often feel that I am hugely intolerant. I am intolerant of intolerance. I sometimes fancy," he continued, "that we are getting more bigoted than we used to be. Once we employed visible instruments of persecution,—

> The lifted axe, the agonizing wheel,
> Luke's iron crown, and Damien's bed of steel;

we persecuted frankly and openly then; and I am not sure that the moral nature of a nation suffered so much when thus relieved. But those who now wage war with intolerance do not require to destroy iron or wooden instruments of torture, but what are much more difficult to get at,—shades of feeling, a habit of thought, prejudices that are inwrought with the finest textures of the conscience. Our civilization is getting every day more impersonal; we seldom come into healthy collision; the oiled wheel slips past the oiled wheel smoothly and noiselessly; and our animosities, though less loud, grow more inveterate."

"Yes," said Miles, wearily, "I fear it is so. But it is an old complaint. Euripides felt it as we do. 'Alas! no mortal is there who is free. For either he is the slave of money or of fortune; or the populace of the city, or the dictates of the laws, constrain him to adopt manners not accordant with his natural inclinations.' That is the sense of what he says, I think, in the *Hecuba*."

"The older I grow," resumed the Dean, "the more do I feel that the only thing very much worth fighting for in this world is—freedom; freedom of heart, freedom of thought, freedom of conscience. What miserable stunted beings we become when we cease, either from fear or shame, to obey our honest convictions! Nothing has a more fatal effect on a man's nature than this base compliance. And yet some really admirable people fancy that free inquiry on any 'shelved' topic is pernicious, that vast fields of speculation, like the snowy slopes of Monte Rosa, are not to be trodden by mortal feet.

"I never argue with such people," said Miles; "I simply avoid them."

"It is well," replied the Dean, "if you can do so. Argument on such men is thrown away. It only renders their hostility more bitter. But when you must not avoid them, when they belong to your own household, then comes the tug to the heart-strings. I tell you," said Leighton, sadly and earnestly, as if stirred by some deep and painful feeling, "there is nothing more miserable than to find ourselves becoming day after day more widely separated from those we love; to know that explanation is fruitless, that it can only widen the breach; to feel that never in this life can we be completely reconciled, that even in the presence of death no understanding is possible, and that the parting breath conveys a veiled reproach. The alienation of the understanding is more hopeless than the alienation of the heart." He paused a moment, and then continued, more calmly: "The only remedies for this household scourge are manliness and affection; the manliness to dare to believe at any risk, and at whatever cost, and that rare instinct of love which penetrates through the superficial environments of creed to the sound heart behind. No love is worth the name which cannot do this; but even this love is sometimes powerless. It is not, I think," he went on, "so much the aggressiveness of the heterodox that is to blame, as the ungenial narrowness and want of hearty bravery which is the fruit of bigotry. It is impossible that the moral lungs can respire freely, that the heart can beat with healthy vigour, in the foul air of intolerance. No; it poisons affection, and stunts the heart."

The Dean had almost forgotten the presence of a listener, and Miles did not care to interrupt him.

"Ah, well," he resumed, "that old grief is nearly dried up now. And God was very gracious to me in his own way. Miles, when you marry, seek out such a wife as Heaven blessed me with—a woman capable of a large tolerance, yet withal noble, generous, and devout."

"Perhaps I have found her already," Miles replied, with a confident smile.

"What are you fellows up to?" exclaimed Darcy, coming up with the terriers at his heels. "We have run you down. Your cigars betrayed you. Now, Tartar, pitch yourself over the rocks, if you please; but in that case the sharks will get you. Talking scandal against Queen Elizabeth, are you? Just let me know, please, and Tartar and I will get out of earshot, as we don't wish to be compromised."

"What were we talking of?" asked Miles. "The virtues of intolerance, I think. Have you any views on the matter?"

"I am all for intolerance," said Darcy. "Tartar has no tolerance for a *foumart;* neither have I. Let us worry the vermin out of creation. Persecution is one of the original instincts of the race."

"The difficulty is to find out who the *foumarts* are," replied the Dean. "The chance is, if you begin to worry, that you worry a respectable tabby, or a domestic tom. Better leave worrying alone."

"Not a bit of it," said Darcy. "I'll do nothing of the kind. I think your modern philandering is hopelessly wrong. You have got so wretchedly temperate and rational that you have lost all manliness. You think nothing of showing up your native land, and exposing the nakedness of your friends, because it's your duty to be impartial, and to love mankind as a brother, and all that kind of drivel. No, no, give me the patriotic fire, the tender piety of Burns.

> The rough burr-thistle spreading wide
> Amang the bearded bear,
> I turned the weedin'-heuk aside,
> An' spared the symbol dear.

Besides, I object to the principle. People are always repeating parrot-like nowadays,—Why should a man be shunned by us for holding any opinions, if he holds them honestly? That is rubbish. Suppose they are opinions contrary to decency, what do you say? Right and wrong, and the moral sense of mankind, must come in somewhere, even in the region of opinion. You wont leave Petronius Arbiter on your drawing-room table, and I wont admit a man into my house who holds that there should be no limitations on murder or adultery or theft."

"And he replies," said Miles, "you are an intolerant bigot."

"And I return him no answer except this practical one,—I disagree with you; I think your opinion leads to certain consequences of which I disapprove. I don't wish these to occur in my house; accordingly, have the goodness to leave it. I exclude him, as the Church excommunicates him, or the State hangs him. Both in public and private it is the same consideration, How am I to secure my own safety? The State says, by penalties; I say by exclusion; and there the matter ends."

"You have fallen on one of the stumbling-blocks," answered the Dean; "I confess I never very clearly saw the answer to what you urge, though I feel that it hides a fallacy. Self-preservation is a law, no doubt, both to society and the individual; and it may be right to enforce the law more strictly in the one case than in the other. The State has nothing to do with opinion; but *you* may have. Every one is the best judge of what is required for his own safety, and entitled to take the precautions which he deems fittest. But perhaps we may go even further. When the natural repugnance to an opinion is so keen as to make intercourse unpleasant, then let association cease. But a true tolerance makes these repugnances as few as may be. Testing every opinion nicely, closely, conscientiously, only when we find that it is utterly obnoxious to our moral sense, should we fence it out. And even in the most extreme case, having perfect confidence in the actual rectitude of the man, we may feel that the opinion does not infect his life, and that by associating with us he comes under an implied contract, an engagement of honour, not to attack the code we adopt."

"But opinions about the supernatural," said Miles, —"and it is against these that war is exclusively waged by the intolerant,—are not of a kind that can do practical hurt? Yet the *odium theologicum* is bitter as gall. Why should a man be excluded from our society because he believes in the Unity and not in the Trinity, in feasting and not in fasting, in the Thirty-nine Articles and not in the Confession of Faith?"

"Darcy's definition of liberty," said the Dean, "comes in effect to this—Remove those restrictions, and those only, which prevent me from doing *what I ought to do*. A very good definition, as far as it goes; but it can work in that society only where God is the visible arbiter. *Here*, who is to be the judge of the 'ought?' To what tribunal can you refer the cause? When we step in with our rude verdicts and our coarse penalties, be sure that in the long-run we do more harm than good. We kill the heretic, but we fan the heresy."

"Settle it between you," cried Darcy; "but, with your leave, I shall continue to worry my *foumart* whenever I get the chance. Ah! Tartar, lad, what are you after?"

Tartar, with his hair on end, was glaring, red-eyed, into a badger's hole. The short, sharp, vicious bark, indicated an enemy not distant. Occasionally he made a dash forward, and then suddenly backed out, casting, like the old Northmen, the earth over his head as he retreated.

"He has got his *foumart*, at last," said Miles. "Can't you fancy him a Grand Inquisitor? Does not that bark of his say as plainly as words can, 'You and I, sir, cannot exist together; there is not room in the world for us both, and as I am the stronger of the two, I will put you out of it? You do not smell well; you are a nuisance; you come between the wind and my nobility; I am convinced that it is my duty to worry you, and, please the Immortals, I will do it. Our theories of the universe, sir, are naturally incompatible, so come out and be worried at once!'"

# VI.

## DEFEAT.

# CHAPTER I.

SPRETÆ INJURIA FORMÆ.

> Only I discern
> Infinite passion, and the pain
> Of finite hearts that yearn.

THE lovers had had an angry contention.

"Weel, Peter," said Elsie, "ye may gang your gate. I dinna mind whether ye like me or no."

"I dinna doubt you," replied the giant, angrily. "Is't Tam Hewison ye're foregathered wi' noo? Are ye trysted wi' him the nicht?" he asked, scornfully; and Peter was not pleasant in his scornful moods.

The little gipsy flushed up. Her whole face glowed with the disdain which her soul felt; and Peter's eyes, giant though he was, fell before the angry lightning he had evoked.

"Tam Hewison!" she said, throwing back her head with a bright and indignant expression of surprise. "Tam Hewison! na, na, Peter, he's ower like you for me to court him."

Peter stood before the little tormentor a moment irresolute. He was hurt and sore, and was on the point of retorting bitterly; but the bright and angry gleam in Elsie's eyes arrested his speech, and he only said, in a constrained voice—

"Aweel, aweel, Elsie, tak your ain way. I'm aff. The boats 'ill be starting shortly, and they'll be needin' me to stow the nets. Gude een to ye!"

Oh, Peter, Peter! have you indeed gone? Not one little word of endearment for this last greeting; not one expression of unconstrained tenderness; not one smile or embrace. Relent and come back; could you see her now you could not but relent. All the bright, beautiful, panther-like mockery has died out of the face, which is no longer flushed, but very pale and wan. Yes, she cannot be angry any longer; she must weep to ease that sharp pain at the heart; and laying her head down upon her arm, she sobs sorely and bitterly. He was unkind, she thought; but she herself was to blame too. She would tell Peter that on the morn when he returned. Yet why not tell him to-night? Why not be reconciled at once, and weep all bitterness away upon the faithful and manly heart which, she knew, loved her so well?

Stirred by this new longing, Elsie wrapped her plaid round her head, and ran down towards the harbour. As the tide was ebbing, the boats were being towed towards the point of the pier; the crews, bearing nets and small barrels of water, were hurrying to the beach. The whole place was alive and bustling merrily, as it always is before the departure of the fleet. Elsie stopped short on the hill-side that overhangs the harbour; she could not face the crowd; if she met Peter, she must needs throw herself into his arms, and she could not do so among these strangers. So she sat down and waited, hoping that he might notice where she sat, and come to her. She saw him distinctly; saw him casting the nets into the bottom of the boat with his brawny arms; saw him with the huge oar pushing his craft away from its neighbours towards the harbour mouth, and then—ah, surely they were not starting yet?— the mast was raised and fixed, and the sail slowly and laboriously hoisted. She could doubt no longer; they were gone: and forgetting everything except the passionate desire to receive but a single word of forgiveness, she ran down the steep pathway to the beach. Peter, Peter, do you not hear that imploring cry? No, he hears nothing, save the waves as they plash against the sides of his craft. The boat beats strongly and lustily out to sea before the fresh evening breeze.

'Tis a pretty sight enough, for one whose heart is not too heavy. The rough weatherbeaten forms of the sturdy tars; the monotonous beat of the long oars, and the heavy lurching of the craft, when they meet the ground-swell outside the harbour bar; the creaking of the mast and tackle as the sail rises heavily from the deck. It is hard work, you see, to force the inert monster into motion; but at length, touched by subtle force, he digs his keel keenly into the hissing foam, and meets proudly the chill kiss of the autumnal breeze, which freshens the water, and deepens the frosty green on the sky, and drives away the slanting gleams of the sunset.

Elsie sat down on the hill-side, and watched the fleet depart. They crowded out; but her eyes were fixed on *one*, until its brown sail mingled with the brown of the twilight. Then she rose and walked home very wearily. Her heart felt very empty. With that boat the hope that had buoyed her up departed, and she returned faint and desolate. Janet had got back from the "toun;" but old Peter had not returned. Janet noticed Elsie's pale cheeks and red eyes—

"What maks you look sae white, Elsie?"

Poor Elsie, she could restrain herself no longer; a passion of tears choked her, as she turned her face to the wall, and murmured—

"That I had said but one word!"

The twilight had deepened into night—the cold clear night of the late autumn—as Miles smoked a meditative cigar along the castle cliffs. Though the sea was perfectly smooth, its roar was loud and defiant—a reminiscence of past storms, it might be: a presage, perhaps of storms to come. Otherwise, the night was very beautiful,—still and lustrous, with flitting gleams of fire in the north. That pale and silent array of warriors, on what mission is it bent?

> Their helmets gleamed white through the vapour,
> In the moonlight their corselets did shine,
> As they wavered and flickered together,
> And fashioned their solemn design.

Swiftly the fire of fight gathered along the northern horizon—swift charges—swift retreats—a kindling onset, as the northern chivalry swept the field, and the arrowy shafts of the archers rang against their burnished corslets, until the battle streamed away, and was lost upon the distant firmament, behind the Northern Star! There was scarce a breath of wind; what there was felt cold and chill for the season, and came direct from the east. "There will be more wind ere morning," Miles said to himself. "I hope the boats are within hail." As he spoke, he looked across "that wan water," and saw, or fancied that he saw, the lights on board the fleet twinkling in the distance, many miles to the south.

Miles went to bed, and slept soundly. About four next morning his servant wakened him—

"It's blowing a gale," he said, "from the sea; and the hail country-side is down on the shore. The boats are trying to weather the Borough-head."

Miles rose, and dressed himself hurriedly. The wind howled among the turrets, and by the grey light of the dawn he saw that the sea was already fiercely agitated. Huge white breakers, running across the whole bay, roared in hoarsely upon the shore. Here and there amid the tumult, a solitary boat was visible,—a scrap of sail hoisted on one of the masts, the other bare of canvas,—plunging deeply and heavily among the waves, and vainly attempting, by lying close to the wind, to escape the rocky headlands.

"God help them!" said Miles; "for man can do little for them this night."

## CHAPTER II.

A GALE FROM THE EAST.

This ae night, this ae night,
   Every night and alle,
Fire and sleet and candle light,
   And Christe receive thy saule.

When thou from hence awaye art past,
   Every night and alle,
To Whinny-muir thou com'st at last,
   And Christe receive thy saule.

If ever thou gavest hosen and shoon,
   Every night and alle,
Sit thee down and put them on,
   And Christe receive thy saule.

BEFORE eleven o'clock the wind began to rise, and a little later the pier-head at Ashton was crowded by those who began to look anxiously for the return of the fleet. One or two of the crews —more cautious than the others—about this time reached the harbour in safety, and were warmly greeted by the watchers. But this happened before midnight, and for two hours thereafter, the wind continuing to rise till it shrieked and howled among the shrouds of the vessels in port, no more appeared. The night had become very dark; it did not rain, but a thick murky cloud stretched across the sky, and blotted out the stars, and it was impossible to see any distance seaward. Only the white fringe of surf, which indicated the line of rocks beyond the bar, grew every moment more fatally distinct. Ah! that wild waste of waters out yonder in the stormy gloom, what hapless struggles, and gallant toils, and bitter throes of anguish, does the darkness veil this night!

"Where are the boats?" was the question that many an anxious heart in the crowd asked fearfully; for it was a crowd composed principally of the wives and daughters of the fishers. But there was little said, the anguish was too profound for noisy demonstration. A bright light flashed out a little way into the darkness, and struck clearly against the massive wall that protected the entrance to the channel from the east. On this a harbour pilot was stationed, and as his shadow wavered and flickered in the glare, they could see distinctly the tough and weather-beaten form of the old tar, in his round hat and pilot jacket, peering curiously into the night. The town clock was striking two, when a hail from the opposite side told them that the first boat was in sight. In another second it came within the flash of the light, and an interval of intense suspense to all who stood there followed. The blast was blowing right in-shore, and the weather-pier of the harbour had to be fairly rounded before the sheet could be lowered—a feat which required no little nerve and hardihood. They were evidently brave and skilful fellows, however, who worked this boat. Through the heavy swell that would have borne them to destruction, they held their own gallantly, and though they came in at prodigious speed, urged on by the swell, and their great sail, which had only a single reef, they were past the light, and the pier-head, and the troubled faces, before the sheet came down.

A hearty cheer, through which the pent up feelings of the crowd first found vent, greeted the men; but this was only one of a hundred boats that were still out in the stormy darkness, amid the angry waves, and the same deep and painful silence again ensued. A few minutes passed, and one by one, four black sails struggled out of the profound gloom, and three of them succeeded in making the harbour. But the last was not so fortunate. It was evidently steered by a good seaman; two heavy swells that broke close upon its bow when it first came in sight, being very skilfully avoided, and no one doubted that it would be equally fortunate with those which had preceded it. But as it approached the mouth of the harbour, the rope that held the sheet was either unskilfully loosed, or gave way under the strain; and in a moment the unlucky craft was at the mercy of the breakers, which carried it like a cork towards the white line of surf. An involuntary cry of horror scaped from the crowd. They saw the steersman rush from his seat in the boat and make a vain attempt to clutch the sheet as it escaped, ere the wind tore it away in shreds; they could almost hear the deep and bitter curse which broke from his lips at the ill luck or folly which had delivered them up to death. They could note this, but little besides, for the tragedy was consummated with terrible rapidity. The oars of the men were of no avail against the deadly gripe of the current, and although they strove gallantly for life, it was clear from the first that they were drifting hopelessly to death. A rope, as they were hurried past the pier-head, was flung to them, but it snapped like a reed before it could be fastened. Past the sickened onlookers they went, not thirty yards away, the light streaming on the white horror of their faces as they struggled helplessly with their oars. The next wave that broke upon them bore them out of sight, and shivered the craft against the Witches' Rock.

"Merciful heavens!" some one exclaimed, as the light fell upon the steersman's pale, resolute face, "it's young Peter Stephen."

What cry is that? It is the cry of a despairing woman, of a woman whose heart is broken. Poor Elsie!

Elsie had gone to bed after her aunt had administered a strong cup of tea, and quickly sobbed herself to sleep. The sore smart of the recent quarrel, the sense of an impending calamity, were forgotten, and the girl dreamt of her lover, and a bright smile played about the rosy lips as she dreamt. About midnight she wakened suddenly, with a feverish start, the wind was howling round the little cottage, and old Peter was moving about the room with the lamp, which he had lighted at the embers of the peat fire on the hearth.

"What's the matter, uncle?" she asked, wearily.

"It's a bad nicht come on, my lassie," said the old man; "I'm gaun doun till the pier-head."

Elsie sickened with fright. Her presentiment of danger, then, had been too true. "Tak' me wi' you, uncle," she asked.

"Na, na, you're best in your bed. There's na fear o' the boats—leastwise o' the lad; he kens hoo to tak Ashton pier, if ony ane kens, I warrant."

The old man put out the lamp, and cautiously opening the door, went out into the darkness. The dying embers on the hearth gave out a dreary and forlorn light. Elsie could endure the suspense no longer; hurriedly throwing on her dress, she wakened her aunt, and they went down together to the pier.

She crouched among the crowd. The wind blew her long hair about her face unregarded. Terrible to the strongest man in the crowd was that silent suspense; an agony, a fever of misery, to that poor girl. Above the roar of the wind, above the tumult of the waves, a refrain rang in her ears, " That I had said but one word." Never, never, never, can that one word be uttered now; not till the great day when they shall stand side by side before the Judge, will she be able to ask him to forgive her.

She did not faint or go into hysterics, as fine ladies would have done. She stood pale and tearless among the crowd. Her uncle was by her side, and she slipped her cold hand into his. There the two watched without speaking or moving; the girl waiting her lover, the father his son. A lusty cheer greeted each boat as it ran into the harbour, but *the one* for which they waited did not come. At length Elsie felt old Peter's hand clutch hers convulsively, but he said nothing. Another moment, and the unlucky boat and its ill-fated crew were being dashed among the waves and the rocks.

She had seen *his* face for a moment as the light fell upon it. Pale and resolute, but full of anguish; she could read its every line, as though he had been standing by her side. It was a terrible vision; so close to her, and yet separated for ever by the great gulf. Her head swam round. "Let me go to him," she cried, in wild unconsciousness, and then, staggering forward, fell stunned and helpless into the old man's arms.

## CHAPTER III.

**THE ELECT.**

Is there no pity sitting in the clouds?

A DEEP grief had fallen upon Peter's cheerful dwelling. Little Elsie had been struck down, and was now lying in a state of feverish insensibility in her lonely little crib. His son, the brave, honest, simple-hearted giant, the pride of his old age, was dead, drowned in those treacherous waters which had already proved fatal to so many of his hardy race. The body, however, had been recovered, and this was a great source of comfort and consolation both to Peter and Hester. The devouring sea would not prevent them from paying their simple charities to the dead—their homely homage to death. The scarred features had been carefully composed—the wet seaweed had been combed out of the yellow curls—the linen winding-sheet which the mother had prepared for the husband had been appropriated to the son—the body had been laid decently in the plain coffin, with its simple "P. S., aged 25," on the lid, and the coffin had been laid decently in the old churchyard among the windy bents on the shore, "which twice a day with his embossèd foam, the turbulent surge shall cover." All was over and finished, and Miles had ordered a plain slab to be laid above the dust of his simple-hearted friend; but Elsie still remained in the same state of bewildered unconsciousness. Old Hester hobbled about the cottage, old Peter sat over the hearth, gazing into the embers; but Elsie would not waken out of the strange and perilous sleep which had overtaken her. At length, weeks afterwards, Corry's low voice penetrated the dulled ear, and sank into the sad, sore heart. The spirit roused itself, cast off the ghastly winding-sheet of seeming death in which it had lain, and then the body quickly gained strength, and Elsie—a very different Elsie from the radiant Elsie of yore—was able once more to attend to the aged couple, to whom she was now doubly dear.

Old Peter was an office-bearer in the little Methodist conventicle built on the shore in front of the village; and on the Sunday following the funeral, Miles met a party of fishers returning home, who informed him that the Rev. Mr. Sturmup had that morning preached a "gran' discourse" on poor Peter, and that the close of the sermon had been reserved for the evening service.

"Let us go," said Darcy, "and hear him. I want to see what this wild people of yours really believe in."

"I am told he is a vehement bigot—loud, long-winded, and intolerant. However, the evening is fine; it will be a pleasant walk across the bay."

The twilight was falling ere they passed through the deserted streets of the deserted village; for the entire population had already crowded into the little chapel. Only as they passed Peter's cottage, they heard old Hester, as she sat solitarily by the fire, "crooning" over the words of some half-remembered text or hymn. The light played upon the withered features of the old crone, and into the little crib where Elsie, pale and smooth as a marble figure, lay in her unquiet sleep. As they approached the conventicle, they found that the service had commenced, and the words of the grand sea-psalm, sung gruffly and rudely, but heartily, by every one present, greeted them as they entered.

The floods, O Lord, have lifted up, they lifted up their voice;
The floods have lifted up their waves and made a mighty noise.
But yet the Lord that is on high is more of might by far
Than noise of many waters is, or great sea-billows are.

The building was quite crowded, and Miles and Darcy had some difficulty in finding an unoccupied pew. The preacher was a long, dark, bony man—middle-aged, apparently—the expression of his face harsh, and at times even repulsive. That he was a man of no inconsiderable ability was evident from the first sentence he uttered, and his opening prayer consisted of a very clever and elaborate account to the Almighty of the object and character of the scheme of salvation which He had invented, and with which therefore He might have been presumed to be tolerably familiar. Instead of those simple, touching, and beautiful confessions of sin, and dependence on the Divine Mercy, with which our ritual has made us familiar, he indulged in elaborate argument and rather boisterous declamation. Still, it was an able and impressive performance; though undoubtedly, whatever it might be, it was not prayer. It was rather an ornate Confession of Faith immediately addressed to the Almighty; with this effect, that it made, or seemed to make, the person to whom it was addressed, a witness to the truth of what it asserted. As such it had no doubt a certain impressive solemnity, and prepared the hearer for the peculiar and powerful discourse which succeeded,—a discourse, like the creed it represented, gloomy and fanatical indeed, but rendered striking and picturesque by its scent of the sea.*

---

\* The sketch in the text is a by no means exaggerated report of a "revivalist" discourse preached by an itinerary "revivalist" which the author had once the fortune to hear. Some of its darker features — the minute narrative, for instance, of the profligate life from which the preacher had been rescued — have been purposely omitted "as unfit for publication." I may add that Mr. Sturmup's doctrine has been coarsely but vigorously caricatured by a well known Transatlantic poet :—

*Ye shall all likewise perish,* was the brief, and characteristically misshapen, text from which it started.

### ITUR AD ASTRA.
#### (Our Confession of Faith.)

The mighty dome of heaven is quaking;
The round earth, like a bubble, breaking;
And we before the Throne do stand
On either hand.

The goats are cast into the fire,
For ever burning higher;
But the sheep feed upon the lea,
And fatten through eternity.

Impartial justice shall be shown,
By the great Judge who rules alone:
The mother and the babe she nurst
Are both accurst.

Who listens to the brazen trumpet
Blown by the Roman strumpet;
But stops his ears when humble Cumming
Begins his drumming;

Who joins the throng when wanton eyes
Inflame the carnal vanities;
Or sits with half-dressed foolish things
While Patti sings:

Who knows by rote the lusty rhymes
That Shakespeare made among the limes
On Avon's banks: these ghosts perplext
In hell are vext.

And he who deems that Mighty Love
And Mercy, infinite will prove,
Shall find that he without his host
Has reckoned—to his cost.

With joyful hearts the Elect shall raise
Perennial praise;
"Duly let us His grace extol—
He *might* have damned us all."

"Men," the preacher began, "are born in sin. They are rotten to the very core. They are not, indeed, devils—no, they are not devils *as yet*," he repeated, emphatically; "but to the natural man good is as hateful as it is to the devils in hell.

"The Almighty," he continued, "had it seemed good to him, might have left us to perish utterly. We could not compel Him to save us. He is the All-powerful. We are not necessary to His happiness. He is the All-happy. We had no claim upon his mercy—whatever He has done for us, has been done out of His own infinite beneficence."

"No claim?" muttered Miles, uneasily. "Was He not their Maker? He who had implanted these capacities for sinning, permitted these possibilities of evil! Have they not the claim which the weak have upon the strong? Not necessary to His happiness? Has the Divine Purity, then, no satisfaction in the diminution of pollution?"

"Hush!" said Darcy; "let us see how he gets them out of the scrape."

"But, my brethren, He did not leave all to perish. He chose to save some from the wrath which is to come. Not, however, for any goodness or virtue of their own, but out of His own free choice, are the elect redeemed. And who are the elect? Nay, my brethren, let us not inquire too urgently. We cannot tell who they are—we cannot penetrate His decrees—we cannot explore the depths of His sovereign and almighty will. This only do we know, that these are they which have come out of great tribulation. Be patient, therefore, my suffering and sorrowful brethren! Be patient and endure to the end, until the old heaven and the old earth have passed away, and ye behold that new heaven and that new earth, where," he added, as he gazed down on old Peter and the vacant pew, "where there is no more sea."

He paused a moment as if to realize the vision he had summoned up. For a moment it seemed to cast a certain grave beauty around the harsh features—for a moment only. When he resumed, the lips were hard and stern as ever.

"Of those who are left to perish what shall we say? They are abandoned to destruction by an infinitely wise and holy God,—is not that sufficient for us who believe in Him? And yet we need not doubt that they justify their damnation. They break the tables of the law, the commandments of Sinai; they are murderers, adulterers, fornicators. On the Sabbath-day, on the day when the Maker himself rested from his labour, they eat and drink, and make merry. O stiff-necked generation! who shall deliver you from the wrath to come? Know you not that this is a holy and divinely consecrated season? When on this day I behold the sailor or the husbandman walking heedlessly along the shore of the ocean which encompasses us even now, I hear from out of heaven the menace of an angel-voice. 'Know you not,' it asks, 'that you are walking on the shore of the boundless ocean of Hell? Do you not see its molten waves of devouring fire? Do you not feel the scorching blast that fans the smoke which rises from its dreadful waters? Are you not blinded by the glare which reddens the adamantine heaven? Hear you not the trumpet of the destroying-angel, the shrieks of the damned, the anathemas of devils? Ay, there they writhe in torture. The souls of strong men are torn asunder in their agony; their sisters and their wives clasp imploring hands, and ask God to save their tender limbs from the fire which burns and yet consumes not. Ay, God save them! But even the Lord of Hosts cannot do it. Even the Omnipotent cannot rescue them from the lake. His hands are powerless. Justice, which sits above the Throne of God, has set fast its decrees. The worm dies not: the fire is not quenched. We are lost—*lost*—LOST. Heaven and earth shall pass away, but Hell shall endure for ever."

Overcome by excitement, his black hair lashed back from his pallid brow, the sweat falling in great drops from his face upon the Bible, his voice quivering with emotion, he paused a moment as he closed the volume, and then opening the little hymn-book that lay below it, said in a low and exhausted voice, " Let us praise God for his infinite goodness, by singing together the Sixty-second Scriptural Paraphrase, beginning at the seventh verse." And then the rough voices took up the hymn.

Reserved are sinners for the hour when to the gulf below,
Arm'd with the hand of sovereign power, the Judge consigns his foe.
Though now, ye Just, the time appears protracted, dark, unknown,
An hour, a day, a thousand years to heaven's great Lord are one.

"A verra comfortable discoorse," said Widow Bodie, an old lady in a red cloak and white mutch, as she accompanied Widow Buchan to the door of her cottage.

"That exhibition is immoral," said Darcy, as they left. "I have felt Rachel's unholy fascination. I felt it again to-night. The man is possessed by a demon. But he is a great actor," added the politician, "and worth gaining."

The shadows of the autumn twilight lay upon the bay as they strolled home across the sands. How grand and peaceful the sea was that night! The ripple broke noiselessly upon the beach at their feet; but away out yonder in the gloom, they heard the voice of the great Deep, — "Deep calling unto deep."

"No," said Miles, "such convictions as that man enforced to-night would make life intolerable, were they credible. But no one believes in the eternity of his own misery. Hope is the heaven-touched instinct which tells him that out of this evil must issue an ultimate good. It is the finger which points to the hidden blessedness. What heart could utter the 'Vale, vale, in æternum vale!' without breaking? If misery be eternal, then hope is a lie."

Overhead spread the infinite spaces sown with illimitable systems. Can it be that behind the starry silence rises an angry Olympus? Do Odin and his fierce warriors still quaff the bowl sweetened with the bitter tears of mortal men? Thank God that it is not so. *As for all the gods of the heathen, they are but idols: it is the Lord who made the heavens.* Odin and the Olympians have been abolished.

> The goats may climb and crop
> The soft grass on Ida's top,
> Now Pan is dead.

We are no more the victims of vindictive malice or of aimless caprice; but the worlds lie in the hollow of His hand, and in His encasing spirit we live and move and have our being.

Homer is not to be blamed for the unseemly tumults which convulsed Olympus, seeing that the Thunderer himself had to strain every nerve to prevent the wrath of Achilles from thwarting the Supreme design.

> Lest, frantic for his loss, he even pass
> The bounds of fate, and desolate the town.

But it is difficult to extenuate the British Christians who endow the Lord of Hosts with the frailties of mortal combatants, and attribute to the Almighty in his government of the universe the policy of a parish beadle.

## CHAPTER IV.

### A REPULSE.

> That is said
> Austerely, like a youthful prophetess,
> Who knits her brows across her pretty eyes,
> To keep them back from following the grey flight
> Of doves between the temple columns.

"ONE lady," says Heine, "did not shed a single tear—in that lies the whole catastrophe." Bitterly true.

What avails it to go on writing? The races of men make haste to destruction, and will not be stayed. No warning of mortal wisdom is heeded: the menace upon the angry heaven is scorned. Men are hard, obstinate, exacting; women fickle, capricious, perverse: so they were when paper was made of the Nile reeds among which the daughter of Pharaoh found the deliverer of Israel; so they continue to be when it is made of the dirty rags collected by his despised posterity. Perversity is in the blood, and no amount of schooling can eradicate the taint. We see every day the life-long woe that an idle word may breed: the sharp undying sting that a momentary miscarriage inflicts; the heavy retribution that silly pique or light caprice exacts. But the warning is disregarded; and even when the tragedy is enacted before our own eyes, and on our own little stage—even when we note how the swift and fleeting alienation of the lovers has been frozen by the hard hand of death into a form of enduring pain,—it does not make us pause. We would not repent though one rose from the dead.

Alice sat on the terrace at Hawkstone which overhung the sea. It was the afternoon, and the drowsy hum of the bees among the fox-glove mingled with the languid beat of the fisher's oars on the motionless water. Alice in her breezy summer muslin looked delightfully cool and sylph-like, and Darcy seemed to think so as he seated himself by her side.

"That wide-awake of yours has caught a charming curve—the white feather is exceedingly becoming."

"I am sorry I cannot say the same of yours," retorted the little lady. "How is it that you men can't dress yourselves now?"

"Because it bores us, I suppose," he replied languidly. "We haven't time for the milliner."

"And we have, while you waste yours on frivolities. Well, I confess I did look at myself for an hour or two in the glass this morning."

"You could not have been better occupied."

"Thank you; I think not. The white feather," she replied, taking it off and looking at it, "is worth the time. It reminds me of Marie's, in the opera. Piquant and soldier-like, is it not?"

Darcy did not reply. He was looking at the light-frilled curls — the Devil's frills, I think they have been irreverently termed—through which, now that they were released, the breeze, and the sunbeams wandered distractedly.

"Where did you get that thing you wear?" she continued, with mock gravity. "Its curves, as you call them, are fearful and wonderful. Do you sit upon it?"

"That must be it, I fancy," he said, absently; "Miss Evelyn—will you favour me with your opinion on a point I am considering?"

"I have no opinions—only one or two fancies which I like to keep to myself. Besides, I thought you were paid for it."

"I will send you my fee—if the opinion is not against me."

"No, no; you must take it whether you like it or not. I hope it is a very intricate point; I won't say anything unless it is."

"Well—it's just this. A friend of mine has done a very foolish thing—he has lost his heart. And he comes and asks me what he is to do?"

A slight blush flitted across Alice's transparent

cheek as he began; but before he had finished the red lip curled rather disdainfully, and the eyes sparkled with malice.

"He must be rather a—a—spoon—is not that the word?—this friend of yours. Being so, I think he had much better hold his tongue. That's my opinion."

"But you see he has made up his mind."

"Of course he has done that, and then he comes to ask what to do."

"He has made up his mind to tell her—if there be any hope of winning. But they are very good friends just now, and he would not like to do anything to hurt her. He thinks that she likes him well enough, but he doesn't fancy that any young lady now-a-days would choose love and poverty—and that sort of thing, you know."

"Oh, yes; I know perfectly well. He must be an excellent judge of women, and let him be satisfied that in this case at least he is right. Love and that sort of thing, you know," she went on in a mocking tone, "is quite an old-fashioned complaint, and nobody takes it now-a-days. He had much better be prudent—a virtue, indeed, that he don't neglect, seemingly. Tell him so, please. Tell him that no woman marries for love—that unless he has ever so many thousands a year it would be absurd to suppose that any woman could love him. We are excellent judges of what suits us best, and none of us care for a man who lives in a garret. We must have our carriage and our house in the Square, and our account with Howell, which would probably be three times as much as he is worth. Without these none of us can fancy being happy—of course not. Tell him so, please, from me."

The little lady spoke with decision—somewhat scornfully too; and Darcy did not like the mocking curl of the red lip,—not quite so red as usual it was now, perhaps. He looked at her doubtfully for a moment, and some words trembled on his tongue —but he said nothing.

And then the little lady looked at her watch. "Dear me! how late it is," she exclaimed; and making him a little scornful curtesy, she walked away, leaving him seated.

Darcy sat there rather disconsolately. She had seen through his sorry artifice, he thought, and had rejected him not only without kindness, but with scorn. Well, perhaps he deserved it; and he continued to brood rather gloomily over the situation. His reveries were at length interrupted:

"Darcy, where is Corry? Have you seen Corry? Where can Corry be?" and little Effie ran up to him in breathless haste, and seated herself by his side.

"No, my princess. May I help your ladyship to look for her?"

"Oh, I don't mind. I am too tired. I must rest. Tartar has run away from me—I think he saw a rabbit—and he has gone into a hole. Do you think he will get out?"

"He will prefer to stay with the rabbits, I suspect."

"Then Corry will be so sorry. But where can she have gone?"

"Ask Miles; perhaps he knows."

"Oh, I can't find Miles either. Miles has not been attentive to me," she added, in an injured and stately tone; "I am not pleased with him."

"Then your ladyship will make Darcy her knight, will you not?"

"I am afraid I can't do that," she replied hesitatingly. "That would not be right. You know," she continued, confidentially, "that I am Miles's little wife."

"And you won't take me then? It's very unkind of you."

"I like you very much, Darcy, indeed I do," said the child, clambering up on the seat, and putting her arms caressingly round his neck. "Do you think I might take both of you? I'll ask Miles."

"Hullo!" cried Miles, who, with Corry leaning on his arm, had approached unperceived by them; "what are you about Effie? Kissing Darcy, I do declare," he cried, with affected horror.

"No, I was not," she said, poutingly; "no, I was not kissing him, and it's very naughty of you to say so."

And then she retreated with great dignity and put herself under Corry's protection.

"Oh no, she had just rejected me," said Darcy, "and in your favour. Let me congratulate you."

But little Effie would make no reply to the accusation; but, taking hold of Corry's hand, she affected not to have heard, and entered into a confidential communication about Tartar, who just then made his appearance covered with mud. He lay down before them, panting as if he would burst his sides, and wagging his tail faintly.

"Tartar," said Effie, solemnly, "where have you been, sir? How could you——"

But Tartar looked up impudently and confidentially into her face, and allowed his red tongue to hang out of his black muzzle with provoking composure.

And then they went in to dinner. I am afraid that Alice was a thorough flirt. She was never more lively than during the evening; and when Sir Maxwell asked her for a Norland ballad—he would always have one before going to bed—she sang the most coquettish of songs with the most provoking tenderness.

> O dinna ask me gin I loe thee,
>   Troth I daurna tell,
> Dinna ask me gin I loe ye,
>   Ask it o' yoursel.

> O dinna look sae sair at me,
>   For weel ye ken me true;
> O, gin ye look sae sair at me,
>   I daurna look at you.

And thereupon she cast at Darcy a look of saucy and laughing defiance that fairly belied the words. I wonder if the little tormentor had a soft place anywhere about her heart? I fear not. Darcy at least looked very glum upon it, and (while Corry still fluttered round Miles like a butterfly) moodily retreated to his pipe.

# CHAPTER V.

VAE VICTIS!

So evil wounded was the knight,
That he behoved to dee.

"MISS EVELYN," said Darcy, firmly, when he found himself alone with her in the conservatory next morning, "I cannot bear this any longer. Pardon me, but I must speak frankly with you for five minutes."

"What do you want?" she replied, petulantly. "You are getting quite annoying. I wish you would leave me alone. Corry wants her geraniums watered."

"Please listen to me for one moment. You cannot have misunderstood what I said yesterday, however clumsily I put it. And now let me say it as plainly as I should at first: Miss Evelyn, I love you—love you with my whole heart, with a love as deep and constant, I believe, as man ever felt for woman."

She sat down. For a moment she turned very

pale; for a moment, I believe, she felt inclined to obey the honest impulse of her heart, but the old spirit of perverseness returned, and she would not own the "weakness," as she called it to herself.

"I like you very well, Mr. Langton," she replied, lightly; "but you are not nearly so amusing as you used to be. You get more tiresome every day. Do, please, change this foolish talk; we shall get on much better if you do."

"We shall not get on at all. I am not any longer able to bear this," he went on with unwonted passion; "I thought I could yesterday—I find I am mistaken. I say once more that I love you—that I would have you to be my wife. Tell me if you will be so. I must have an answer, yea or nay."

Somewhat rough wooing, I fancy, and so Alice thought. The defiant spirit kindled up in her, more especially as she felt, or seemed to feel, that she was yielding. It became a matter of honour with her not to give way. She was piqued into obstinacy.

"Upon my word, Mr. Langton, you are somewhat peremptory. I am not used to be spoken to thus. Really, it seems to me that you are becoming very disagreeable."

Darcy looked at her grimly in silence for a moment.

"Am I, then, to understand that you do not care for me—that you will not consent? Do not throw away the heart that is offered to you," he said, almost bitterly. "Such love is perhaps worth even your acceptance."

The bitterness grated upon her ear. All the perverseness in the little woman's nature was thoroughly roused.

"Don't suppose," she exclaimed, scornfully, "that I am not duly aware of the honour you design. The sense of my unworthiness must excuse me to you. Make no sacrifice, sir, on my account, I beseech you."

The tone in which the words were spoken stung him to the quick.

"Thank you, Miss Evelyn, you have undeceived me," was all he said; and turning quickly on his heel, he left her.

Alice lay back in her seat and covered her face with her hands. She was glowing all over with excitement. What perverse demon had taken possession of her soul, and made her thus reject the man she loved? For be it spoken frankly here,—I hate all deception and mystery,—even while the sharp bitter words were falling from her lips, her heart thrilled with tenderness.

Are we our own masters, my masters? If we are, why are we so often prevented by aimless pique or objectless obstinacy from doing that to which our whole soul prompts us? When the very blessing for which we have prayed is granted, why do we turn from it and affect to wish that it had not been granted? A jest, an idle word, has changed the destiny of an empire. It was a taunt from Cassius that sent Cæsar to the Capitol. And it happens also in the lives of most men and women that a momentary impatience, a passing pique, an unaccountable perversity, renders the whole after-life barren, fruitless, and unblessed. Our free will and our free reason are no better than philosophic watch-words; for constantly in the course of life we find that we have been the mechanical slaves of motives that cannot be sifted, that will not bear analysis. A trifle that cunning fate leaves in the way turns us aside from the engrossing desire of our hearts. A trifle at the time—but oh! how tragic the trifle, when three-score years of vain repentance have failed to redress the sorrow that has drained the springs of hope, and spoiled *one* life at least.

Life must be taken on its own terms; but there are times when one does feel inclined to throw up the bargain. It is sometimes such a weariness. When ambition and love withdraw their urgent motives, when the fervid pulse beating high with excitement and hope abruptly stops, or creeps on so feebly that its dull and languid life grows more intolerable than the sharpest pain, we are often tempted to wish that it might cease altogether. "O that I had the wings of a dove, that I might flee away and be at rest." Beyond the dawn-struck summits of the snowy hills, in the silent places of the heavens traversed only "by morn, and even, and the angels of God," peace is to be found, perchance. God knows! But here at least we can only chase the phantom of a hope, and happy are they on whom the phantom does not cease to beckon. But few of us are permitted to keep even the illusion. Ambition becomes powerless, and love is wrecked. When we have received our sentence, when our most passionate prayers have been heard unheeded, when the wonderful eyes into which we have piteously gazed will not answer our appeal, when the sweet lips have told us with cruel calmness that there is no hope for us any more, how the charm is taken out of work, how bleak life becomes from henceforth! Cynics tell us that such sorrows do not kill, that the sharpest pain loses its edge and ceases even to hurt. It is false. Such misery is immortal. We may plod on; the mild happiness and the common joys of middle life may make us content; but a light has passed out of our lives that can never be restored; the mainspring has snapped; we are never again quite what we were before. Had our prayer been granted, would it have been otherwise?

And no pain stings like unrequited love. The separation of death is easier to bear. Innocent is dead. The white and stainless lily could not outlive its spring. And so the pale cheek gradually lost its faint, delicate, zephyr-like bloom, and the soft eyes their earthly light, and a shadow fell upon the white brow, that, had it not been for the deep love in both your hearts, would have made her almost strange to you, even while she stayed beside you. But she died in your arms; your name was the last upon her lips; and the strong instinct of immortal love binds you deathlessly together. When Christ who is our life shall appear, then shall she also appear with him in glory; and in that great city, the Holy Jerusalem, descending out of heaven from God, the vows that were cut short will be renewed. But Mabel still lives. All the wealth of your heart has been laid at her feet; all the memories of her sweet girlhood have been invoked; piteously you prayed her to have mercy—in vain. She turned her head aside; she told you haughtily or kindly (upon my soul, I forget the tone—but what does it matter?) that your love stirred no echo in her heart, and—she married your rival. Upon him her eyes shed a light that never fell upon you—though you dreamed it, fool that you were. Yes, death's sting is not the sharpest. To know that you are an alien from the heart which you have made your home, that its household gods can never be yours, is more bitter than a dishonoured name or a bankrupt ambition.

"I have made one cast for happiness," said Darcy;

"now I will go in for ambition—a wealthy wife and the woolsack."

As for Alice, she went on with tearless eyes watering the geraniums, but she saw the flowers no longer.

## CHAPTER VI.

### A NIGHT IN VENICE.

Here you come with your old music—and here's all the good it brings:
What! they lived once thus at Venice, where the merchants were the kings;
Where St. Mark's is; where the Doges used to wed the sea with rings.

DARCY was to have acted as "best friend" at Warrender's marriage; but the wounded hero had not the heart to stay. "Oh! how bitter a thing it is to look into happiness through another man's eyes!" Darcy disappeared for six months. I cannot say where he went. Some one had seen him at Venice with Lord Ashton,—Lady Beatrix's eldest brother, and the heir to the Dukedom. A member of the Alpine Club was said to have met him on the North Pole. Another had hob-nobbed with him in the Great Geyser. I incline to believe that he spent his time mostly among the Lagoons. His name, at least, frequently occurs in Sedley's *Souvenirs from the South* which were published a year or two thereafter, and rather ruffled—for ten days—the English proprieties. Sedley avers that the lawyer fell madly in love with the great singer Catarina; but I suspect that Sedley himself was the victim. Darcy may have flirted with the Gipsy Queen in passing,—*que voulez vous?* Can a man live without bread, or without love? We must eat or die. At any rate—if we are to credit the Confessions—they had rather a wild time of it. They shot wild-duck among the islands during the day; they bathed, they danced, they eat ices at Florian's; their black gondola, with the eastern battle-axe, ominous and menacing, at the prow, stole like a water-snake through the dim canals. I do not know if my readers (those who survive the joltings of this infernal machine) will allow me to wander so far away; yet perhaps they may relish—after these haggard northern coasts —a breath of air from "the sweet South," and a fugitive glimpse into the festive life of the Adriatic.

---

*THE FENICE.*

O father! what a hell of witchcraft lay
In the small orb of each particular tear.

"Catarina has come back from Milan," said Darcy, looking up from the shabby Venetian newspaper he had been diligently perusing; "she sings tonight at the Fenice. We must go."

When we entered the house they were at the end of the second act. I forget now what the opera was named, but I believe it was an Italian adaptation of

## A NIGHT IN VENICE.

*Macbeth*—very characteristic in its way; for a certain Carlotta, amid a cloud of white-bosomed nymphs, in extremely transparent gauze, was skipping over the floor, to the unbounded amazement of the good Duncan, who had probably never seen anything of the kind before. I secured a comfortable position in the *fauteuil* which Darcy, with the connivance of the box-keeper, had conveyed into his box, and glass in hand leisurely surveyed the beauties who lined the principal tier: women with their golden hair in sunny ripples, like the ripples that shine on the Adriatic. Titian painted their mothers.

But Carlotta had skimmed off the stage as a seamew skims the waves, " now wafted through the air, now moisting the tips of its wing-feathers in the violet-coloured sea;" the simile, dear critic, is old as Homer, who applied it to the swift-footed Hermes, and therefore, though not original, must be good; and ere the burst of applause that followed her performance had ceased, Catarina stood suddenly before the people, and hushed the tumult. Like most opera-goers, I know nothing of music; but I fancy that her voice was not one of great extent or compass, as they call it. Still, there was passion, expression, natural music in its tones, which made it infinitely more persuasive than a more powerful organ. It was, of course, a contralto,—no profound emotion can receive adequate expression, except through these rich notes. Depend upon it that in such a voice Sappho carolled her exquisite little scraps,—sharp, luminous, and radiant as diamond-chips for ever and ever,—and Troy would never have been sacked had Helen, as she hung over her golden shuttle, expressed her passion in a soprano. We reverence the tenor; for in a tenor (so a great commentator assures me), Achilles was singing the deeds of heroes when Ulysses found him among his ships; but the contralto, doubt it not, is " *the* most excellent thing in woman."

Still Catarina was not a great singer. There she was matched often—sometimes probably excelled. But as an actress she stood alone. In this second scene she had little to say—a few passionate words of anger and entreaty. But the vignette was perfect in its way; an elaborate picture could not have been more curiously finished. She stood before the house for one breathless moment, a white-armed fury. Very beautiful, but fierce and merciless as the panther, as raising her white arm she points pitilessly to the chamber wherein lies the king. Such an arm! I have never seen its match. It spoke to the people expressively, eloquently as her face. What often becomes an incumbrance to an inferior artist, was with her the highest spell of her craft. In its strained and agitated muscles you could read anger, contempt, defiance, detestation; most womanly weakness, when at the end it dropt exhausted and helpless by her side. She cast it up to heaven, and its grand vehement curve invoked the vindictive gods; it clasped the neck of her Roman lover with the passion and tenderness of an Italian Aphrodite.

When the curtain fell, I found that Darcy had quitted the box; so I lay back and ruminated on this ireful apparition—this deep-breasted Roman matron.

But Catarina's triumph was reserved for the last act. The general conception of the act was unsubstantial enough; but her acting redeemed it. She has taken off her jewels and the rich robes which befit a noble's wife; there is nothing save her white night-gear around the queen. Her small feet are bare; and though they are blue with cold, the marble floor does not chill her. She advances coldly, calmly, stilly—like the visitant of a dream. What wants the queen? She knows well, no doubt; for there is neither hesitation nor embarrassment in her gait. But look into her eyes. They are blank, expressionless, like a statue's. The lamp is there, but the light has been extinguished, or rather inverted, turned in, to illumine that inner life men call the conscience. For see, a spasm of pain contracts the pale lips, and the white hands wring each other in a fierce pressure. "Out, damned spot." 'Tis in vain. That white arm and that little hand, all the perfumes of Arabia will not sweeten again. Ay! she knows it. She will give up the fight. The

T

fever has devoured her life, and the damned spot has eaten into her soul. What a sigh is there! 'Twas that sigh snapped the heart-strings. Back to bed, fair queen, an you list; but it matters not. The hours are numbered. No man or woman could groan that bitter groan and live. So the pale apparition passes away to her doom,—pale, but with the flush of pain still upon her cheek.

"Catarina wants us to sup with her," whispered Darcy, as the curtain fell upon the funeral train that bore the queen to burial.

"Where? In Hades?" I asked, for the spell was not yet broken.

"By no means," he answered, laughing, "else had I declined the invitation with thanks. No, no! at the Palazzo Soranzo, a much nicer place, and pleasanter company, I take it. At least, she has the best *chef* in Venice, a real artist, like his mistress. There is a delicacy," he continued with animation, "a subtlety, nay, at times a grotesque oriental richness in his conceptions, that become Venice admirably. He is one of the masters; B—— says he belongs to the chosen people."

"Let us go."

And we went.

### THE SORANZO.

*Hebe, when her zone
Slipt its golden clasp, and down
Fell her kirtle to her feet,
While she held the goblet sweet,
And Jove grew languid.*

The Palazzo Soranzo, on the Canale Grande, is one of the most sumptuous in Venice.

We were led through the central sala, which was, *more Veneziano*, filled with flowers and vines, among whose branches a few lamps were suspended, along the grand balustrade, to Catarina's own room. The other guests, two or three Italian gentlemen and a brace of Englishmen, Lord Ashton and Mr. B——, had arrived, and the party was at supper. Darcy mentioned my name: Catarina bowed and smiled. The pallor of the spectral sleep-walker still haunted my mind; I saw before me the rosy revel of a Bacchante. The contrast was effective and striking. Could this girlish form assume the superb matronhood of Rome? could the merry and mocking eye, the mischievous smile, pale their lustre at will under the pressure of an intolerable woe?

The style of the room added to the contrast. It is a thousand pities that so little remains of the rich interiors of the old Venetian life. San Marco and the Ducal Palace may survive for another generation; but those domestic adornments, not less, nay, even more characteristic of the genius of its people, have been either destroyed or dispersed. At home the Venetian noble was the most luxurious of men, a luxury ministered to by a taste sumptuous in its simplicity, refined in its caprice. His was a civilization which combined a Roman manliness with an Oriental languor. Massive couches, gigantic cabinets, mirrors framed in columns of jasper and porphyry, benches at which the sons of Anak might have supped, were overrun with the whimsical fancies of the Moor. When I first knew Venice much of this remained; but thirty ruthless years have left scarce a single trophy behind them. Catarina's room retained its antique magnificence. There had been no change for a century; none perhaps since her fair namesake, Catarina Cornaro, "a widow, but no wife," came back from Cyprus. The transparent floor of cool and snow-like marble; the elaborate carvings of the antique high-backed chairs; the fantastic cupids around the mirror from Murano; the walls hung with the celebrated cloth of gold, which weavers of Bagdad wove for Alraschid, and merchant-princes bore from the Tigris to deck their palaces on the salt Lagoons. The ceiling was painted of a sky-like blue, with fleecy patches of vapour, and behind the clouds, roguish and rosy-cheeked, the fair-haired Venetian children lurked and smiled. But the crowning glory of the room was the cinque-cento frieze, with its quaint border of grotesque satyr and purple grape-crowned faun, circling the immortal gods of Giorgione. For lo! the Immortals.

With ruffled plumage the kingly bird nestles in the unwary breast of Hermione. Apollo strings his lyre beside the banks of the Amphrysus, and night after night, upon old Latmos, Diana stoops to kiss the dead Endymion. Here the smiling Hebe fills with flowing nectar the cup of an enamoured god; and Bacchus, flushed with the grape-juice and crowned with the vine-leaf, springs lightly from his chariot,

———while his eye
Makes Ariadne's cheek look blushingly.

Death itself is changed by the magic pencil into an influence graceful and endearing. Hyacinthus forsakes not the beautiful world, and the pleasant sunshine that he loves: but, as a delicate flower, still communes with the god. The melancholy tree is charged with the drooping spirit of Cyparissus; and in the feathered anemone Adonais blooms into a purer and gentler life. But now bow down, bow down; for lo! Aphrodite in her immortal girlhood woos the young Anchises among the sheep-cots on Ida—Ida, that looks down on windy Troy!

We gathered round the open window which reached to the floor, and admitted right into the midst of us the full sweep of that glorious outer life. The moon had scarcely risen; the warm haze of the summer night hung over the city: innumerable lights played upon the rippling water. In the pauses of the talk we heard the lapping of its waves on the palace walls; for in Venice the sea is never still. Through the most sequestered canal the tide of the Adriatic ebbs and flows. Among its palaces and its tombs, its marts and its churches, there is the unresting murmur of the very sea.

> Through all the isle
> There is no covert, no retired shade,
> Unhaunted by the murmurous breath of waves.

The talk turned naturally upon the fortunes of this strange people.

"Ah!" said Catarina, "I wish I had lived two hundred years ago. What a famous life I should have led then!"

Darcy was very glad that her birth had been postponed.

"We could not have spared you," he said.

Her male friends—and she had none of the other sex—addressed the actress in a certain tone of freedom, the inevitable result of her equivocal position; but it never degenerated into grossness or indelicacy. Catarina was not exactly what she should have been, certainly: but one felt when with her that this was more the accident of her position than her choice. She could not have been naturally vicious. The slight child-like form, with its indefinite and impalpable grace, was the incarnation of innocence,—on the surface at least. And if her language, the tone of her thought, the consciousness of her smile, the wild levity of her manner, at times

insensibly produced the conviction that there was
a taint somewhere, the sensuousness of her constitution was so bound up with and disguised under
a bright and sparkling intellect, a restless and sensitive imagination, that it rather added to her charm.
Hers was the moral languor, the spiritual *abandon*,
of Aspasia.

Catarina used to remind certain people of Alice
Evelyn: yet was she formed upon an essentially
different type. Richer instincts, more delicate insight,
on the whole a finer organization; but slight, sensitive, and tremulous, as a flower. She might
have been a poet had she learned to rhyme, or an
orator had she not been an actress only. But as it
was, the poetic temperament in her spent itself in
gay, sparkling, sarcastic sallies which young Mr.
Sheridan might have envied, and during graver intervals communicated to her character a ripe and
prodigal pensiveness, like the purple leaves and sun-
sets of autumn.

Her eyes were hazel—people said so at least; but
the colour changed continually in them, as it changes
on the sea. It was never exactly the same for ten
minutes together. And it was a wonderful eye that
lay in wait behind the long dark lash,—so long that
cast a shadow on the transparent cheek; an eye
that expressed with curious mobility every change of
feeling, every phase of passion. Now it overflowed
with dreamy and voluptuous tenderness, then it

sparkled with bewitching mockery and charming malice; now still and ominous, it crouched like a leopard in its lair, then flashing as a sabre-stroke from its silken sheath, it smote the beholder along the face, so that even a strong man would grow pale and embarrassed before the sovereign lustre of her scorn.

Her cheek,

> White as the consecrated snow
> That lies on Dian's lap,

had that transparent delicacy of hue which we associate with disease. One could look into it as into the veins of serpentine and agate that wander round the sepulchre of the merchant-dukes at Florence. Yet it generally retained a rare flush of colour; a flush like that with which the Greek stained his marble of Psyche or Latona; a flush which woke up and wandered fitfully along, as though the breeze fanned it; a flush like the rosy bloom caught of a strayed sunbeam by a pearl or a shell below the sea.

The mouth was quite in character with the rest of the face; delicate, tremulous, the lip cleanly cut, and indicating a quick, nervous, susceptible temperament. The smile that played around her mouth was, like Undine's, white and wave-like. The hair, "brown in the shade, golden in the sun," and among whose fretted network all day the sunbeams strayed, rippled around the low Greek brow; rippled around the white, proud, defiant little throat; and fell at length in a cloudy cataract over the white peerless curve of the shoulder.

The same type was predominant throughout; a charming uncertainty, an exquisite indecision, each trait so subtle and evanescent as to baffle classification and defy analysis. One felt disposed to lay hands on the fairy creation—could such a gossamer be touched by mortal hand without breaking—and forcibly prevent it from turning itself, as seemed inevitable, and perhaps most meet, into a hare-bell or a sunbeam.

"Who could I have been?" she asked; "I am not quite sure."

"Bianca Capella," Darcy suggested.

"Catarina Cornaro," said B——, one of the Englishmen present.

"Bianca, no; Catarina, yes. Yes, I should have been the bride of Cyprus. Besides, I was named after her."

"Catarina let it be," answered Darcy, twisting some vine-leaves that lay round the fruit, into a wreath; "may I crown your queenship?"

"We thank our loyal servant," she said, inclining the little head to him with grave condescension. He twined the green leaves into her light hair. "Green on gold," he said, "the colours of the Cornari."

"Just so, and the Doge—Marino Faliero, is it not?—welcomes us home to Venice." "Nay, my lord, we cannot enter Bucentaur. We are a daughter of Venice. 'And Queen of Cyprus,' replies the stately gentleman in his noble way, as he leads us to his barge. I should have kissed him ere we landed, I know I should: Catarina did it."

"Happy man," murmured Darcy.

"Yes," said B———, "those old merchants understood the grand courtesies of national life. We have forgotten the art. The antique gentlemanliness has departed. I too belong to a merchant people; but it deals only in the retail trade. We are a nation of shopkeepers."

"We always did these things well," said the Padre; "it was natural to us. The effect, indeed, was studied with an artist's eye; but there was a true gentlemanlike spirit, as you call it, at the root, we may be sure. The most graceful courtesy the Republic ever paid, I think, was when, during the war of Chioggia, in calling on the citizens to contribute, it specially excepted from the tax 'Tiziano Vecellio, that marvellous painter, and Jacobo Sansovino, the great architect.' What a masterly tribute of admiration!"

"Only fancy," exclaimed Darcy, "the uproar such an exception would make in England. Favouritism! Corruption! It would be denounced as a ministerial job from every hustings in the country. How the economists would fume! How the working classes would be required to rise as a man, and resist these iniquitous burdens! 'Walter Scott, that great poet, and David Wilkie, that memorable painter,' would be made to pay up to the uttermost farthing."

"I trust when minister," said B——, "to teach our islanders a more generous respect for genius."

"You believe in the Millennium?" Ashton inquired, somewhat sceptically.

"We shall see," was the confident rejoinder. "I admire the Venetian policy immensely," he went on. "It was the most subtle and sagacious that modern Europe has yet developed. What in its machinery was capable of being exposed to the daylight, was exhibited with supreme ostentation; what was narrow, vindictive, pitiless, they inexorably concealed. An Oriental Machiavelli must have devised it. Bolingbroke is the only English statesman who has understood it."

"Yet," said the Padre,—the Padre, I say, for it was the Church official who spoke,—"it was founded upon a lie, and so—Delenda est Carthago."

"Let the gods decide," answered B——.

> "Ilion is fallen, and they who dwelt therein
> Are as they are before high-judging heaven.

I speak only of its policy; and good or bad, no policy, down to the minutest detail, was ever executed with more consummate ability. A governing oligarchy and a popular republic! That was the central idea, and you trace it everywhere. In its huts and in its palaces, in the haughty reserve of the Broglio, in the frank fraternity of the Piazza. It exacted the funeral simplicity of the gondola; it dictated the black domino of the noble. The mask was not a mere cloak for intrigue or adventure. No, it was a national institution, essential to the economy of Venice. For it preserved that mystery and *prestige* to the governing classes which such a constitution imperatively required."

"Don't you think," said Darcy, "we had better import it into England? The governing classes there seem to be rather in need of it."

B—— was a remarkable man in his way. There was an exaggeration, an epigrammatic bombast in his talk at which many wiseacres grinned, and which Catarina mimicked to the life. But he was a remarkable man—much more so than his critics. His political and historical creed was no doubt partly fictitious: it smacked of the insincerity which must always attach to the creed of the mere artist; but he construed it at least with the breadth and generosity of a poetic intellect. His nature was large and unselfish. He was insanely ambitious, but never base. He could abandon his principles; he never abandoned his friends. And his persevering *insouciance,* his obstinate *nonchalance,* were indomitable. Nothing could shake him from his purpose: he held on to it like grim death or an English terrier. And he did not exactly fail. He was first minister of the *République Occidentale* when he died.

As the night wore on the Padre disappeared: Lord Ashton, engaged elsewhere, had left earlier. The mirth became fast and furious. Catarina was brilliant and bewitching — saucy, bitter, tender, pathetic, as the mood changed. Her vivacity was not the wild effort men can make to smother a rooted sorrow; there was not room for any deep misery to take root in her heart, and she had none to conceal. No doubt some bitter memories now and again jarred against the heart-strings, but they did not abide long; and when they did recur she made no effort to hide them, but gave expression to them with passionate directness. At such moments one feared to say what this angry child might *not* do: children have fired temples before now.

We went out on the balcony. We heard the plash of the water below our feet, and a hundred church-bells answer each other through the mist. The grey ghost of the morning lay along the northern sky over the Euganeans. It was two o'clock.

"Let us see the Duomo," cried Catarina, suddenly, clapping her hands. "Let us go," we all echoed. We were excited, and we entered readily into the whim. "The sail will be superb."

Catarina wrapped her opera-cloak round her, and drawing the white hood over her head, greeted us with one of her grave smiles. "I am a sister of the Carthusians," she said.

Our gondolas were lying at the door, and wakening our men, who were lying in a heap fast asleep in the bottom of the most commodious, we bore down the Canale for the Piazza.

Catarina was in great spirits. In her white hood she was the most charming nun the moonlight ever looked on. Her eyes sparkled with glee at the frolic on which we were bent, and at length she burst into an Io pæan of victory. It was the fierce Osmanli chant in *Mahomet*, which in the opera is chanted to the menacing music of barbaric cymbals. We joined in the chorus, gondoliers and the rest of us, and from among the hoarse male voices rose, like the spring of a crystal fountain, rejoicing, triumphant, the liquid notes of the great singer.

"The infidel is at the gates, and the senators of the Republic are a-bed," concluded Darcy, in a sort of Runic chant. "We will hang the banner of the Moslem on the vanes of St. Mark. We must humour her," he whispered to me as we landed at the stairs of the Piazzetta; "but it is more than likely we shall spend the morning with the Austrian police. We are in for a row, you may be sure; but here goes."

However, we met no one. Two or three sleepy gondoliers raised their heads as we passed them from out the forest of gondolas which were moored at the stairs; and between us and the Lido the painted sails of a few fishing craft bearing up from Chioggia were dimly visible. But the great square was silent as the valley of death. Not a creature stirred, and the Infidel were masters of the situation. Catarina insisted upon another Saracenic chant in celebration of our victory as we marched round the Piazza; but no one interrupted us, though we saw a black-bearded Jew thrust his ugly head out of a little window near the summit of the orologio. The head retreated hastily when B—— solemnly adjured it in what we took to be the Semitic tongue.

"We must say good morrow to his Saintship," exclaimed Catarina when we reached the Duomo. The great gates were closed; but a small door at the west angle stood open, and we entered the famous cathedral of the Lagoons. During the brightest sunshine the interior oppresses one by its gloom; now it was mirk as the day of judgment. Our mad gaiety vanished. The gloom sobered us. It was too solemn for our infidel scorn. We groped our way quietly through the darkness to a chapel near the high altar, where lamps were burning, and two old priests muttering the service for the dead. I leaned against a pillar, a square massive column that could have borne Ossa and Olympus on its sinewy shoulders, and enjoyed the Rembrandt-like effect. The lamp-light peered into dark and mysterious vaults, played upon vast gilded arches, discovered the rude and quaint character of the gigantic figures in mosaic capriciously scrawled over the spacious domes, and revealed above the altar one glorious woman-face by

Tiziano Vecellio, "that marvellous painter"—a sinful woman at her Redeemer's feet, washing them with her tears and wiping them with her golden dishevelled hair.

> Pone luctum, Magdalena,
> Et serena lacrymas;

said the scrawl below. But now when my eyes turned from the picture they fell upon another figure with as fair a face, weeping tears as scalding as any Magdalen ever shed. It was Catarina. The awe of the darkness had fallen upon the child's heart, and in a sudden revulsion of feeling she had sunk upon her knees before the shrine, and now sobbed sorely and piteously, like one whose heart is broke,

> "Pone luctum, Magdalena,
> Et serena lacrymas."

I do not know how long she remained. Slowly the daylight gathered into the edifice and subdued the darkness, revealing as it came the alternate pauses between the triple domes, the radiant angels, and the BENEDICTUS QUI VENIT IN NOMINE DOMINI, on its golden ground. Then slipping quietly away, I bade Catarina's gondolier wait her return, and reached home as the market-boats, with their purple and crimson colours, crowded on to the Rialto.

## CHAPTER VII.

HYMEN, O HYMENÆE!

> My royal head when weary
> In my queen's arms softly lies;
> And my endless broad dominion
> In her deep and gentle eyes.

THIS chapter is the shortest but the most emphatic of my book. I wish the printer would put the whole of it in italics or Roman capitals. It is composed exclusively of materials borrowed from the *Ashton Tomahawk* of the 25th December, 18—.

*At the chapel of Saint Ursula, Norburn, by the Very Rev. the Dean of Ashton, Cordelia, only child of Sir Maxwell Menteith, Bart., of Hawkstone, to Miles Warrender, Esquire, of Carlyon, M.P. for the Ashton burghs.*

# VII.

## THE SETTING SUN.

# CHAPTER I.

### AGAMEMNON.

His voice is silent in your council-hall
For ever; and whatever tempests lour
For ever silent; even if they broke
In thunder, silent; yet, remember all,
He spoke among you, and the Man who spoke.

WHEN a politician's watchword is "Measures, not men," he is presumed to be patriotic. The truth is, that he is often less so than the most selfish place-hunter. Most of the existing vices of our public life are to be ascribed to an ignorant belief in this fallacious and pernicious maxim.

I say, with Fox, "Men, not measures." What healing virtue is there even in the wisest measure? What influence can it exert over the national heart and the national conscience? Does it purify the one or arouse the other? A measure is only a machine: beneficial to organise, powerless to inspire. The impulse, the motive-power, for good, must be derived from THE MAN.

It matters little to what party *the man* may nominally belong. The statesman great enough to arrest sympathy and command obedience, must be great enough to give a nation its principles and a party its creed. He is no authentic leader unless he can mould his followers, and modify their traditions. To become the exponent of a stereotyped and fossilized policy is the ambition of a mediocre intellect.

Mowbray's career had been a striking illustration of this truth. By tradition and sentiment he was attached to the most frigid of political parties: the men who voted along with him were of the straitest sect of the Pharisees, of the haughtiest connexion of the patricians. He had a genuine dislike to many of the stock watchwords of the party which monopolized to itself the credit of political progress. He hated, indeed, every restriction on the liberty of individual action or thought; and he had done more than any man living, either among his friends or foes, to break the narrow and oppressive yoke which his ancestors bound round the necks of themselves and their children. But the official policemen of freedom were always arrayed against him. He came into public life a Tory, and a Tory he remained to the end.

Yet this representative of political sectarianism commanded the sympathy and support of the strongest, ablest, and freest men of his time. The most generous and the widest-hearted Englishmen recognised in Mowbray their fittest leader. How was this? He did not affect the slang of political liberalism: he did not carry the measures which his opponents had invented. Mowbray never courted popularity; he did not care much for fame, at least for the fame whose echoes do not stir St. Stephen's. The tribute to his power that he relished most was the profound silence of the House when he rose to speak—to charm them by his wit, to rouse them by his invective. How, then, did he who was *de jure* monarch of the Tories become *de facto* the leader of scientific Liberalism?

The answer is not difficult. It was felt that this was a man who, whatever political nickname he might choose to assume, *really loved liberty*. This was the spell. Other men might prate about the great principles of civil and religious freedom; but it was shrewdly guessed that to them these watch-cries had practically lost their significance, and had become the mere symbols of party organization. What had been living truth, most living truth worth fighting for, and praying for, and dying for, to Hampden and Locke and Sidney and Russell, had ceased to be intelligible to their descendants. They believed in the principles of the Revolution Settlement as they believed in the Settlement of the Thirty-nine Articles. In other words, attachment to the principles of progress had become a mere mechanical habit of the mind. All earnest men saw this; and saw that it was quite otherwise with Mowbray. Let his enemies call him what they liked, the nation had learnt that to this man freedom of thought and speech was as needful as "the encasing air;" that he was one who resented, as morally hateful to his highest instincts, any interference with either—who detested social and ecclesiastical slavery with his whole heart —who loved liberty with a true and irrepressible fervour, and bowed before Her as before a crowned queen, with loyal and reverent obedience. Compared with his natural and inborn sensitiveness to her honour, the frothy protestations and empty symbols of official patriots seemed mean and tawdry to observant eyes.

This was the secret of his power. A liberal people knew that the statesman who best represented them —who, because he was their greatest man, was also their freest and broadest—was in the camp of the Philistines. But they did not hesitate, and the choice they made was a sagacious choice. They said frankly, "Men, not measures." Measures, they had discovered, were powerless to cure the profound intolerance of their social system: the inspiration of one great man would do more to relieve their life and widen their code than any amount of parliamentary legerdemain. And they were right. There was never more real liberty in England than under Mowbray's Administration. He was great, honoured, beloved: and the influence of his example penetrated the land. His countrymen hung upon the terse and pregnant words which fell from his lips. It was a thing to be proud of that England should speak to the nations in that ringing voice, and that the most potent monarchy in Europe should be identified with the logic and vigour of that unrivalled intellect. Red-tapists sneered when a ray of genius lighted up a Diplomatic Note or a Royal Proclamation; but the heartfelt words stirred the hearts of the people, and bound them at once to the man and to the official. Few Governments have been stronger than Mowbray's; for it rested upon the strength and the integrity of a great man. Since his death all sorts of liberal measures have become law. The constitution is tinkered every ten years: and whenever one costermonger licks another, an act to amend the laws relating to the liberty of the person is solemnly introduced by Lord John Bustle. But is there less intolerance in our society, less sectarianism in our life, than during the Iron Age when Agamemnon reigned in Argos?

## CHAPTER II.

#### VERE NOVO.

*The moan of doves in immemorial elms,
And murmur of innumerable bees.*

"I SAW," says Heine, "the young Spring-God, large as life, standing on the summit of an Alp." Beautiful and charming picture, which no painter has yet succeeded in painting. Among the pale snows, and the rocky scaurs, and the morning silence of the uncovered hills, stands the rosy God in the flush of his fresh, glad, scornful boyhood—one foot resting lightly upon the topmost crest, the other raised for swift flight down into the valley—crowned with the lily, and the orchis, and the anemone. Hear our petitions, Boy of the Violet Crown! May these hearts that hail thee now never grow dry and seared and withered, never lose the capacity for loving, never cease to stir with the old triumphant, rejoicing gladness, with the early exquisite life, whenever the birds and the green buds welcome thy return. Nay, the prayer is already too long delayed.

"Already I discern a winter on every hand." No longer is it possible for us to believe in this seeming gladness. It is hollow, artificial, insincere. Shine as thou wilt, O Sun in Heaven, the too cunning eye detects the coming cloud. Bud and blossom as you will, O murmurous elms, the prophetic ear hears the autumn winds warring among your desolate branches. The unquiet heart, the unstrung nerves, the overwrought brain, are sceptical of happiness. Only the Sunshine that lies upon the child's heart is without its shadow to warn and menace.

Yet Spring in England is lovely — where more lovely? As the cripple to the pool of Siloam, as Arthur's knights to old enchanted fountains, go and bathe the soiled and tainted soul in that serene and tranquil haven. By her blue lakes, on her breezy downs, amid her hedgerows and orchard-blossoms,— everywhere, like Raphael's blessed mother, she is pure and calm and beneficent, and everywhere she is alike. Amid the still cathedral cities, amid the grey ancestral homesteads, amid the rook-haunted elms, and not least, but most of any in Thee, thou fair and indolently graceful city, lying, swan-like, along the margin of thy belated river—where the shadows drift lightly across the green meadows of Christchurch—where the ivy clusters and the apple blossoms, white and scented, around the quadrangles of Merton—where the deer roam, and the sturdy oaks force their reluctant leaves, and the sunlight crosses the radiant angels that veil their faces before the saint-like tower of Magdalen—where the spirit of one age has been roused into life by the skilful hand and faithful heart of another—where Hughes' black-stoled weeping queens mourn for the wounded Arthur, and the sad Guinevere of Rossetti warns back the sleeping Launcelot from his quest, and Merlin, as he nears the oblivious waters, listens to the notes of the beguiling lute; a city where abbots have prayed, and poets have rhymed, and scholars have disputed, and nobles have fought, and kings have governed; an illustrious and venerable city, which the inventive intellect of Müller, and the mild wisdom of Jowett, still dignify and adorn. Abolish whatever else you choose, vulgarize and secularize our society in every way which the mechanical invention of the mill-owner can suggest, pare our imagination and clip our wings, stifle our public spirit by the ballot, and extinguish our local nationalities in electoral districts, make Frederick Peel a Chancellor of the Exchequer, and Mr. Bright a Lord of the Admiralty,—do all this if you will, but leave us at least the monastic and beautiful life, which impresses the most careless mind, falls with the quiet power of the unforgotten and unforgettable dead on the most reckless heart, and encompasses with the silent strength of a rich, energetic and vivid organization, the most fickle temper. All monopoly and exclusion are hateful : but surely a nourishment like this must make finer men and better citizens than the ignoble scramble of a metropolitan university or an industrial school. Only leave us this, and we will yet undertake to raise a race of statesmen and gentlemen fit to govern their country.

It is pleasant to think that there are certain districts of England, where science has not yet made much way, where the people do not use the dialect of the Seven Dials, but a Saxon, on the whole, not altogether unfamiliar to Alfred, where no profane hand (for the urchins who scramble through the branches after the sparrows' and the linnets' nests, are privileged neophytes) has disturbed the hedgerows since Cromwell posted his Ironsides behind them, and where each inch of the green bank at their roots nourishes a group which Millais or Hunt would take a year to copy. I know one of these banks by heart: we sat upon it years ago, and *she* pulled an ivy-leaved snap-dragon to pieces (how well I recollect the fall, one by one, of the blue and violet flowers from her nervous hand!) as the colour came, and went, and came again upon her cheek. I could describe it to you at this very moment, I solemnly believe, though I have not seen it since that day. I wonder if the same flowers grow there now as used to grow there in the old time? So much is changed and altered since then—so much is lost and destroyed—so much blighted and soiled—that I cannot fancy that the place quite retains the look I remember, that the ox-lip still peeps through the grass, or that *that* flower still hangs out with serene indifference its blue and purple banner. Did these timid witnesses escape the blow? did they not feel the pang which hurt our hearts for ever?

The city is not very beautiful in itself; a few houses in the Close, built in the old English cottage style, are very quaint and charming; but the dwellings in general are sombre and mean. But as you wander through the dirty and narrow streets, you look up at last into the sky, and lo! a painted cloud lies softly on the heaven, rapt, serene, and spiritual as a dream by Angelico. And a fair and exquisite piece of dreamwork it is; all the more so from the contrast between its wonderful and rare purity, and the homely and harshly-coloured buildings among which you stray, and over which it rises. As when gazing on the dying splendour of the summer sunset, you fear to close the eye for a moment, lest when you look again, the aërial fabric may have fled. But do not fear; you may advance, and yet it will not retreat; it stands firm against the breeze; it has been framed by human hands, and fashioned out of a human heart; it is the noblest memorial that remains to England of what England was, of the free strength and rich simplicity of happy and pious men.

On the outskirt of the town, but in sight of the cathedral, whose massive towers are visible through the budding elms of English May, buried in a little clump of brushwood, which fringes the lawn down to the river's bank, Marley Lodge forms a delightful retreat for the wearied lawyer or the jaded statesman during the rest-day of the week. Miles has taken it this year for the spring months; so that Corry may escape from the glare and fever of the metropolis when she likes. Corry affects to hate London, and she divides the season pretty impartially between the cottage here and the great house in Tudor-square.

The rustic drawing-room, with its softened glow of colour, is not quite empty. Did you ever see lovelier children? Seraph faces, worthy of Greuse or Murillo. The twins are three or four years old, I fancy (children's ages have always been a mystery to me), and both are dressed exactly alike; so piquantly dressed, that in their little red cloaks, and bright pink tasselled Turkish smoking-caps, you might mistake them for little Eastern princesses, from Bagdad or the Bosphorus, or the Arabian Nights. I never could make out which was which; but the tiny fairies would resent any confusion of identity, and one or other would elaborately explain, "Me not Minnie, me Doe." When the one took ill, the other did likewise; when Minnie laughed, Doe would laugh in sympathy; and they had a genuine sense of the ridiculous, and enjoyed any kind of fun with infinite relish and tact. Doe was a satirist from her cradle, a flirt from the day her blue eyes opened;

it was said that she solemnly mocked her sister before she could walk; Minnie was graver and statelier, a coquette of another order, who tried different arts on her admirers, and captivated them by her pensive affectation and sweet deprecating smiles. Bewitching is the half-hidden side-glance which steals so coquettishly to you—withdrawn suddenly, indeed, if you show too plainly that you are conscious of it, withdrawn for a moment as the little hand rises nervously to the mouth, but still the merry eyes— for the eyes are always laughing, and disavow the pensive mouth—will not cease to gaze at you, and keep you captive. Ah! little rogues — blue-eyed banditti, as Mr. Longfellow would call you—how many hearts you will break ere the noonday! But as yet the kittens are quite content where they are; in their soft furs, and in the midst of this happy, warm life; and each toddles after the other, and each rolls over the other, and gets up again in a quiet, unconcerned way, as if tumbling were natural and inevitable to men and kittens.

The little fairies are listening to a fairy tale, and the fairy tale runs thus:—

"Once upon a time two boys were playing beside the banks of a river, and as they played they saw the fairy who lives far away down below the blue water rise to the surface of the pool. She had a harp in her hand, and her yellow hair was long and wavy, and her eyes sparkled like dewdrops, and her voice

was as sweet as Alie's. It was such a lovely place—
tall green trees grew round about, and their shadows
rested on the smooth water, and delicate mosses and
white lichens clung to the rocks that rose from the
water-side. You would fancy that the Necke—that
was the fairy's name—would lead a happy life in
such a bright sunshiny spot, for though it was shut
in by the rocks and the trees there was plenty of the
warmest sunshine inside—and so she did, and she
sang so sweetly it might have made you cry, and the
burden of her song was always, 'And I hope, and I
hope that my Redeemer liveth.' Then one of the
boys,—he was not a cruel boy, only he had been
badly taught at school, and did not know that the
birds, and the bees, and the flowers are loved by the
good Lord who made all these beautiful things; and
he was a brave boy, as all English boys are, and not
a bit frightened,—he said to the Necke, 'What is the
use of your singing and playing, Necke? You will
never be saved.' And the other boy, who was the
smaller of the two, said rudely—I don't know why,
perhaps because he thought it manly to speak
roughly, like his big brother—'No, Necke, you will
never be saved.' When the poor Necke heard this,
she began to weep bitterly, and then she flung away
her harp, and sank down under the water. But when
the boys went home they told their father what they
had done, and their father, who was a kind old man,
like Effie's papa, said to them, 'My children, it was

wicked to make the poor Necke cry; you must go back and comfort her.' And when they went back they found the Necke sitting upon the water, and sobbing as if she would break her heart, and they said both at once (for they were sorry for what they had done), 'Necke, do not grieve so; our father says that perhaps your Redeemer liveth also.' You should have seen how bright the Necke looked when she heard this, and she took up her harp again, and, as they went home, they heard her singing as only fairies can sing when they are happy, and after that she sang joyfully the whole night through,—for fairies don't care about going to bed till morning."

Within the policies, but on the margin of the sluggish river, stands a miniature temple; call it what you will, a temple, a chapel, a cell, nay, rather the inverted bell of a beautiful flower—a foxglove, or a convolvulus. Do you know the chapter-house of the cathedral of Moravia? Well, this is a model of it—such a model as Doe is of her mother. The inverted bell of a beautiful flower, I say; but a lily-stalk rises from its centre, and then the ascending and descending cups lightly kiss, and mingle lip to lip. The building grows and expands like a flower, and must have risen as the lily rises. There is not a straight line nor a sharp angle anywhere; but an exquisite curve is caught throughout, which I do not think stone or lime ever caught elsewhere, except, perhaps, in the arched roof of the chancel at Peterborough, and the secret of which the birch and the acacia now keep to themselves.

"I like it," said Mowbray to Miles. They were standing by the bank of the river; "I like to catch a glimpse of our old Norland work here. Strange where our rough ancestors could have got these exquisite proportions and that rare beauty!"

"From the sea," said Miles.

"They got their cod and mackerel there; I doubt if they got their churches."

"I think they did—their churches and their ballads. The sea is in them both; its misty solemnity in the one, its fresh breezy scent in the other. A man needs to live by the sea ere a building will grow out of his mind, as a flower grows out of the soil. The sea harmonises and attunes his powers. I never heard of a man who did anything great, who had not known the sea."

"You harp upon the sea," replied Mowbray; "and yet—'tis a grand master, after all. I remember how, Greek-wise, I used to harangue it in the old days; I think some of the best speeches I ever made were addressed to the bay of Ashton. Sydney says that whenever I get into a passion with the House (which of course I never do), I remind him of a storm in the Atlantic. There is perhaps more in it than he thinks. I once tried hard to catch the moan, or sob, that the waves make in the Earl's Cave. I never quite succeeded myself, but I took Benoni there one summer-day, and he gave us its liquid gurgle afterwards in a surprising way, in *Bombastes*, I think. But the old ballads—yes, they are full of the sea, and you are saturated with them. Give me a cigar, Miles, and we will talk about them in the temple. What has come of the Solicitor? I thought he was to be here."

"He was to row up," replied Miles, as they entered the lily-like shrine; "but I suspect he is *courting*, as we say in the north; and a man in that state is not to be relied on."

"Fickle as a patriot," said the Minister.

Yes, the old ballads are full of the sea, and, like the sea-shell, they carry their scent along with them. Not of the soft blue Adriatic which touched Horace and the Hellenics, which runs through the *Odyssey*, as the Ægean runs through Greece, but of the grim, rough Northern sea, which laps the feet of Odin and the Gods, do the old ballads smack. It is no summer breeze, no Mediterranean "white squall," that blows through Sir Patrick Spens, but a black "norwaster" straight from the pole, that will blow till the masts are bare, and the waves are black, and the very midday welkin itself dour as night or death.

> They had na sailed a league, a league,
>   A league, but barely three,
> When the lift grew dark, and the wind blew loud,
>   And gurly grew the sea.

It is always on the sea or the sea-like rivers that the

crowning tragedy takes place. The Douglas rides on; but his life-blood runs the while, and stains with a purple stream "that wan water." The death-mist darkens the earl's eyes as he bleeds to death upon the English moors, but his heart is beating with the wild northern breakers—

> For I hae dreamed a dreary dream
> Ayont the Isle of Skye.

And when we come to such lines as these—

> There was a roar in Clyde's water
> Wad fear'd a hundred men,—

we can see and hear the flooded river tearing along as the fevered knight gallops down the hill-side, and we know at once that he will never reach the other bank, though man and horse swim stoutly, as Scottish men and horses do.

"Our fathers were Vikings," said Mowbray, "and that is the reason why these sea-stories stir our blood. But, after all, I am only half a sea-king. I was not born, Miles, among the waves, as you were;

> But it was in the gude green wood,
> Among the lily-flowers,

like brave English Robin. And an Englishman is not such a despicable creature, after all. Look at these towers."

Sharply cut against the encrimsoned evening sky rose the famous towers of that immemorial shrine.

The river flowed between, the town lay between; but the massive pile, like the mountains, dwarfed every other object, and towered right overhead, as it seemed.

"Yes," answered Miles; "but it is from its cathedrals alone that you can tell that a great people once occupied this land."

"And are they not enough? What other people, except the Romans, can show more? And Roman work was barbarous; they were hard-handed soldiers from first to last, and cared for nothing except bulk and strength."

"But what do these tell us of the past? Do they tell us anything?"

"This at least," said Mowbray: "in the complete unity of every feature, in the perfect harmony of every detail, that the men who made them knew what they wished to make, that they were in earnest, that they felt, as Leighton would say, that they were doing God's work, and so did it, as such work should be done, without fear or flaw. But ours is an age of doubt," he continued, in that tone of sarcastic melancholy which was habitual with him, "no, not of doubt—hesitation is the right word (for we do not dare to doubt)—when no man's work lies at his hand, and God's work seems farthest off of any—when no man knows indeed whether what he proposes to do may not be the devil's work. And so, instead of these eternal shrines, we will leave—what?

Our cotton-mills, our plaster palaces, our mud embankments which every flood washes away,—the perishable memory of a wealth which perished in the using! Miles," he said, after a pause, "your architecture is all very well; but you cannot rival this yet."

A ribston pippin grew along the wall, and one of its blossomed branches crept round the doorway where they sat. Have you ever nicely observed a sprig of apple-blossom? One lies beside me while I write this that I would fain describe if I could. There is a bright vermilion glow on the unfolding leaves, like the rosy bloom on the child's face, while the pale and delicate flush on the opened buds recals the faint flush that comes and goes in soft pulsations on the maiden's cheek. But why write about these things? This black ink and dingy paper on the one hand; the radiant white and pink of these blossoms on the other; what affinity can there be between the two, and how is it possible to change the one into a picture of the other? That is a transformation which only the spell of a Goethe or a Tennyson can work.

"These are my rosebuds at least," answered Miles, as Corry slowly approached, with the children clinging to her knees.

"You gentlemen can never think of anything except your work. I know you have been talking politics," she said.

"No; like Falstaff, we babbled o' green fields," replied Mowbray. "I hope it is no proof that our wits are going."

"I misdoubt you, my lord, and so does Doe. She avers you have not spoken to her to-day."

"My dainty little tyrant, come and play the coquette to me."

But the little coquette, with affected timidity, hid her face in her mother's lap, and would not listen to the statesman's flatteries. At length, the beguiling voice, potent with men and gods, won its way, and Doe, mounted on his knee, lisped in broken words how angry she had been with him for his unfaithfulness, and how she had determined never to forgive him. Probably she could not make so long a speech in articulate words; but the large reproachful eyes may have said as much.

Mowbray, when he unbent, was fascinating. Could his enemies have watched him as he sat there, with the child nestling upon his knee, and heard him with mingled tenderness and *naïveté* win his way to the little heart, perhaps they might not have hated him so fiercely as they did. The great satirist was hardly to be recognised at such a moment, except perhaps in a tone of ironic sadness, which tinged his most familiar talk. But the irony was not unpleasing; it was the irony which lies deep, I think, in the English character: the surface-play of a temper habitually grave. The intense reserve of an intellect which protects itself even against its affections, could find no more characteristic defence. And with Mowbray, time had mellowed its bitterness and taken away its sting. It was rather "the wise sad valour" of a man who has seen many cities and men; who has found when at the summit of a career that success is not such a very successful thing, after all; and who, as he witnesses the eager scramble of the crowd, is content, not indeed to laugh with Swift, but to smile with Horace. He had many very deep and hearty convictions; if he had not, I honestly believe that he would have given up public life; though no doubt the charm of vivid action was profoundly felt by that active and sleepless intellect. But when he unbent, he unbent wholly; a certain indolent listlessness and *abandon* succeeded the keen energy of work: his repose was as complete as the repose of a Greek statue, and as graceful. Indeed, the Minister was always graceful; his Latin was graceful; his epigrams were graceful; I have no doubt that even his dressing-gown was not inelegant, and that its folds were studied. But this gracefulness was neither affected nor shallow. It was the genuine and deeply-rooted instinct of an intensely refined and fastidious intellect, and therefore was quite free from affectation. Nor was it a proof of shallowness any more than the clumsiness of W——d is a proof of depth. The grace was not incompatible with the keenest and most passionate energy of feeling and thought.

"The daintiest little angels out of heaven," said Mowbray, as the children played about his knee. "Let us lie down, my pets, on this grassy bank, and you shall teach me the innocent secret of childhood."

And so the spring sunset fell upon the group of to-day, as it fell upon the great Minster of a perished race, upon the yellow girlish curls, upon Corry's pensive beauty, upon the worn but noble face which once hung in the boudoir of every Englishwoman,— who recognised in the Great Commoner the sole representative, in an unchivalrous society, of the antique grace and gallantry.

# CHAPTER III.

### THE JEBUSITES.

> And when religious sects ran mad,
>   He held—in spite of all his learning—
> That if a man's belief is bad,
>   It will not be improved by burning.

MOWBRAY had now been Premier for nearly six years. During that period his administration had been constantly gaining ground in the confidence and the respect of the people. In the House, also, its position was respectable. Around the Minister sat a group of illustrious colleagues—men who for tact, zeal, and administrative capacity, have seldom been rivalled. Behind him were ranged the rank and file of his own party, and a band of untried politicians—men then little known to fame, but who have since proved that the generous chivalry and imaginative enthusiasm which bound them to Mowbray had not disqualified them for the graver responsibilities of office. On the Opposition benches those statesmen were gathered before whose compact organisation and bitter hostility a greater minister than Mowbray had fallen. Their ranks, moreover, had been recently recruited by various Tory deserters, who hated their ancient leader with the zeal and venom of apostates. It was a powerful Opposition, —such an Opposition, that only the high personal character of the Minister had kept the Cabinet in place so long. The vehement Barton, the wary Orange, the subtle Halifax, all the representatives in the Commons of the great Whig connexion, were united by a common tie—hostility to the untitled "adventurer" who had braved their displeasure, and whose wiry and tenacious hands held the reins of government. But the opportunity to wrench them from the plebeian dictator had now apparently arrived, and it was eagerly seized.

In the strange society of whose characteristics I have been writing, a small sect of religious enthusiasts whose tenets are, to say the least, eccentric, had long maintained a torpid vitality. They believed that an old lady, who was said to be no better than she should be, and whose scarlet petticoats were of the deepest dye, was the divinely appointed head of the Church. A hundred and fifty years before, a great poet had ridiculed with less, perhaps, than his usual keenness of satire, the other article of their creed:—

> The Egyptian rites the Jebusites embraced,
> Where gods were recommended by their taste.
> Such savoury deities must needs be good,
> As served at once for worship and for food.

Ridiculously absurd, no doubt,—though indeed many of the finest intellects in Europe did not hesitate to accept, and with keen logic to defend, the thesis,— but not demanding more than the loud and vacant laughter to which the great nation treated it. Not content, however, with intellectual dissent, the leaders of civil and religious liberty had prosecuted the professors of this doctrine with all the industry of the Inquisition, and the gall of their bitterness still infected and disgraced the Statute-book. Because the Jebusites supported opinions which were speculatively absurd, they were excluded, for instance, from the general Legislative Council, an assembly which professed to represent every class in the community. To the genial and high-bred temper of Mowbray, the vulgar disabilities of sect were peculiarly obnoxious. He was by temper, as I have said, essentially tolerant. The zealots of either party beheld in him the political Gallio, "who cared for none of these things." The judgment was as false as it could well be; for the large tolerance of his nature was not the offspring of indifference, but of an intellect at once keen and equable. To erase from the Statute-book the sullen animosities of creed, to free the Constitution from the impurities of fanatical intemperance, was, of all the measures which the Minister contemplated, the one which lay nearest to his heart. During his administration many minute but irritating sores had been cautiously removed, and he had now ventured to introduce a sweeping measure, and to try conclusions with an arrogant and intolerant Propaganda. In inaugurating a policy which offended many of his own followers, he had to rely to some extent upon the support of an Opposition which had condescended to become the champion of the Conscience. These very disabilities, indeed, had been created by the ancestry of the Opposition, and had been criticised and condemned by their rivals of the hour,—for the Tory of King George was the Radical of Queen Anne; but times change and parties revolve, and the Whig who in power had persecuted was the Whig who, when persecuted, eloquently protested against persecution. And so long had his exclusion from office now lasted, that by the mere force of assertion the nation had been led to believe that "Liberty" was the peculiar dowry of a party which history declares to be narrow and selfish at heart, ungrateful to friends, ungenerous to foes. Mowbray was thus entitled to expect, that for shame, if not for love, a measure of emancipation would be welcomed by Emancipators.

## CHAPTER IV.

#### LADY WINDERMERE'S.

Where throngs of knights and barons bold,
In weeds of peace, high triumphs hold;
With store of ladies, whose bright eyes
Rain influence, and judge the prize.

THERE was a crowded assembly at Lady Windermere's.

"Why do our young men," said Mrs. Warrender to Alice, "so resolutely strive to look like fools? Nature is strong enough unaided."

"The labour is thrown away, certainly," was the reply; "it is gilding the gold."

"It is the morale and not the physique," said Lord Maurice, "which has deteriorated. They are splendid fellows at a hedge or a six-barred gate. Let them go at the French or the Cossacks, and you will see what pace is. The pluck and the stamina are as good as ever; but, as you say, they are fools. I dine with some of them, for my sins, once or twice a year—it is awful work. Anything more utterly feeble, I defy you to find in Christendom. 'Tis a moral and intellectual paralysis."

"Very long words," said Alice; "but why do you do it?"

"Why, as Congreve says—'I please myself: besides, sometimes to converse with fools is for my health.'"

"You take rather too gloomy a view of our admirers, don't you? But who is that?"

"The fat little man with the sharp face? That's the new Judge. His father was a publican in the Isle of Dogs. What right have they to put such men on the bench? They can't be judicial: they have not the inborn instinct which keeps a thoroughbred intellect in the straight path of logic and reason."

"Don't speak so," said Mrs. Warrender; "you know we are all for the people."

"The people are very well in their way—but why make heroes and martyrs of them? I believe they are pretty much like the rest of us, and don't want to be canonized."

"Ah! you are an infidel, Lord Maurice, and don't believe in the saints."

"I do—in one or two," he replied, bowing to them in his courtly way. "But saints are common among the lower orders only in that visionary world where Walpole is a philosopher and Wood a wit."

Lord Maurice, who knew everybody, and everybody's father and grandfather, continued his commentary as the guests went past. That was the new Bishop, and that was the new Poet. That was a Reformer of provincial manners, who had cured the provinces, by showing them his own. That was a strenuous Defender of the Faith, who, privately, did not believe much in anything except whisky-and-water. That was a parochial Satirist, who wrote terribly severe epigrams about the doctor and the clergyman when they neglected to ask him to dinner. That was a Classical Editor, who had taken to the dead languages late in life, and had begun to learn when his contemporaries had begun to forget. "It's rather a bore," said Lord Maurice, yawning. "He is under the impression that the rest of the world, like himself, are still being birched. So he fills the morning paper with Greek verbs and exercises in Latin syntax—much to the edification of the general reader." That was the Historian of the aristocracy, who was as familiar with the peccadilloes of the Roses as with the *Chronique Scandaleuse* of the Regency. "He fancies that he has the blood of all the Howards in his veins," said Lord Maurice; "and his father—decent man!—was a drover in Drumnadrochit."

"I have just left the House," said Charley Latimer, coming up to where they sat. "Warrender has made a first-rate speech, and come down upon Trelawney in style. The House was quite with him. Are any of our men about, Maurice? I am beating them up."

"Are you going to divide?"

"In an hour. Monmouth was winding up when I left, and Mowbray is not to speak thirty minutes. Ah! there is Lord Bustle with the Baroness—I must waylay him."

And the whip disappeared in the crowd.

"Let me congratulate Mrs. Warrender on her husband's speech," said Darcy, who had come up. "'Tis a great success. Mowbray is immensely pleased. The House was taken by surprise. They didn't know it was in him; he has never cared to strike yet. But Trelawney's attack on Mowbray stung him, and worked him up to the point where anger gets eloquent. The severe and weighty indignation of his rebuke made a profound impression. Sir Jasper didn't like it, I can tell you."

A glow of gratified pride tinged Corry's cheek.

"I am very happy," she said, in a low voice, that was audible only to Alice; "I should so like to have heard him."

"He didn't mean to speak. Mowbray will make a great reply. Miles sent me along to try and get you to come down."

"Charming. Will you go, Alice? But how are we to get there?"

"Leave it to me—I will manage. Will you take my arm?"

## CHAPTER V.

### APOLLO'S LYRE.

> " We, we have seen the intellectual race
> Of giants stand, like Titans, face to face—
> Athos and Ida, with a dashing sea
> Of eloquence between, which flowed all free,
> As the deep billows of the Ægean roar
> Betwixt the Hellenic and the Phrygian shore.

THEY drove quickly through the streets, which, late as it was, were still crowded and brilliantly lighted. The political clubs were astir and excited; members hurried in to learn what even yet hung in the balance—the fate of the great Minister. For, after considerable hesitation, the Opposition had resolved to fight. But as Emancipators could not with seemliness defeat a measure of emancipation, considerable circumspection was necessary to give a decent colouring to the assault. So, instead of a direct negative, they asked the House to affirm that certain things were out of the Bill which ought to have been in it. The Jebusites, at the time the penal statutes directed against them were passed, had declined to use the hair-powder then worn by the loyal subjects of the monarchy. Political motives were supposed to be involved; the tax on hair-powder was an important source of national revenue; and thus unpowdered cues became the cue of the disaffected. The result was, that a Whig minister carried a measure which declared that whoever was guilty of wearing his head as God made it, should be visited with the pains and penalties set forth in the statute. Men in the old days had died at the stake to assert the lawfulness of unpowdered hair. But these days were past; the nation had changed its mind, and left the finance minister to discover other sources of revenue; the distinction had been abolished and forgotten. The obnoxious statute was perfectly obsolete, and its existence was only known to a few constitutional antiquarians. Mowbray's measure, intended to redress practical grievances, had neglected to deal with penalties which public opinion had repealed. Here was an opening for the Opposition! The ministerialists vainly attempted to explain that it was unnecessary to repeal a forgotten and fantastic disability, and unsafe, by such an association, to discredit the relief that was urgently needed. It was of no avail. The Opposition had got their grievance, and they worked it like men. The measure was a sham—a Tory intrigue—a fraud, which pretended to enfranchise, but virtually enslaved. Not repeal this odious and despotic law! True, nobody wears powder now;

but the principle is at stake. There is no difficulty, besides, in getting quit of a practical grievance; it is the invisible and intangible, those which hurt no one, and which no one resents, that the true friends of freedom must watch most narrowly.

The Jebusites unfortunately were not able to rise to the height of this great argument. They were quite willing to take the Bill as it stood. It liberated them from many irritating restraints; it conferred upon them all the rights of citizenship. Nobody wore powder that they knew of, and nobody that they knew of had ever been prosecuted for not wearing it. "But," replied the jealous guardians of freedom, "it is the principle we fight for, not the wretched details. It is your duty and your privilege to suffer in its vindication." But the argument did not disturb their ignoble content. They wanted to be made justices of the peace, and members of the senate; and they could not be got to entertain right views upon the hair-powder. Fortunately for themselves, however, they were not enfranchised as yet, and so could not vote against their friends.

This was the High Debate, on the issue of which the fate of the Ministry depended.

"Did you ever hear such rubbish?" said Darcy, as they rolled along, and he described some of the speeches. "The little statesman struts about on the constitutional dunghill, which he wants to keep all to himself! Like the hero of the old song—

> Aye cacklin' like a clokin hen."

It was a mild spring night, and the round moon rested serenely upon the towers of the Abbey. Black, massive, silent, the huge pile rose into the sky, and cast its cold shadow upon the neighbouring chapel. Darcy and his companions passed quickly through the hall, where a large crowd awaited the issue of the debate, and in another moment, from behind the latticed screen, they looked down upon the famous arena.

It is a grand spectacle, that simple assembly. The entire absence of ceremonial or parade adds, I think, to the effect which it produces on the mind. There is no deception, no artifice. It is an unpretending meeting of English gentlemen. Yet what can be finer than the chivalrous courtesy? How the rivals hate each other, and yet the noble politeness never fails! Only centuries of high breeding, of guarded honour, of inherited tact, could preserve that voluntary restraint. How bitter is the sarcasm, how cutting the irony; but the speaker never uses an expression which a society of gentlemen can resent, and the victim never winces. Self-command and self-respect are the secret machinery which gives to this unimpressive and unambitious assembly an authority which the most splendid despotism does not wield.

Every bench is crowded, every seat occupied. A former colleague, who had recently deserted the Minister, is speaking. Calm, insidious, and studiously moderate, it is yet obvious that he hates his old friend with more than party bitterness. Mowbray feels it, they say; is wounded by it to the quick; but will not notice it, will pass it by with a silence that is more expressive than any words could be. Even the Opposition are conscious that the speech is somewhat ungenerous; still it helps them, and they cheer it lustily; the oily orator concludes amid a shout of applause that contrasts with the silent and stern dissatisfaction of those among whom he lately sat. It is a triumph of a kind, a triumph that, even at the moment, could barely have gratified, and which, years afterwards, was bitterly avenged.

As you enter the antechamber of the new Houses, the two great orators of a generation that has passed away stand upon either hand; the spare and attenuated minister, and his jovial and rotund foe, the most eloquent and simple-hearted of Englishmen. Their successors preserved many of the old contrasts, though traced in less marked and decisive lines.

"I see Mr. Mowbray," whispered Alice; "but where is Mr. Barton?"

"There," said Mrs. Warrender, pointing out the leader of the Opposition.

Ay, there they sit, one on either side of the House, and respectively in the van of the famous historical parties, which for two centuries have governed this famous England. Men not lightly to be forgotten. Mowbray, the great commoner who has refused the blue ribbon, and would not exchange his simple "Esquire" for any title on earth, keen, clear, commanding, thoroughbred, a fitting representative of a temperate people and an historic monarchy! Barton passionate, generous, warm-hearted, logical, vehement, a fiery orator, a courageous tribune!

Very fierce to-night were his words; and, feeling perhaps that his argument would not bear much handling, he gave more than usual play to the sweep of his rich and fervid invective. And yet even the argument was conducted with infinite ingenuity; it coiled itself around the foe; it twisted and untwisted its links with surpassing dexterity; it was impossible to sift these passionate sophistries. Sustained and searching argument, clothed in rapid, vehement, nay, almost boisterous declamation—that was his peculiar gift, a gift bestowed upon no other orator I ever heard, at least in the same measure. For men are for the most part divided into the two classes; the logical and the rhetorical; and rarely, very rarely, once in a century or so, are the two found united. But logic was the very soul of Barton's eloquence.

Amid the tumult of cheers which greeted the

peroration of their chief, the Minister rose, and immediately, in a still and unimpassioned voice began his reply. From the turbid mountain torrent to the azure and many-dimpled smile of ocean—from Barton to Mowbray—the contrast was sudden and striking. Exquisitely poised as a Greek capital, every syllable was effective. The art was perfect—perfect because so artfully hidden. Each successive sentence was a step to the *dénouement*; but the path was studiously concealed; he seemed to toy with his victim, and dally with his argument; and the ringing invective or the winged jest startled, at last, with all the suddenness of surprise. The burnished shaft had pierced the quarry ere it was seen that the bow was bent. He spoke without pain, and without passion. With mellow laughter, he ridiculed the pretences to which the Opposition had had recourse. Then he alluded slightly, but in a graver tone, to the charges which had been hurled against himself. "Some of them," he said, calmly, though the bell-like notes did not ring quite so clearly as in the passages of fun and irony that had preceded, "might have been spared, if only for the ghost of a departed friendship." Then amid the touched silence of the House, he went on to vindicate his consistency. "If anything has been dear to me since my boyhood, if anything will remain dear to me till death, it is — liberty. That birthright of the sons of England is the peculiar heritage of no party in the State. An aristocratic connexion has, indeed, vouchsafed to it an exotic patronage; but I take leave to doubt the genuineness of the homage. At all events, I will permit no party to enjoy an exclusive monopoly. Statesmen, as well as patriots, may assert the excellence and vindicate the integrity of English freedom. As for myself, I regard not the bitter words that have assailed the "ambitious adventurer." They do not hurt me now, they will not disquiet those to whom I bequeath the justification of my ambition. True, I am ambitious; it is an early frailty; a frailty which, even to-night, I am not solicitous to disown. That it has been altogether gratified I do not presume to affirm, for I have desired something more than even the confidence of this great assembly. My ambition, my sole ambition, has been to gain a place in the hearts of my countrymen, and to leave a name, not altogether unbeloved, nor unfamiliar to the English race."

He spoke calmly, but the words thrilled his hearers. The solemn accents, the calm reproach, were affecting at the moment; *now* they are touched with enduring pathos and a sad immortality. The nation has not forgotten even yet—amid futile politicians and feeble statesmen—the dying appeal of the great Minister.

A few minutes of keen anxiety—for the division was expected to be very close—and then the result was known. A majority of twenty-nine for the

Government — narrow, but sufficient in the then balanced state of parties. In fact, after the ominous prophecies of the past fortnight, the numbers were regarded as a triumph by ministers.

One clamorous cheer, and the House rapidly emptied. Leaning on Miles's arm, Mowbray walked along the hall, which was still crowded—crowded by those who had waited to greet the triumphant Minister. As he passed by they pressed around him; the antique rafters echoed their acclamations; it was a great popular ovation. Mowbray was evidently affected; he trembled with unusual emotion; Miles had never seen the reserved and haughty Minister so visibly moved.

"This is the recompense," he muttered as they drove away; and the unwonted cheers startled the empty streets and the grey dawn.

# CHAPTER VI.

### DOWNING-STREET.

He is all fault who hath no fault at all;
For who loves me must have a touch of earth.

MOWBRAY sat in his office in Downing-street the morning after the debate. The room was simply furnished; the walls lined with blue-books and works on foreign and international law; a massive writing-table of oak occupied the centre. A print of Pitt hung over the mantelpiece.

The Minister was dictating a diplomatic despatch to a clerk who sat at his elbow. It was a communication addressed to a foreign and not very friendly court, and every sentence required to be weighed and measured with the nicest attention. Mowbray's exquisite tact was never more conspicuous than when thus occupied. If the balance wavered a hair's-breadth on either hand—if a word hinted too little or implied too much—the unfaltering instinct was awakened and the slip at once repaired. Not a line passed from that room which could not bear the scrutiny of the keenest intellects in Europe. His despatches were addressed at once to the closet and to the forum. The hostile diplomatist read them, and admired their wary and sinewy discretion; the people read them, and felt that in the hands of this fearless moralist the honour of the country was secure. He never committed himself, though to the uninitiated and on the surface the words often seemed wonderfully frank and unreserved. But it was not so. Foreign ministers scanned them eagerly, to elicit from any unguarded phrase the secret wishes of the English Cabinet; parliamentary opponents dissected them with critical animosity; but the more they were handled the more intangible they grew. I know that some wiseacres are rather disposed to underrate diplomatic address; only the unwise and ignorant can do so. The subtle and vigilant diplomatists of Continental Europe acknowledged that Mowbray was a master of their craft—almost the only master the islanders had produced—and the opinion of the English monarchy, always exerted in behalf of "truth, peace, freedom, mercy," had never more weight with the world than during his administration.

He continued to dictate; it was a grave State paper, and required even more than ordinary deliberation. A deputation was announced.

"Let them in. Wait, please," he added to Miles, "they won't keep me five minutes."

The deputation had come to advocate the abolition

of certain import duties. Keen-eyed Manchester cotton-spinners, Sheffield cutlers, as sharp as their own blades, professional agitators, and honest tradesmen from the country, who looked rather afraid of the Minister.

"Well, gentlemen," he said, rising and standing before the fire, "what can I do for you?"

A spare, hollow-chested man, with a very long and sallow face, who stood in the van, acted as spokesman. With remarkable clearness and precision he explained the nature of the changes which they desired. The Minister listened attentively, thanked the speaker, with the grace peculiar to him, for his lucid exposition, and then briefly indicated his own sentiments—

"I am opposed," he said, "to all restrictions upon trade, thought, and speech. As to moral and political restrictions, I think we are in a fair way of getting quit of them, because nobody is peculiarly concerned in their retention. But it is quite otherwise when we come to deal with the restrictions that affect our trade and commerce: powerful classes are interested in their maintenance; their abolition cannot be secured until after a protracted, and what, I fear, will prove a fierce and obstinate struggle. Now the nation is unprepared for the step you ask me to take. No Government would be powerful enough at the present moment to carry such a measure. Twenty years hence all this will be changed. I make no doubt that then you will have the nation with you; but till then it would be madness for any Government to undertake to change the law."

The deputation, after the manner of deputations, thanked him for his courtesy, and withdrew. Two or three more followed in rapid succession—one about a new pump, one to have the drinking of strong ale made a capital offence, one to see about getting the Established Church repealed.

"Do you really think so?" asked Miles, alluding to the answer he had made to the first body of malcontents.

"Certainly," was the answer. "I do not doubt it. Why should we produce a state of artificial poverty? Whenever the nation sees this as clearly as I do, or as that fellow does, it won't stand it any longer. But it does not see this yet; unfortunately, its selfish instincts—short-sighted, because keen and intense—will prevent it from doing so for a generation yet."

"But if we think so," said Miles, doubtfully, "is it right to go on as we are doing?"

Mowbray was silent for a moment.

"Why," he said at length, "every measure that I have passed paves the way to this conclusion. To me it is as clear as day that the Bill we carried last night involves these others. They are all component parts of a policy to which the nation is becoming *familiarised*. But not till it has grown familiar as a household world does any policy obtain popular sanction here. Neither you nor I may live to see the change. But are we to fold our hands and do nothing, because we cannot get all? Even as it is, we are somewhat in advance already: I don't believe that a majority heartily likes our work of last night. It is carried by the sheer intellect of a minority."

"But must this always be the way? Is truth not to be fought for? lived for? died for, if need be? Are we never to hail her, until the populace acknowledge her? How, then, is truth to work its way, how force itself into the daylight? Are we only to register the decrees of the mob? There must surely be something better for us to do."

"Miles, I am not a philosopher. I cannot deal with abstractions. I must have real men to work with. I must have real work to do. I can honour the men you speak of—men who in an age of falsehood are bold to appeal to the truth. Their protests are invaluable—their protests lie at the root of any practical work we achieve. I can believe that unless Milton had written his *Areopagitica* two hundred years ago, we would not last night have carried our Bill. But these men do not make statesmen,—they are not fit for practical politics. The politician does not protest—he registers, as you call it. An inferior work, it may be; but still needing to be done, and done well. I am a politician, Miles. Were I to bring in the measure these men want, I should be out of office to-morrow. But I have many things to do," he added, with a smile, "ere I die."

The smile vanished, and a sudden paleness succeeded. Mowbray pressed his hand to his side, and for a moment breathed with difficulty.

"What is the matter?" Miles exclaimed, starting up. "Are you ill?"

"No; it is nothing. A slight spasm—I have them at times. I am better now."

There was a knock at the door: a courier entered.

"Ah," said Mowbray, quickly, "from Vienna already?"

"I left last Friday," was the reply, "and have just arrived."

Mowbray took the despatch, and, as the messenger left, opened it with visible eagerness.

"No; he dare not do it. I will be even with him for this. Write a note to Bourillon, Miles, and ask him to come here this afternoon. An alliance between them now," he went on, in a low voice, as Miles wrote and despatched the note, "would be fatal. But they cannot do it. I know too much."

He said no more; on foreign affairs Mowbray was singularly reserved, and even Miles was not admitted to his confidence. He held each mesh of the web in his own hand, and played every move himself. Miles knew that for weeks he had been engaged on it night and day, and that even the great Home

z

Debate had occupied only a subordinate place in his thoughts. Two of the great Continental despotisms were understood to be bitterly hostile to the English Minister. It had been a hand-to-hand fight hitherto; but Mowbray, it was whispered, had played his cards so well, that he had disconcerted the alliance.

Miles would have liked to gain Mowbray's confidence. He saw that the strain was beginning to tell even upon that nervous intellect, and that he could not bear it with safety much longer. Perhaps the Minister felt so too; but he made no response. Only as Miles finished the despatch on which they had been engaged, he lay back in his chair, and closed his eyes for a moment, as if to rally all his faculties.

"Give me another week," he murmured, "and they will know who is master."

"Come and dine with us," said Miles, as he rose to leave. "Corry is enraptured with last night, and won't be pacified till she sees you."

"No—thanks—I can't to-night—I am busy. But give her my love, Miles," he added, softly, "and the little doe too. Ah, Miles, you are a happy fellow. God bless you. I wish I could come."

Miles paused.

"I don't wish to force your confidence," he said, anxiously, struck by Mowbray's tone, "but I think it would do you good to have some help with this business that bothers you so."

"Would that I could," he answered. "But the

skein is so tangled, that I could never unravel it to you. No, even to speak about it confuses me. I can only just *see* my moves, and play them in silence. But I will have a talk with you to-morrow."

A servant entering announced, "The French Ambassador."

"I am happy to see you," said the cold, calm, courteous voice. "I trust my request has not inconvenienced you. My kinsman, Mr. Warrender. Don't let me keep you, Miles."

Miles bowed and disappeared.

"Another move in the game," he said. "He will win, I dare say, but it is killing him."

# CHAPTER VII.

#### THE PARK.

> Love here blindfolded stands with bow and dart,
> There Hope looks pale, Despair with rainy eyes.

MRS. WARRENDER and Miss Evelyn had visited that morning the studio of a very great and famous artist, and were returning through the Park on their way to Tudor-square.

He is a very great painter; perhaps as a colorist he has had no rival since Titian and Veronese,

> In that lost land, in that soft clime,
> In the crimson evening weather,

revelled in the mellow and lustrous life of the Venetian Archipelago. Though the world scarcely knows or honours him rightly yet, it will come to do so before we die. There is a Saint Catherine or Saint Cecilia of his which actually glows with colour, with such a glow of gold and amethyst as sometimes burns upon the sunset Atlantic. But he is great not alone as a colorist. He has drawn with exquisite feeling that vision of Queen Guinevere which arrests Launcelot as he seeks the San Greal. The sad woman comes between the knight and the mystic quest. The head is not averted,—the look is still and passionless, though sad. Passion is buried and dead, and it is only a pale spectre who warns the warrior back. It would be difficult to express in words all that that visioned face expresses. There is none of the old love and tenderness (that was over when she turned away from his caress at Arthur's grave); there is the sense of the inevitable sorrow, of the incurable shame; and yet, through it all, in those calm, pitiful eyes, a profound and womanly compassion for the man who had shared her guilt, and partakes her punishment. Such a look—straight from the inmost soul as that— is greater than any victory of colour.

I have sometimes deemed it strange that this man can turn from his Hebrew kings, and his old romance, and his prostrate angels, and his golden skies, to the commonest and most simple aspects of this mean, modern life. It startles at first, as though we were to find Angelico and Hogarth working together. Here David, the kingly minstrel, amid orange and golden blossoms, strings his harp, and Arthur sleeps beneath the yellow leaves; there between the sun and shade the wounded woman revels in a ghastly festival, or on the cold London pavement, in the chill London dawn, shivers drearily, as the peasant—fresh from the breezy meadow-lands among which the child played in her innocent girlhood—drives his team into the sleeping city. And yet there is nothing discordant in this: both aspects are consistent with plain truth. One is drawn from the deep fountains of historical and religious feeling, where the boldest and most unreserved conventionalisms may be admitted: the other from the present, where nothing except simple transcript is possible. In the antique, all the suggestions of the imagination may be introduced under abstract and formal forms,—like the chorus in the Greek drama, an embodied commentary upon the passing transaction; while in the modern the same law dictates the frankest and most conscientious adherence to reality. "Signs and wonders" were familiar in the old ages of faith; but we have no creditable witches or miracle workers now, no angels resting on the rosy clouds, no "spears arrayit" upon the menacing heaven. Our story must be related, as it relates itself in the life, and from the hidden face and the averted gesture alone can the shame, misery, humiliation, and swift remorse be gathered.

But Corry and Alice are driving as aforesaid in the Park, and æsthetic discussions are neither relevant nor gallant. And indeed no painting that Raphael Sanzio of Urbino painted is sweeter than that of those two girls.

Alice's face was full of life. The light auburn hair in its breezy ripples; the swift shafts of mockery and ridicule that shot from the blue eyes; the tremulous delicacy of colour on the white blue-veined cheek; the slight curl of defiance on the watchful lip;— every feature was impressed by the keen and dominant life that animated the whole. The Greek would have desired more repose: the perpetual unrest would have fatigued him.

But Corry would have satisfied him,—satisfied the soul even of the unrivalled artist who *dreamt* the pensive Antinous of the Borghese. The rich brown eyes, sleepy and soft as the fawn's; the drooping eyelash; the mouth, content with its own sweetness; the regal gait which dignified the maiden, and which had now matured into the superb sweep of beautiful matronhood; the dark lustrous twilight in the hair,— why, Velasquez, did you not paint her in her prime? How languidly the eye travels, and yet how delicious its languor!—how indolently the swan-like neck sweeps round, and yet how noble that indolent grace! But there is no haughtiness nor scorn, such as curves the heavy lips of Antinous: only the sweet meekness you see in the brown eyes of the oxen which pasture below the Apennines.

Both had changed since we knew them first. Corry had grown less serious. The grand gravity of the girl could not resist the little lips that babbled on her knee, and pressed her bosom. She was no longer abstracted and absorbed. She was a proud wife and a happy mother; and such happiness, charming away the solitary romance of girlhood, fills its place with less romantic and more active sympathies. Alice, on the other hand, had become more pensive. The ceaseless vivacity, which would have driven an Oriental lover distracted, had disappeared. When serious she was more tender, when gay more bitter, than she used to be. The bright content of the old time was gone. There was a sharp and unquiet restlessness in her manner, very different from the light-hearted mockery of the past. Her life somehow had not rounded its orbit serenely. Something—some care or woe—had contrived harshly to arrest it. At least, so I felt. She used to honour me by flirting with me at that time—the world said she was a tremendous coquette; but a sharp pain hurt her often, and the anguish would sometimes drive the colour from her cheek, spite of all her bravery.

Corry had long felt that something was amiss. But Alice would make no confession of weakness. When there came a sharper twinge than usual, it was still "the tooth-ache only"—never the heart-ache. No doubt she was an intrepid little soul, and bore her pain—wherever it gnawed—like a martyr.

"How you start, dear!" said Corry, as they drove along below the budding elms; "you are getting quite nervous. Dear Alice! there is something wrong with you—what is it?"

"Yes," said Alice, trying to laugh it off, as the

colour went and came again with a richer bloom on her cheek, "I think I am getting nervous. How stupid of me! I believe I will take to fainting, like a fine lady, one of these days. There is some one bowing to us—who is it?"

"Why, Darcy, of course; don't you know him?" Corry replied, looking keenly at her friend as a new light broke upon her. "We must get him to dine with us."

She stopped the carriage. Darcy came up.

"You must dine with us. I have so much to say to you about last night. There is no one with us— only Alice. You are not engaged?"

Darcy was not, and would be delighted.

A carriage swept past them. A haughty recognition from Lady Beatrix Trelawney was vouchsafed to the party.

"Poor thing!" said Corry; "how ill she looks! I wonder if she is happy?"

"She looks miserable," said Darcy, "and I don't wonder. What between her own and her husband's temper, she must lead a wretched life."

"You politicians always dislike each other. I used to like her, but she seems to avoid me now. I fear her husband does not admire mine."

"After the drubbing he got last night, I should think not. The man is so oily and so implacable, no wonder he is hated. But I think he regards

Mowbray and the Mowbray connexion with peculiar bitterness. Do you know how it is?"

"No," Mrs. Warrender replied, with a little hesitation; then she added, "I have heard that there was some old love-affair in which Mowbray was the fortunate rival."

"I recollect something of the sort. You never saw Mrs. Mowbray? I knew her when I first came up here. She was very beautiful. They said she was the most lovely woman of her day. She was the idol of her husband: it nearly killed him when she died. Do you know, I sometimes fancy that you are like her?"

Mrs. Warrender blushed slightly, but she only said, "It is dreadful to think of such bitterness."

"I have heard," said Alice, in a low voice, "that men are very bitter about these things. They never forgive."

Darcy looked quickly at her: she could not bear the look; again all the blood forsook her face; and it really seemed as though she were about to make good her promise, and faint in grim earnest at last.

Mrs. Warrender noticed her agitation. "Till seven," she said to Darcy, and the carriage drove on. Alice lay back, and after a moment's silence, during which she seemed trying to subdue the hysterical affection that was mastering her, burst into tears. Corry soothed and petted her, as she would have petted a child.

"Alie," she whispered at last, "I see how it is. You love him."

"I once told him that I did not," was the sole reply.

## CHAPTER VIII.

### THE DYING LION.

> And the poor deities, high in the heavens,
> Travel in sorrow
> Endless disconsolate journeys;
> And they are immortal,
> Still bearing with them
> Their bright-gleaming sorrow.
> But I, the mortal,
> Planted so lowly, with death to bless me,
> I sorrow no longer.

MILES had occasion to call at the Foreign Office before returning to Tudor-square. He was then informed that shortly after he had left, the Minister had been taken ill and had been instantly conveyed home.

Miles, much alarmed, at once followed. "Thomas," Mowbray's butler, an old family domestic, met him in the hall.

"Oh, Mr. Warrender," said the honest fellow, with tears in his eyes, "I am glad you are come. Mr. Mowbray has been very bad to-day. I have never seen him so long of coming round."

## THE DYING LION. 341

"Is he better?" asked Miles. "Can he see me?"

"He asked for you a few minutes since. I will let him know, sir, if you please."

Miles waited in the spacious antechamber, which was furnished with almost monumental simplicity; only above the hearth hung a single picture, ordinarily concealed by a curtain of crimson velvet, which to-day was partially withdrawn. Mowbray must have looked at it before he left for the day's work; perhaps he had gazed at it in the grey dawn-light, when he returned from his triumph. Two as lovely women faces as Sir Peter or Sir Joshua ever painted—the elder very high-bred, noble, and thoughtful-browed, the other full of soft vivacity and *espièglerie*. The matronly sister leans upon the other, bends over her fondly, caresses her with sisterly caresses. She is cheering the "wee pet" of their flock, telling her that she must obey the true instinct of her heart; that the untitled adventurer who loves her will make a nobler mate than the most noble Plantagenet of them all; and in reply a shy glad smile, you see, crosses like sunlight the long-lashed violet eyes. Ay, the potent voice has won its way to that proud heart, and tamed it into beautiful obedience.

"Mr. Mowbray will see you now," said Thomas, opening the door that led into the study.

Miles entered. There sat the Minister, pen in hand, a great heap of papers beside him. He finished the sentence he was writing before he looked up. He was somewhat pale; but the eye was clear and penetrating, and the voice did not shake. Miles could not have guessed that he had been ill.

"I am glad to find that you are no worse," he said. "From what they said at the Office, I was rather frightened."

"The blockheads," said Mowbray, "it will be all over the town to-morrow that I am dying. However, Miles, I have had a sharp bout of it this time. Sir Benjamin very nearly gave me over, I can tell you. I suppose they will say that that spiteful speech of Trelawney's has killed me. Well, it was base in him to say such things behind my back. But take my word for it, were there no other wound than he can inflict, I should live till doomsday. As if his insolence could touch ME," said the Minister, with his superb scorn.

"I am gathering up the woof," he continued, pointing to the pile of papers, "so that you or some one else may hold it. I fear me it is too late."

A weary sigh that was almost inaudible escaped from him. Miles heard it, however.

"You should rest to-night; you will never get round, if you treat yourself thus. Put away your work and rest this one night."

"I must work while it is day," replied Mowbray, with a somewhat sad smile. "The night when no man can work will come soon enough. But I promise you I will not sit long. Just let me get this business put right, and then we will take a long holiday.

Where shall we go, Miles? Oh, I must see Carlyon and the grand old sea once more. You were a mere chit, Miles, when I was there last, and here you are —one of the senators of our great Babel! It will make me a new man to go back to the old place. I remember it all—the day I first went there, as well as if it were yesterday; your father, a youngster like yourself, and that superb old heathen of a grandfather. We have no such heathen now. It is a perished race. They were too sinfully jolly for this morose generation. Ah, Miles, won't we enjoy ourselves?" Had the Minister cheated his fancy with the picture he conjured up? I think not. At least there was something—a rich swell of sea-like sadness in his voice—that did not assure Miles.

"Now go," he added; "don't scold me any more. I shall be in bed in an hour, I promise. True Thomas will see that I am punctual. Take my word for that."

## CHAPTER IX.

#### PEACE.

And away through the mist of the morning grey
　The spectre and horse rode wide;
The dawn came up the old bright way,
　And the lady never died.

THEY had a very pleasant party at Miles's. He said nothing about the Minister's illness or of his apprehensions regarding him. No sense of an approaching calamity lay upon their hearts. Darcy was good-naturedly clever as usual. Alice had recovered; she looked languid and subdued, but tranquil. Some drops of summer rain had fallen upon the thirsty heart.

They spoke of the artist's life; the girls' visit to the studio brought that topic into the talk.

"Do you know," said Darcy, "that I am a devoted adorer of Velasquez? It was that picture at Lord H——'s which first opened my eyes. I take a look at it every afternoon, almost. It puts me straight after the dirty work of the day."

"How beautiful it is!" said Alice. "It is like a bunch of grapes."

"Yes; and what a charming notion it gives one of the life he led. Any mother and any ragged urchin that he found sunning themselves upon the hot sierras, and any group of peasants or beggars at the wayside albergo—the picture is nothing more; but then it discloses such a richness and vivid vital strength, and such an abundance of the ruddiest juice of human heartiness in the man, that it charms and enchains. Your comparison is admirable, Miss Evelyn. The picture is ripe and fruity—a basket of golden peaches or Spanish grapes kissed by the sun."

"How he must have enjoyed such work," said Miles; "so simple and natural and gloriously indolent. The artist life is after all the best. It is the green spot in this desert—the resting-place amid the tumult."

"We go at a desperate pace, truly," replied Darcy. "Somebody says, 'we need to struggle to stand still.' Do you know who said that, Mrs. Warrender? I have quite forgotten."

They had all forgotten, as the present writer has; when the author claims it, his property will be restored to him.

"It is too true," said Miles, "but at least the artist on his hillside or seaside can keep aloof. But the torrent will carry him away with it some day, or leave him stranded without a vocation."

"How do you mean?"

"I was talking with old Snarleyou the other day, and he said, truly enough, I thought, that the theatrical age was past, that we had arrived at one that was 'intolerant of form.'"

"My dear Miles," said Darcy, "if you comprehended him, it is more, I am sure, than I do."

"We did not expect that you would," exclaimed Corry, with her peerless smile.

"If you are not understood in this world, the next best thing is to be utterly misunderstood," remarked Darcy, in a resigned tone. "I detest compromises."

"Of course there is something in it," said Miles. "We don't go to see the drama now; we prefer to read *Cymbeline* at home. The sermon, which was quite a necessity of life to our forefathers, is now regarded as an absolute nuisance. Our culture has been so much extended that these forms have become less able than they used to be to serve any practical purpose. We are taught every day their inadequacy. Painting, which is one of them, may suffer the same fate. Who cares now for Aurora, or the Graces, or the Seasons? No one except some old China collectors, and yet these abolished forms are just a shade more artificial—more *formal*—than those which still obtain in art. Painting must become more nearly identified with life, if it is to live."

"And why should it not?" asked Darcy. "Why should it not become a perfect transcript of life, of our life, of the life of nature? I think the man you saw to-day will teach us that that is not altogether impracticable. As for sermons, I can't give them up either. Many a sound sleep, many a blessed dream, do I owe them. It is only then I see angels."

"I wish you wouldn't talk so," said Corry, gently; "I know you are both longing to hear our dear Dean again."

"One good man can't save a city. I go to church to worship, not to hear *preachments*, as old Jeremy Taylor has it. The Prayer Book does me good, but the sermon leaves me just where I was. Not only so, it positively hurts. I often leave church a perfect Pagan. How can it be otherwise? When you are forced to sit for a good hour, listening to the rhetorical rubbish of an ineffable idiot; to foolish and illogical argument which you are not allowed to refute!"

"Wouldn't you like to have one of them in the house?" asked Darcy. "How you could demolish him!"

"Come, Alice," said Mrs. Warrender, rising, "we will leave them to their politics."

"One song, Alice," Miles pleaded, in the drawing-room. "I will ring for lights."

"Please don't; this dim twilight is so much nicer," said poor Alice plaintively; "I can't sing to-night, I am too hoarse."

"Only one—we won't ask for more."

Alice went to the piano, near which Darcy was seated talking to Corry.

"Sing that old dirge," said Miles; "you know it by heart, I am sure."

Alice tried, and though the notes trembled a little doubtfully as she began, she contrived to finish it. The subdued pathos of her voice made its wild sadness most touching. For it is, indeed, one of the saddest and eeriest of ballads.

> They shot him dead at the Nine-stane rigg
>   Beside the headless cross;
> And they left him lying in his blood
>   Upon the muir and moss.
>
> They buried him at the mirk midnight,
>   When the dew fell cold and still,
> When the aspen grey forgot to play,
>   And the mist clung to the hill.
>
> They dug his grave but a bare foot deep,
>   By the edge of the Nine-stane burn,
> And they covered him o'er with the heather-flower,
>   The moss, and the lady-fern.

A fitting dirge for the gallant soldier, "who died, and died so young."

Miles was called out of the room ere the ballad was finished, and Corry followed him. When Alice finished, she found that Darcy was by her side alone. She trembled—every drop of colour left her cheek.

"May I say again what I said once before?" Darcy began, with hesitation; "I have loved you always—

I love you now—more, if it be possible. Oh, Alice," he continued, passionately, "why may we not be happy?"

She did not answer at once; she trembled so violently, that he thought she would faint. But she did not; she looked into his eyes so full of love, and then said, in a low, penitent voice, as if the thought of the old girlish wilfulness that had made her cast away in caprice the treasure-trove of her heart, had come back upon her again, nay, had never been absent from her memory since she had turned away from him long ago,—

"I do not deserve this. Can you forgive me, Darcy?"

Ah, well; let us be thankful that there are some griefs which death does not freeze into despairs.

# CHAPTER X.

### THE GATES OF DEATH.

—◆—

>   Most like the roar
> Of some pain'd desert lion, who all day
> Has trailed the hunter's javelin in his side,
> And comes at night to die upon the sand.

—◆—

THE end had indeed come. The overwrought brain can sustain the pressure no longer; the nerveless fingers drop the pen; the web which the great intellect had woven is unloosed. Though Europe be wrapped in flame to-morrow, the master must die to-night. What he might have done had he lived to complete what he began, no man can tell. This only we know, that when he died at forty-five, he was the first man in the freest and most famous monarchy in Christendom.

When Miles, who had been hastily summoned, arrived, Mowbray was still conscious. He held out his hand with a faint smile to his kinsman. "It has come at last," he said.

Then the keen eye brightened strangely, the fine

intellect began to wander, the lips, so often touched with authentic fire, were silent, or only spoke foolish words more painful than the silence. The fever-tide had caught him, had torn him away, had hurried him along with it in its black anger. Once, and once only, the torrent seemed to abate, leaving its exhausted victim weak and stranded on the bank; and then the blinded consciousness slowly, very slowly, aroused itself, and looked out keenly once more at those who stood around. The lips tried to articulate; Miles bent his ear close down; he deciphered a single sentence,—only one; even that iron will, that eloquent tongue, could not master another word—

"Tell Leonardo I will never consent."

Leonardo was the Imperial ambassador.

"Well, it does not matter much; we can do without his consent now," the polished courtier inwardly surmises; "there will be a new minister at the Foreign Office to-morrow."

These were the last articulate words that Mowbray uttered. The pause in the fierce race did not last long. Again the devouring waters close over his head, and bear him with them until they near the sea, and cast the naked body lifeless upon the beach.

# CHAPTER XI.

### THE EUMENIDES.

The old miraculous mountains heaved in sight,
One straining past another along the shore,
The way of grand dull Odyssean ghosts,
Athirst to drink the cool blue wine of seas
And stare on voyagers.

THE Great Minister died. Without the master spirit the Cabinet could not hold together a day. So the King requested a nobleman who had translated a tragedy, and written a review, to look after the monarchy on which the sun never sets. The Premier, who loved his jest, appointed Trelawney a Lord of the Admiralty (Sir Jasper being always dead sick when at sea), and then dissolved the Parliament. Trelawney posted down to Ashton and commenced a vigorous contest for his old seat. The Duke exerted his influence: there was a controversy about the PARISH PUMP which divided Miles's supporters; and a month after Mowbray's death Miles Warrender, Esquire, had lost the burgh, and Sir Jasper Trelawney was elected to sit for Ashton in the new Parliament.

My history stops here. I am sorry for it. The retributive "thunder and lightning" which overtakes the villain in the third volume, is no doubt effective. I cannot help it; my work is not in three volumes. Considered as a mere question of art, I admit that my *dénouement* is decidedly tame—not by any means striking. But English life is not striking. In English life "justice is not vindicated, nor virtue rewarded," in the broad visible characters that the patrons of the drama demand. The mystic *Mene, Mene, Tekel, Upharsin*, is not written upon the walls of our houses. So far as my observation has extended, indeed, the villain—I don't mean your housebreaker, but your heart-breaker; not the thief who steals your spoons, but the thief who steals your honour and your happiness—contrives not only to escape unpunished, but to secure most of the honours and emoluments which a grateful people provides for its best men. If you force me to go on—to anticipate another ten years or so of the century—I am afraid that your theories of atonement will not gain much by any facts we can collect. Lazarus never succeeds to the purple and fine linen; he continues to eat the crumbs, and sees nothing more of the loaf. On the contrary, his sores grow so offensive that even the most charitable dogs are forced to avert their noses. Dives, for his part, speculates successfully on the Stock Exchange; goes into Parliament; is made a member of Government; dines with royalty, and "falls asleep in the bosom of the House of Lords." Miles continues plain Miles to this day: I don't suppose there are a dozen people in the metropolis who know him by name now; while Sir Jasper is a Secretary of State and an oracle of the May meetings. Leighton was not made a bishop. In the old kirkyard of Kinkell there is a simple slab, "To the memory of a brave and devout Christian gentleman." That is all. It was put up about the time that a virulent partisan—a man who had abused Mowbray like a pickpocket, before the breath was well out of his body, for having treated fellow-Christians like fellow-creatures—was preferred to the richest diocese in England. Don't you think that the "villain" has the best of it? Let us all be rogues.

But it may be admitted that there is another side to the picture. Lazarus, I have heard, is now in Abraham's bosom. And Miles at least was never so happy as when he found that he might, with a clear conscience, retire from public life. Corry was charmed to get back with her "bairns" to the old Norland home, to the dear Norland faces. Nor did Leighton dissuade them.

"I feel glad," he said, in one of the last letters he wrote, "that you are coming back; Effie bids me say that she is "so glad." I think you are right. You can work better through private than through public ties. It is what the age needs,—visible sympathy between man and man, not legislative association between classes. We must rise from the family life to the national life; work through the one into the other. Religious ascetics and theoretical politicians make the same mistake. The Apostolic life is no doubt the model. But are we to become pilgrims and martyrs before we become Christians? No. In old days a supreme necessity forced earnest men to cut asunder the domestic ties; *we* are to make these very ties the means of work. The aim in either case is to keep the life true; the form will follow. The power of the domestic life as a political force has never been rightly recognised; and, in an age of constitutional reconstruction, we are in danger of losing sight of it altogether. Come soon; I would fain see you again."

And so they came back, and tried to reform the nation by reforming themselves, as Leighton had recommended. No doubt the world said that Warrender was a man whose career had failed, and it looks upon him somewhat sourly in consequence at times; but I cannot say that he ever manifests any violent symptoms of chagrin; and if he has failed, as is alleged, the spectacle of honest failure—

> The long war closing in defeat,
> Defeat serenely borne—

has always seemed to me much more "interesting"—in much better taste—than the coarse clap-trap of success.

And what of the other compartment of the picture, as it represents the Right Honourable Dives, M.P., Q.C., D.C.L., K.G., and so forth? I am sorry to record that Lady Beatrix ran away from her husband the day he was made Home Secretary. Sir Jasper, who was a crack shot, followed the fugitives, made up with them at a miserable albergo on the road to Madrid, sent a bullet through the young Guardsman's brain, and left the wretched woman without a sixpence, to beg or starve in a strange land. And here, within brackets, or without them, let it be remarked that it is the villain who is commonly most anxious to see justice summarily vindicated, and whose keen eye and ready hand are most successful in exacting a speedy settlement of accounts—a fact which may start certain reflections in the reader's mind regarding the tardy vengeance of the Immortals. Was this the sole plague-spot in his life, the only skeleton in his house? Apparently so: the world at least never heard of any other. But true it is,

> the gods creep on with feet of wool
> Long ere with iron hands they punish men,

and the menace of the overhanging evil—of the cloud charged with death—often infects the soul with a chill and undefinable horror months and years before it burst. Was Sir Jasper pursued by the invisible Eumenides? I fear he was. This is why I think so.

And yet what good to tell of the blank dread I once saw depicted on that man's face? It is all over now,—the stars and the ribbons have been put away, and the moths eat them. The Earl of Ravenscraig died last August, "universally regretted."

He has gone to his last account; he has answered at the tribunal of the Judge. It may be that little Katie is avenged above,—if the vengeance of Heaven be any recompense for a broken heart below.

# CHAPTER XII.

#### WAITING BY THE WAVES.

I shall be married shortly.
      To whom?
To one whom you have all heard talk of.
Your fathers knew him well; one who will ne'er
Give cause I should suspect him to forsake me.
A constant lover—one whose lips, though cold,
Distil chaste kisses; though our bridal-bed
Be not adorn'd with roses, it will be green—
We shall have virgin laurel, cypress, yew,
To make us garlands. Though no fire do burn,
Our nuptial shall have torches, and our chamber
Shall be cut out of marble, where we shall sleep
Free from all care for ever. Death, my Lord,
I hope will be my husband.

*THALATTA! Thalatta!* We are once more beside the ancient sea. Still it murmurs solemnly and peacefully upon "the ribbed sea-sand" of the moon-like bay,—solemnly and peacefully, as if a great man had not died, and an historic empire perished,—solemnly and peacefully, as it has done any time these thousand years or so.

A bright jagged coil of red granite runs into the green water at that point. 'Tis the vanguard of the iron-helmeted host who guard our sea-nursed nation. A stormy place in winter, when the fishers come during the northern storms to watch the long lines of Arctic birds that the fierce sea-wind drives before it. But now the crimson autumn sunset rests peacefully upon the bright plain of waters underneath, and dyes the red granite with a yet deeper carmine.

One solitary watcher haunts that solitary spot. A draped woman-form, with clasped hands folded upon her breast, is clearly outlined against the white sky above the sea-line. The face is sad but composed, —the yellow hair is drawn back from the fine brow, that yet bears the traces of an old pain. The sharp pain stings no more indeed,—God has healed the bleeding heart; but the cheeks are thin and faded, and the blue eyes are very dim now. If you look curiously at these dimmed eyeballs, you will understand how last night, as the village children played gleefully about them upon the soft yellow sands, Elsie hid her face in her sister's lap, and moaned,— " Oh, that I could see!"

But these bursts of passion are not frequent now. Her life is calmed into a sad content. She is willing to wait; to wait in blindness for the hour when her eyes will be opened; to wait in loneliness for the day when at eventime it shall be light. Still, the poor child's heart is very empty—at times; and she longs with inexpressible longing for "The Order of Release" that is to liberate her. *For ye are not as yet come to the rest and to the inheritance which the Lord your God giveth you.*

When the men are on the sea, and the women at their household work, she steals away unnoticed to her lonely watch-tower above the waves. She hears their tender moan in the long summer twilights; she listens to the dreary wail they make when the keen winter wind strikes stormily against the granite headlands. And though her eyes be veiled, still, as she feels the sea-breeze wander across her face, that glorious spectacle is not altogether hid from her. In memory, the golden-lighted main burns below the blue horizon, and she sits and gazes on the smooth and treacherous water,—breathing quietly as a child, smiling peacefully as a saint,—" where he she loved was drowned." Oh, empty heart, wait in patience.

> A little longer ere life, true, immortal,
> Not this our shadowy life, will be thine own;
> And thou shalt stand where winged Archangels worship,
> And kneeling bow before the Great White Throne.

# EPILOGUE.

> And Autumn with a noise of rooks,
> That gather in the waning woods.

THE Norwegian rivers were in bad trim this year; so we turned the *Lily* homeward before the days began to darken, and sailing up the beautiful Bay of Ashton, anchored the other evening below Carlyon, where we still lie.

We have had a glorious autumn week. Warrender's water and moor have been both in first-rate condition. I cannot tell you how many sea-trout have been landed—how many black-cock and wild-fowl have fallen upon the heather and the mere—since we came. Their name is legion.

The Teal-Moss is a capital locality for wild fowl; but there is another station which, for duck-shooting, an indolent man prefers. The wild duck commonly pass a number of hours during the day at sea (where they are out of harm's way), returning at sun-down to the stubbles and the inland marshes. They follow the same route with great punctuality—across a ridge of sandy bents, then across the barley-fields, and so up to the lonely sides of the valley. Donald and I conceal ourselves among the long grasses on the downs as "the gloaming" approaches, and wait the evening flight. Nothing can well be pleasanter during these soft autumn afternoons. You smoke, of course—everybody does. You hear the reapers at their work, the laughter of children and sweethearts, the tramp and neighing of the horses as they wend home from the watering-place—all the cheerful sounds of farm life. The shrill and plaintive call of the partridge sounds from the fields, and now and again a covey sweeps swiftly past to its roosting-place on the links. The hoarse rattle of the corncrake— no, the corncrake has lost his voice by this time, not to recover it again till spring returns, and the earth "renews its ancient rapture." Then, while the soft mist rises from the heated ground, and the lark " in a privacy of glorious light " chants his evening song, but ere the rosy flush has faded from the sky, or ceased to rim with gold the phantom island-shores that float along the horizon, the wild ducks, in companies of twos and threes, begin to whistle overhead, and ever and anon a brace comes within range of our fowling-pieces. And as we sit and watch, Donald favours me with his notions on men and manners, old-world stories, and "the clash" of the countryside. Donald is a great institution. He is as old and as wiry as the Prime Minister. He has consumed oceans of whisky in his time. I believe, had it been properly mixed, that, like the Celtic son-in-law of Noah commemorated in the famous ballad, he might have drunk up the deluge. Donald was a mighty poacher in his youth—the dread of all the game-keepers and game-preservers in the neighbourhood. But he has become a privileged character in his old age, and is permitted to land his salmon, or bring down his brace of "deuks" without molestation. His fly falls on the water like a midge; he is a dead shot at a seal; and, in the less reputable branches of the craft, I have heard that he is as accomplished as his namesake, Sir Walter's friend.

> Donald Caird can wire a maukin,
> Kens the wiles of dun-deer stalkin'
> Leisters kipper, makes a shift
> To shoot a moorfowl in the drift.
> Water-bailiffs, rangers, keepers,
> He can wauk when they are sleepers;
> Not for bountith or reward,
> Daur they mell wi' Donald Caird.

A shrewd, douce, "pawky" old gentleman is Donald, not without a vein of romance either. Moon-lighted nights, forays after wild duck and ptarmigan, the moan of the western sea on the shore, or its whisper among the reeds, have enriched his character. Like all sea-born and sea-bred men, he is a bit of a poet. The ballads of these sea people, you must have noticed, are seldom coarse in feeling or prosaic in expression. There is a natural melody in them; they rise and fall with the waves. But their sympathy with nature, though intense, is not cheerful. It is touched with the sadness and the dread of men who know what death on the winter sea is like. They love, but they fear her.

"There's a loon," said Donald yesterday afternoon, as we lay in our hidingplace among the bents—a hidingplace, however, from which a glimpse of the bay could be obtained. "Shall I gie him a shot? He's no aboon a hundred yards, and I've a charge o' heavy leads in."

Donald never shoots with anything smaller than No. 2, so that his "heavy leads" must be like small cannon-balls.

"For the Lord's sake, sir, haud doon your head: there's a sealch makin' this way. It's a pity I've no a bullet in my pouch."

"Gaudebant carmine phocæ. Try him with a song, Donald."

"The brute's aff," said the old man, after a pause and a long look. "I ken that fellow's nose weel; he's as keen as a whitret, and as wily as the Laird o' Braxy."

"Don't speak evil of dignities, Donald. I thought you and Braxy"—Braxy is a neighbouring laird—"were fast friends."

"Hoot, sir," he replied, "I canna thole him. He's racked the rents, and turned a wheen o' the puir bit cottar bodies into the muir. Ye'll mind Andrew MacTavish? A canny auld chiel is Andrew; sair

## EPILOGUE. 365

hudden doun wi' the rheumatiz, and aye grumblin', as he micht indeed, and his leg as stiff as the funnel o' the loch steamer, but wi' sense and spunk eneuch, and likin' his snuff verra weel," said Donald, as he took out his "mull," and thrust a huge spoonful or two up either nostril. "Andrew was swear to gang; he had lived in the place for forty year. The wife had deed in it, and three o' his bairns; guid bairns they were, and weel liket in the country. So Andrew puts on his shoon, and hirples across to the Laird. 'Deed, Laird,' says Andrew, 'I canna look to bide lang noo, and ye'll let me dee in the auld hoose.' But he wudna, for he's a dour and greedy body, and wanted a langer rent; so Andrew was forced to pack. Faith! I wish we had the auld Laird back; he was a *raal* gentleman. Deil a berry from the Ha' garden was selt, as lang as he was maister. They didna mind then if a lad was whiles seen in the gloamin', wi' a maukin at his belt and his gun under his shouther. But the law's changed noo. New maisters, new men; and troth, sir," Donald continued, waxing confidential, "if Braxy fa's our the back o' the pier ane o' thae mirk nichts, he wunna be lang missed. What think you tried he last? He wanted the fisher-bodies doun at Norburn to sell him their fish *cheap*, so he gets Sawney to ring the bell, and when they are a' seated in the Kirk—for public worship, ye wud jalouse?—he begins and bargains wi' them like a travellin' packman. Heard ye ever the like?

But they wudna bite. Ae lad—Fluke they ca' him—asked him for a sang: anither wud hae a sermon on greed. And auld Browney gaed up to the pulpit and began a discoorse—for Browney can speak like a buik when he's no blin' fou—on the money-changers in the Temple, and what was dune till *them*."

Donald chuckled over this reminiscence, and took another spoonful ere he resumed.

"And there was Elspit Gray,—ye've seen her aften, I'll warrant?—she was a servant lass at the castle lang syne. Weel, sir, she deed yestreen. She was a gran' auld wife, and keepit up her head till she gaed. The yerl aye said she was born a gentlewoman, wi' her saft hands, and her white mutch, and her glitterin' een, like a kite's. She was blin' for lang, and did na hear muckle forby. So she wud sit ben the hoose for weeks without speaking a word to her ain dochter, as gran' as a queen with her crown on. It was gruesome whiles, though—she's gaured me loup often when I've come on her at orra times—her head turned up, a licht on her face, and her een glowerin' oot into the mirk."

I had seen old Elspit often, and had been struck by her grave and almost solemn cast of beauty. As a girl, she must have been strikingly handsome: but even as a girl, her expression could never have been other than stern. The features had not grown hard as she grew old: they must have been petrified in girlhood. The story of some cruel wrong was vaguely associated with her in my mind; a story which I had once heard, but had long forgotten. So I asked Donald if he knew the details.

"I ken it weel," he said, "and guid richt I have —nane better noo. I was a wean at the time, and she was a bit lassie hersel—a bonnie lassie, wi' bricht een, and curly red hair, that happed her roun' like a hood. It was in the hard time afore the war, when the hail country was fairly wicked wi' hate and hunger. Her feyther was verra chief wi' the yerl,— a strang, stout chiel, that spoke his mind freely. But he was hard on the starvin' folk, and 'the boys' swore that he shudna live past Marymas. Sae it chanced that ae mirk nicht in the fa' a band o' them cam to his hoose—he was a fearless man, and wudna steek the door for a' the deevils oot o' hell, he wad say—and into the room where he was sittin' wi' his wife Marion, and little Elsie upon her lap, beside the fire. There was a dull licht, for the peats were low, and they dragged him oot, and never a word spoken; for man and wife kent what was come upon them, and that it behoved not to pray to them that shed innocent bluid. They stickit him like a stirk at his ain door. Weel, the wife jaloused that they wad finish wi' her (for she had ever backed her man up—he was aye richt, the rest were aye wrang); and when they were awa', she grippit little Elsie, and steekit her into a closet in the wa'. There was a chink in the buird, and she says to her—'Noo, lass, they are killin' your feyther ootside, and when they hae kilt him, they will come back and kill me. Look weel at them when they come, and mind you swear to them when you see them in coort. I'll cast a peat on the fire the last thing to raise a bleeze, and struggle hard that you may take a guid look.' Marion Gray was a keen-spirited wife; she was ane o' the auld Leslie clan, and married her man for luve, but she was noo clean daft, and her last thocht on earth was to hang the loons. Auld Elspit had a picture o' her mither, that was painted by a foreigneer when she was a lass,—a lauchin-face, safter-like than Elspit's. The bairn keeked thro' the chink, and saw them murder her mither. It's a terrible but true story," said Donald, wiping his brow, over which the sweat was running. "But she had marked them weel, and swore to them afore the lords. I was there mysel; and weel I mind it, tho' I was but a wean at the time,—it's sixty year this very fa'. There were the twa lords, sitting crackin' in their red gowns like twa howdies, and a wheen glib lads wi' horsehair wigs, and the prisoners ahint them. There was unca little against them though; and the writer body—a fat man, wi' a red roun' face like a haerst moon—was cock-sure they wad wun aff, till the lass was fetched in. Her face was deadly white, but her een burned like live peats. The writer-bodies were no for lattin' her speak at first; but she was sae quiet, and douce, and keen, that the lords pit her in the box, and speert at her aboot the catechism, and the Testament, and the ten commandaments, and she answered every word freely and fairly. Then she looked lang at the men, and says quite quiet, pointing to ane and anither o' them, 'You were there, and you were there, and you were there.' It was like as if she had spoken in a dwam, or aff a buik: there was nae dauntin' her. The three loons were hangit, and Elspit gaed hame wi' Whitey, that was sib to her feyther's gude brither. She grew lang and bonny, and Sandy Gray courted her; but they say she never leuch again. And 'deed, sir," he concluded, "it was a burnin' trouble for a young bairn."

Having finished his narrative, Donald took a pull at the capacious flask which I handed to him. There are no abstainers among the northern hills. The sportsman "takes his dram" after he has slain his stag on Ben Vorlich. The fisher "takes his dram" when his twenty-pound salmon lies on the grass at his feet. The pastor "takes his dram" after his Gaelic discourse. The bard "takes his dram" when he has recounted the exploits of Fingal and the Fairshon. And each in succession "blesses" the Chancellor of the Exchequer, and "tamns ta whisky tuty."

"Elspit was the last o' the clan," he resumed. "She saw her folk a' oot. Little Elsie bided wi' her, after auld Peter gaed,—but she did na bide lang, puir lass."

"Little Elsie?" I said; "I did not know that she was a relation of the old woman?"

"Indeed, sir, she was," Donald replied. "Elsie was caed after her gran'mither. Hester, her eldest dochter, married Peter Stephen; an' the ither, ye may hae heard tell, gaed wrang—Katie they caed her. Whist! sir,—whist! There's a brace o' deuks anent the burn."

And so musing upon Fate—upon the doom which haunts a fated House, by the shores of the Northern Sea as by the sleepless Cephisus, in the fisher's hovel as in the palace of the King—I prepare at length to lay aside my pen. But this is a book on politics, you say; and you think, therefore, that it might be advisable to point the moral which it enforces. But it points to nothing,—neither to the legerdemain of Whig, or Tory, or Radical. It is a *man* we want, not legislative antidotes. All history has proved, all true religion has asserted, that the form is worthless, if the spirit be dead. Christendom is the life of Christ. The life of a Divine Person, and not the dogmas of priests, lies at the root of all the truth, and goodness, and greatness of eighteen hundred years. Whatever is most characteristic in the life of any nation is due to the influence of some half-dozen men, whose high deeds or thoughts inspired the race,—thereby raising it out of itself, out of its savageness, and its meanness, and its selfishness, to the level of sacrifice,

## EPILOGUE.

and to the sense of duty. I have no confidence in measures: I believe in men. Mowbray was the last of the men who were greater than their measures. He did not enfranchise the ten-pounders, but he stirred the imagination and wakened the faith of the nation. Had he lived the ten-pounders might not have been enfranchised. The people would have been satisfied to be led by one in whom they recognised a chief, a guide, a leader. They would not have required to be saved by an ingenious piece of mechanism. But he died, and as the Whigs, who cultivate "Houses" instead of "Men," succeeded to the Government, and had neither personal genius nor lofty virtue to offer to the people, they were forced to try the ten-pound experiment. Whether it has worked well, I do not stay to inquire. Upon the whole, I am inclined to agree with Darcy, who once said—

"There *must* be a Divine Governor of the world. Else into what a mess we should get when Lord John, for instance, is at the helm. And as long as there is a Divine Leader, it does not, perhaps, matter very much *who* is Prime Minister."

THE END.

LONDON : PRINTED BY WILLIAM CLOWES AND SONS, STAMFORD STREET,
AND CHARING CROSS.

www.ingramcontent.com/pod-product-compliance
Lightning Source LLC
Chambersburg PA
CBHW021338300426
44114CB00012B/991